THE COUNTRY LIFE POCKET BOOK OF
COLLECTOR'S TERMS

THE COUNTRY LIFE POCKET BOOK OF

COLLECTOR'S TERMS

Written and illustrated by

THERLE HUGHES

COUNTRY LIFE BOOKS

LONDON · NEW YORK · SYDNEY · TORONTO

Published by Country Life Books
and distributed for them by
The Hamlyn Publishing Group Limited
London · New York · Sydney · Toronto
Astronaut House, Feltham, Middlesex, England

First published 1979
ISBN 0 600 31968 7

Filmset in 10 lens on 10 pt. Photon Times by
Tradespools Limited, Frome
Printed and bound in Great Britain by
Hazell, Watson & Viney Limited, Aylesbury

INTRODUCTION

Here is a small book, but an ambitious one. In a minimum of words I have tried to supply the basic background facts about more than two thousand items, skills, processes, decorative styles – all the people and places, ideas and triumphs that fascinate collectors of antiques.

Always I have found that new knowledge stimulates a new pleasure in collecting. Just to know the range of, say, Mauchline boxes, or the technique of bat-printing, or the sources of radiant lustrewares, may prompt all the delights of a new quest. The range is endless, whether among teapots or thimbles or Trafalgar souvenirs.

Essentially the survey is restricted to British items with brief glances abroad to cover subjects of international fame. This has meant that I have been able to include many an intriguing minor treasure, tracing the story of shagreen, for example, not just for its old-time uses, but through basic changes in its sources and characteristics. It has been my purpose to sort out innumerable confusions, such as roemer and rummer drinking-glasses, to identify unusual terms such as sheveret, tyg and harlequin table.

Since over-abundant cross-references can prove tedious, a technical or unfamiliar word in a definitition will probably be found in its own alphabetical context.

Assuredly small triumphs may still reward the collector alerted to recognise the clues that others have overlooked – finding maybe a silhouette inside a watch-chain seal, a double fore-edge painting, a telescopic candlestick, a puzzle fan.

As far as possible I have attempted the approximate dating essential to real collecting, but far too often absent in collectors' books even in these fact-appreciating days. (And including brief guidance concerning the confusing dates occasionally offered to the unwary, in ceramic marks, maybe, or even on the coin in a silver punch-ladle.) But, throughout, the first aim has been to ensure that would-be collectors have the quickest, easiest reference to anything and everything; to answer those in a hurry, whether their problem is an inscription under a print or a description in an auction sale catalogue. This surely is the best way to wish any collector 'Good Hunting'.

Abacus Ancient (Chinese) calculating frame with beads sliding on wires. Also the top of the capital of a column. *See* Orders of architecture.

Abbotsford furniture Of *c.*1820. Named after Sir Walter Scott's house at Abbotsford, his novels prompting furnishings in romantic-Gothic mood, such as dark, massive carved oak in ill-proportioned imitation of Tudor and Jacobean work, some made from older materials.

Acacia wood Yellowish with darker veining, used for marquetry.

Acanthus (Fig. 1) Finely indented graceful leaves of *a. spinosus* (bear's breech), in conventionalised form used in classical ornament; in English carving from the 16th century and especially on late 17th- to 18th-century furniture, for example, on cabriole legs.

Acid etching Use of hydrofluoric acid to ornament the surface of late 19th-century glassware, where a pattern had been scratched through a resist substance; recognised by thin shallow lines. Often found on cased glass. Cheaper than wheel-engraving. *See* Etching.

Acid gilding *See* Gilding.

Ackermann's *Repository of Arts* (Fig. 236) Monthly periodical (its subjects including furniture, furnishings, etc.) named after the London building of Rudolph Ackermann (1764–1834), at work in London from 1790, an important publisher of magnificent illustrated books, periodicals and innumerable prints – such as the *Microcosm of London*, illustrated by Rowlandson and Pugin, etc. Encouraged many promising young artists and especially influenced the popularity of hand-coloured aquatints. From 1795 at 101 Strand; from *c.*1830 at 96 Strand and 191 Regent Street where the Sporting Gallery was run by his son (same name).

Acroter In pedimented furniture, a small pedestal for an ornament.

Act-of-Parliament clock *See* Coaching-inn clock.

Adam brothers John, Robert, James and William. Robert (1728–92) was an especially influential architect and designer of interior decoration, popularising his view of the Neo-classical style, 'all delicacy, gaiety, grace and beauty'.

Adams Important family of potters led by three cousins named William. William Adams (1746–1805) is remembered for bone china and fine Wedgwood-style jasperwares, usually impressed with his name. His Greengates, Tunstall pottery, founded 1779, was continued by his son Benjamin to 1820. William Adams of Cobridge and Burslem (1748–1831) introduced underglaze blue transfer-printing to Staffordshire, but did not mark his wares. William Adams (1772–1829) had five potteries in Stoke, making ornamental bone china and much export ware printed with American views. He was followed by four sons, the eldest, yet another William (1798–1865) also running his own Tunstall pottery with a far-reaching export trade. His son, again William (1833–1905) bought back the Greengates factory in 1896 to continue as William Adams & Sons, Ltd.

Adelaide period Now-popular term for the 1830s, named after William IV's wife; e.g., Adelaide chair with balloon back composed of facing C-scrolls. *See* Couch.

Adze marks Ridges and hollows on furniture surfaces that have been smoothed with a type of axe having a curved, dished blade set at right angles to the plane of its handle. On medieval furniture; also on more recent country furniture.

Aerograph colouring On ceramics, delicate background tinting, especially on late Victorian and Edwardian ornaments; achieved by spraying.

Aerophane Filmy fabric found in embroideries, elaborate valentines, etc.

8

Aesthetes From the 1860s considered themselves philosophers of good taste and arbiters of fashion in art, design and domestic decoration, on a basis of mood and atmosphere. Aesthetic became the late Victorian term for fashionable, the opposite being philistine.

Agate Colour-banded form of chalcedony, white, buff, brown, grey-blue, etc.; popular with Victorians for daytime jewellery, snuffbox lids, etc. *See* Mocha stone.

Agate ware Earthenware or stoneware imitating stratified agate, composed of intermingled clays that burnt to different colours, sometimes surface-tinted with pale blue. Associated with Thomas Whieldon from the 1740s and revived by late Victorians.

Aglet. Aiglet In early dress, a metal finial often of gold or silver, attached to the free ends of points or ribbon ties. In 16th-century became purely ornamental.

Agraffe In dress, the hook of a clasp fastening; hence an ornamental hook worn as jewellery.

Aigrette Feather spray worn as a hair ornament or a jewel to hold a feather or imitate it.

Air twist glass (Figs. 102, 103) Internal ornament in smooth-surfaced drinking-glass stems, especially late 1730s to 1780s. A cluster of bubbles drawn out into slender spiralling threads of air, the most perfect being found in stems cut from prepared rods or canes; these included wide-diameter threads in exceptionally brilliant glass (the so-called mercury twist). Similar stems were made with internal spirals of opaque white enamel, wide and narrow, and with colours, especially red and blue. *See* Cane.

Alabaster Soft stone used by carvers, popular in ancient Egypt, a form of gypsum, usually white, fairly translucent with zones of yellow and brown tones, fine grained, uniformly textured, lustrous and taking a marble polish. Harder than the gypsum used for plaster of Paris.

Alabaster ware Kind of bone china or glass with similar translucency.

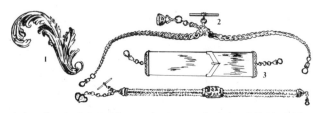

1 Acanthus leaf. **2, 3** Albert and other watch chains. **2** Typical Albert with bar and seal and (*bottom*) 1870s 'leontine' version with movable rider. **3** (*centre*) Silk fob ribbon.

Albert Gold or silver watch-chain with a bar for attaching to a gentleman's waistcoat buttonhole. Named after the Prince Consort. *See* Watch fob.

Alcove furniture Beds, seats and shelves shaped to fit wall recesses.

Alder Strong brown wood with knotty figured grain fading to pinkish tones. Found in 18th-century country furniture, especially turnery.

Ale glass (Fig. 100) Drinking-glass usually with a deep funnel (flute)-shaped or ogee-curved bowl (sometimes bucket-shaped from the 1770s) for the potent drink, strong ale, as is often indicated by hop and barley ornament wheel-engraved on the bowl from the 1740s onwards. Frequently on a tall stem, with the alternative of a similar bowl on a short or vestigial stem – the dwarf or quarter ale which also continued well into the 19th century. *See* Flute.

Ale warmer (Fig. 4) Handled vessel for warming ale in the fire embers. Copper or brass, tinned inside. Cone-shaped for use with a fire in a grate; boot-shaped for the early down-hearth (often reproduced).

Alexandrite Rare precious variety of chrysoberyl gemstone, admired by Edwardians, appearing green or red in different lights.

Alexandrite glass Late 19th-century translucent glass skilfully reheated so that a single vessel showed a range of colours from amber through rose to blue.

Aller Vale Devonshire art pottery from 1868, becoming the Royal Aller Vale & Watcombe Pottery Co. in 1901. Produced ornaments, mottoed slipwares, etc.

Alloy Combination of two or more metals such as brass (copper and zinc) or of a base metal with gold or silver.

Almandine Deep red gemstone garnet found in Victorian jewellery.

Alto relievo High relief or strongly projecting carving, casting, etc. *See* Bas relief.

Aluminium jewellery Around 1900 this metal was used occasionally as a setting for gems and is found in light-weight hair ornaments and in bulky belt buckles in the Glasgow School's style of superimposed rectangles.

Amaranth 1. Palisander or purple wood. Dark brown to dark violet colour with wavy grain, for marquetry. 2. Purple dyestuff made from amaranth wood.

Amazonite Opaque semi-precious stone, brilliant green, popular with Arts and Crafts jewellers.

Amber Fossilised resin of coniferous trees, more or less translucent, mainly in pale yellow to red tones, light and warm to the touch. Found in ancient jewellery and popular with late Victorians, but imitations may also be found.

Ambergris Waxy substance from sperm whales containing fragrant ambrein used in perfumery. *See* Pomander.

Amberina glass Translucent glass containing air bubbles, with reddish to yellow colour shadings. Made in England in the late 19th century, under American licence; usually mould-shaped.

Amboyna wood Golden brown, the grain much resembling walnut but distinguished by 'birds-eye' curls.

Amelia Fragments of paper cut out and gummed to compose a picture, given very slight relief effects by pricking from behind with needles of different sizes. A girls' hobby from the late 18th century onwards.

Amen glass Drinking-glass *c.*1745, its large trumpet bowl diamond-point engraved with a Jacobite paraphrase of 'God save Great James our King' and the word AMEN below the cipher of James III of England and VIII of Scotland. *See* Jacobite glass.

Amethyst Hard translucent gemstone quartz, ranging in colour from bluish violet to reddish purple. Popular in Victorian jewellery.

Amorini Now a popular name for plump little naked 'boys' found in Baroque furniture-carving, silver, etc. Sometimes distinguished from winged cupids (Italian *putti*) and the winged heads known as cherubs.

Amphora Much-imitated ancient Greek earthenware vessel for wine or oil, urn-shaped, with two handles.

Amulet (Fig. 172) Any small item worn as protection from evil by man and his animals; hence forerunner of early sun-shaped horse brasses intended to dazzle the evil eye.

Andirons Firedogs, the pair of log-supports flanking the creepers in the hearth, L-shaped with decorative uprights. Usually made of iron, some of 18th-century steel, some partly silver or bronze.

Aneroid barometer (Fig 19) From 1844, displays on a dial the atmospheric pressure as measured on a partly elastic box, air-exhausted and hermetically sealed; cheaper and more compact than the earlier mercury tube. Often found in the case of an older-style banjo barometer. *See* Barometers.

Angel bed With the tester and its curtains extending over only the upper half of the bed and not supported by posts. From Medieval days; popular with Victorians.

Aniline dyes Chemical dyes associated with much harsh textile colouring, especially reds and purples, from the mid 1850s, such as Berlin wool embroideries.

Anodised Metal work given a hard protective coating by a modern electro-chemical process.

Annealing 1. In glass, toughening by slow heating. Improvements in the 1740s and 1780s, such as using a tunnel lehr to cool the glass slowly, facilitated more ambitious cut ornament. 2. In silver, heating followed by quenching in cold water to render it malleable for further hammered shaping.

Anthemion (Fig. 206) Stylised honeysuckle flower copied from Greek ornament for much 18th- to 19th-century Neo-classical decoration of furniture, silver, etc.

Antimacassar Rectangle of fabric (often embroidered) or crochet work to protect an upholstered chairback from macassar oil, a 19th-century hair dressing.

Antique Term applied by Elizabethans to Greek and Roman antiquities, but now usually signifying any article made over a hundred years ago.

Antiqued Given the appearance of age, not always originally to deceive.

Antiquities Term generally now used to distinguish relics of the ancient world, Greek, Roman, etc., from post-Medieval antiques.

Apostle spoons Haloed figures with their distinguishing attributes, introduced as cast knops on straight-stemmed spoons. Very rare as early christening spoons, but popular in 19th- to 20th-century sets of teaspoons.

Apple wood Hard, pinkish to light brown, long used for country furniture.

Applied ornament Made separately and attached.

In *appliqué embroidery*, motifs in different fabrics cut out and stitched onto the basic material. *See* Card-cut work; Sprigged ceramic ornament.

Apron In furniture or silver, shaped ornament between the front legs immediately below the cross-framing of a table-top, chair seat, tea-kettle stand, etc.

Aquamarine Magnificent gemstone, variety of beryl, its clear pale blue-green colour often intensified by heating.

Aquatint Print suggesting a wash drawing. An acid etching taken from a copper plate prepared with a grained surface of porous resin. Often a basis for commercial hand-colouring.

Arabesque. Moresque Popular Baroque ornament of stylised foliage and flowers, elaborately interwined, but free of the human or animal motifs reputedly forbidden by Mahomet; in contrast to grotesques.

Architect's table Known to the 18th century as a writing-and-reading table. The front pulls forward with part of the front legs as a fitted drawer with a writing slide and out-swinging quadrant ink-drawer; the top can be tilted, this often releasing a small projecting book-rest.

Architectural furniture Furniture and clocks based on architectural design. Associated especially with the massive early 18th-century William Kent style, interpreting Palladian ideals.

Argand, Liverpool and duplex lamps Oil-burning, with a tubular wick for effective air flow and a glass chimney, the Argand was introduced from Switzerland in the mid 1780s and improved as the Liverpool lamp with an adjustable disc to extend the flame. The duplex lamp from the 1860s had two wicks. The sluggish colza oil (made from rape seed) had to be gravity-fed to the wick from a reservoir slightly above it.

Argyle (Fig. 255) Lidded vessel with a narrow spout set low in the

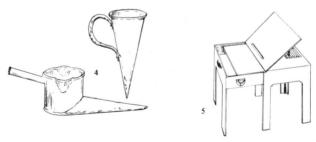

4 Ale warmers. **5** Architect's table.

14

body for serving the best of the gravy, kept hot either by a central box iron or by a hot-water lining filled at the top of the handle. In silver, Sheffield plate, from *c*.1760s. Probably named after the 4th Duke of Argyll.

Arita ware Japanese porcelain from *c*.40 factories in Hizen province brought to Europe from the mid 17th century. Underglaze blue ware followed by Kakiemon and 'brocaded Imari' ornament, and finally wide-mouthed 'Nagasaki vases'.

Ark North of England term for a sloping-lidded chest; made by an arkwright, less skilled than a joiner.

Armada chest 'Armoured' iron strong-box of the late 17th to 18th centuries, the most elaborate being German or Dutch imports with locks and bolts filling the underside of the lid and with hidden and false keyholes, hasps for padlocks, etc.

Armillary sphere From the Middle Ages, a skeleton celestial globe with a series of metal rings representing the equator, etc., revolving on an axis within a wooden horizon.

Armoire Mainly a Continental term for a clothes-cupboard.

Armorials Owner's coat of arms or crest decorating dinner-ware, hall furniture, silver, etc. *See* Lowestoft.

Armorial ware Introduced 1892 by W. H. Goss. His son, Adolphus, copied local antiquities to make small souvenir models in ivory porcelain ornamented with coats of arms – of towns, colleges, schools, abbeys, etc., in many hundreds of designs.

Arras General term for wall-hangings; originally tapestry from Arras, France.

Art Deco Named from *L'Exposition des Arts Décoratifs*, Paris 1925, where harsh, but lively, geometrical patterns and exotic Egyptian motifs influenced English design.

Art furniture Also art needlework, etc. Late Victorian term signifying fashionable good taste in contrast to the ill-designed flaunting vulgarity of much commercial manufacture. Derived from the 1860s aesthetes' assertion that art should embrace all aspects of life.

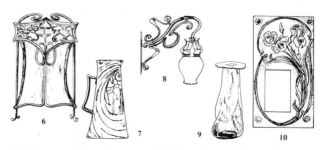

Art Nouveau. 6 Brass firescreen. **7** Minton Secessionist jug. **8** Iron and copper gas fitting. **9** Clutha glass. **10** Pewter photograph frame for amateur tooling.

Art needlework supplanted Berlin wool work by the 1870s, mainly worked in crewel stitch, an irregular stem stitch, in faded 'artistic' colours on linen for furnishings; some in silks on velvet.
Artificial porcelain *See* Soft-paste porcelain.
Art jewellers *See* Jewellery.
Art Nouveau. New art International decorative style of the late 19th century and into the early 20th. Breaking away from historic academic styles in favour of original qualities expressed in asymmetrical shapes, ethereal figures, tall sinous plant growth and whiplash curves on every kind of domestic furnishings, but perhaps most appealing in jewellery and glass.
Art pewter *See* Tudric pewter.
Arts and Crafts movement Late 19th-century support for artist-craftsmen led by John Ruskin, William Morris and such professional designers as C. R. Ashbee, Walter Crane and Lewis Day. Expressed in a series of exhibitions from 1888 and the founding of many local guilds to encourage professional and amateur designer-craftsmen in wood, metals, ceramics, embroideries, etc., aiming for honest work in contrast to flimsy commercial glitter.

Art unions Subscribers participated in annual lotteries for works of art and many specially commissioned minor prizes such as engravings. References are sometimes found among marks on, e.g., parian-ware figures, Doulton stoneware, commissioned prints. From Paris and Berlin the idea came to Scotland in 1834, London in 1836 and was so popular that it spread to other cities.

Arundel prints Engravings and chromolithographs published by the Arundel Society for Promoting Knowledge of Art (1848–97). About 200 were produced (illustrating important architecture, sculpture, etc., e.g., frescoes by Vasari and Giotto). Named after Thomas Howard, Earl of Arundel, 17th-century art patron.

Ash wood Whitish, tough, springy with long fibrous grain, much used in country furniture, tool handles and seats of Windsor chairs.

Ashbee, C. R. *See* Guild and School of Handicraft.

Assay Testing of gold and silver to ensure that it contained no more than the permitted proportion of alloy before stamping it with hallmarks, *See* Carat; Hallmarks; Sterling.

Astbury wares Elusive Astbury family, including John (1686–1743), were reputedly associated with improvements in early 18th-century Staffordshire ceramics such as white salt-

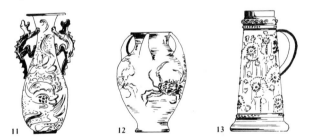

Art pottery. 11 Barum ware. **12** Martin brothers vase. **13** Doulton relief-ornamented salt-glazed stoneware.

17

glazed stoneware and red earthenware and with early pew-group figures.

Asterism Star effect sometimes seen in, e.g., a cabochon-cut sapphire or ruby.

Astley Cooper chair Child's high chair with tall straight back and outcurving legs. Designed by orthopaedic surgeon Sir Astley Cooper (1768–1841).

Astragal 1. Small convex moulding or beading to conceal a join, e.g., edging one of a pair of cabinet doors. 2. Simple framing for cabinet glazing, usually mahogany.

Astral lamp Development of the Argand lamp, with the oil contained in a flattened ring so that light could shine directly downwards.

Atlantes In classical ornament, plural form of Atlas; hence furniture pillars or pilasters in form of male figures or demi-figures, females being caryatides.

Attic From Attica (Greece) or its capital Athens, applied, e.g., to ancient Greek pottery.

Aubusson French town long renowned for tapestries, technically inferior only to Beauvais and Gobelins, and for carpets.

Ault, William *See* Swadlincote.

Aumbry. Ambry Popular 15th- to 16th-century domestic and ecclesiastical term, apparently for an enclosed storage cupboard or storage niche with doors.

Automaton Animated figure (usually clockwork) becoming elaborate in the 19th century with a musical-box accompaniment. Christopher Pinchbeck and James Cox were important 18th-century English makers.

Autotype From 1853, a print facsimile made by a photographic process.

Aventurine 1. Form of quartz crystal (yellow, brown, green or red) glittering with yellow mica. 2. Name taken from early Venetian glass containing brass filings and imitated from the 17th century with fragments of gold wire in varnish and with murky brownish glass (sometimes green) containing golden spangles, found in 18th-century 'toys'; also Victorian glass sparkling with iron filings.

Axminster carpet Seamless hand-knotted pile in Turkish style from the 1750s. In the 1830s manufacture moved from Axminster to Wilton.

Ayrshire work *See* White embroidery.

Baby cage From Tudor days, for toddler to learn to walk. Wooden framework encircling his waist, with splayed spindles resting on wooden castors.

Baccarat, France Fine quality glassware from late in the 18th century becoming renowned in the 19th, especially for millefiori paperweights.

Bacchantes Frequent ornamental motifs representing those taking part at festivals of the wine-god Bacchus (originally only women) with flowing garments and dishevelled hair. Maenads (mad Bacchantes) wore vine leaves and serpents in their hair and carried a cone-topped staff or thyrsus which caused milk and honey to flow from the earth.

Bacchus glass Birmingham firm of Bacchus & Green (George Bacchus & Sons after *c*.1840) were important manufacturers of decorative coloured glassware including millefiori paperweights; also pressed glass.

Bachelor's button Attached by a split pin through a metal shank; (now considered among early 'costume jewellery').

Bachelor's chest Low chest of drawers with folding top that opens as a writing-table. From 18th century onward.

Backgammon board Medieval term was 'pair of tables', the game being called 'Tables' – a folding board suitable for backgammon, draughts or chess.

Back painting Painting on the underside of glass, such as the mirror ornament commissioned from China through the 18th century on glass shipped from Europe and finally silvered in England. *See* Glass prints; Silhouettes; Verre églomisé.

Backstool Stool constructed with four matching legs and an attached back as distinct from a single (armless) chair. Mainly 17th–18th century.

Baguette (Fig. 41) Rectangular cut for small diamonds.

Bail handle (Figs. 25–29) Half-hoop suspended between knobs fixed to a backplate, on drawers, etc. More strongly attached from *c.* 1720s in a sequence of datable styles. Found in silver on table baskets and cream pails.

Bain marie Large flattish metal pan for boiling water to heat food in smaller vessels fitting inside it.

Baleen Whalebone. *See* Scrimshaw.

Ball-and-claw (Fig. 118) Eagle's or dragon's claw grasping a flattened ball. In furniture a fashionable carved foot on a cabriole leg especially during the second quarter of the 18th century when alternatives included a lion's paw.

Balloon back Chair-back popular in the 1820s–50s, shaped as an open or cane-filled oval supported on short nipped-in side-rails.

Balloon clock (Fig. 69) Mantel clock with case shaped like a balloon, late 18th and early 19th century.

Baluster (Figs. 116, 215) Swelling vase-shape or pear-shape. 1. Especially associated with furniture of the late 17th to early 18th centuries, as a turned leg and in flat outline for a chair back. 2. The stem of a baluster drinking-glass (*c.* 1680s–1760s).

Bamboo Giant Indian reed made into furniture, imported in the late 18th and early 19th centuries; copied in beech and other cheap woods, turned and stained. Extremely popular in the late 19th century.

Bamboo ware Made from *c.* 1770 by Josiah Wedgwood, followed by other potters. A fine-stoneware shaped as teapots, etc., suggesting strips of bamboo lashed together with cane.

Banding Strips of veneer usually edging a table-top, drawer front, etc. Included: straight banding cut with the wood's grain; cross banding cut across the grain; feather banding cut at a slant; herringbone banding composed of two narrow strips of opposing feather banding, especially popular in early 18th-century walnut. Corners were mitred in good quality English work.

Banjo barometer (Fig. 15) Wheel barometer in banjo-shaped case, popular from the 1770s. *See* Aneroid.

Banker. Banncove Medieval term for cloth to cover a long bench (bank).

Banner firescreen Pole screen with adjustable crossbar supporting loosely hanging tapestry, beadwork, etc., weighted by tassels. Popular from the 1800s.

Bantam work Originally incised lacquer screens, etc., imported from Java by the English and then the Dutch in the late 17th century.

Banqueting dish Made, so-named, in pewter to the end of the 18th century. A shallow plate, sometimes with a flat projecting handle, for fruit or sweets served at informal parties. *See* Dessert glasses.

Barber's bowl With a section cut away to fit under client's chin.

Barber's chair In the 18th century, usually a corner chair with headrest; in the 19th century developing designs with ratchet-adjustable headrests; in the later 19th century also swivelling and tilting seats.

Barbotine painting On late 19th-century earthenwares, e.g., by Minton's Austrian decorator W. Mussill and on Watcombe terracotta. Birds, fish, etc., painted in bright naturalistic colours thickened with a thin kaolin clay paste.

Barcheston tapestry *See* Sheldon.

Bargello embroidery work. Florentine stitch. Flame stitch
Surface-covering embroidery in a vertical counted-thread stitch, typically in closely related colours forming, e.g. zig-zag or similar repetitive geometrical patterns to cover furniture, etc. from the late 17th century. English embroiderers often used crewels in place of the Italians' untwisted silks.

Barge wares (Fig 283) 1. Metal jugs etc., decorated with bright flowers, castles, etc. 2. Ornately colourful earthenware, suggesting canal-boat painting, popular in the late 19th century. Included gallon and half-gallon teapots, probably from several minor potteries including Church Gresley (Leicestershire). Often with applied ornament such as a miniature teapot as the lid finial.

Barm pot One-piece vessel with a domed top and fist-size circular opening high in the side for holding barm, the yeast formed on fermenting malt liquors, used in baking. When used for salt, known as a salt kit.

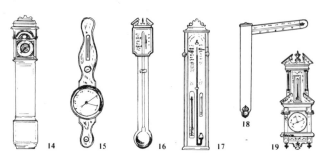

Barometers. 14 Halifax. **15** Wheel. **16** Stick (Regency version).
17 Fitzroy. **18** Yard-arm. **19** Aneroid in Edwardian frame.

Barometer Instrument for measuring atmospheric pressure as an aid in weather forecasting. Made for home use from late in the 17th century using a glass tube of mercury, until the introduction of the aneroid. The vertical mercury tube limited the instrument's shape as the air pressure movements were observed near its top, 28 to 31 inches above its lowest point (a rise in the visible surface level of the mercury foretelling fine weather). Hence the wood frame in self-explanatory stick, banjo, etc. outlines. *See* Aneroid, Fitzroy, Hallifax, Portable, Wheel and Yard-arm barometers.

Baroque pearl *See* Pearls.

Baroque style Massive florid style in revolt against earlier Renaissance classicism, manifest in extreme English fashions of the 1660s–1730s, such as carved cabinet-stands, Caroline silver, engraved maps, etc.

Barrel designs Barrel-shaped with lines suggesting staves and hoops, popular in the 1800s in silver (beakers), glass (decanters), porcelain (tea jars), earthenware (mugs and jugs), etc.

Barum ware (Fig. 11) Art pottery in tall Art-Nouveau shapes with lively ornament in relief and trailed slipwork, from Barnstable, Devon, made by C. H. Brannam (1855–1937) from the 1880s when Liberty's became his London agent.

Basaltes Josiah Wedgwood's improvement on the fine-stoneware known as Egyptian black, for ornaments, medallions, figures, tablewares from the 1760s. The twice-fired ware could be brilliantly polished, decorated with encaustic colours like Greek vases and mould-shaped in sharp detail. Made also by his rivals. Modern term is basalt.

Base. Basse Part of the 'bed furniture', of stiff fabric, three being required to mask the lower bed frame. *See* Bonegraces.

Basin stand (Figs. 22, 62) Bedroom or powder-closet furnishing for a tiny basin and water bottle, soap box, etc. From the mid 18th century it could be a delicate tripod stand (now often mistakenly called a wig stand) with an open ring for the basin. Gradually became larger and sturdier, known in the Regency as a lavabo. A more elaborate wash-hand table from the later 18th century could be closed to resemble a chest of drawers. Marble-topped wash-stands by the 1820s, becoming commodious Victorian furnishings.

Bas relief Ornament in less than half relief. Opposite to alto relievo.

Basse-taille enamelling Ornament hollowed into metal and flooded with translucent enamel to achieve tone contrasts corresponding with the depth of the enamel. *See* Email ombrant.

Bateman silver (Fig. 161) Made in London by the brothers John, Peter and Jonathan and the latter's son and grandson, both William, the business being sold *c.* 1840. Their mother, Hester

Bateman (widowed 1760, retired 1790), managed the firm, but it is unlikely that she worked herself as a silversmith. Unspectacular but often charming domestic silver sold by retailers in London and the provinces, characterised by beaded rims, bright-cut engraving and delicate piercing of the period's simple Neo-classical shapes.

Baton Long rectangular cut for diamonds, larger than a baguette.

Bat printing Comparatively slow, costly ceramics ornament developed around the 1800s to 1830s from transfer-printing, being used for small, fine detail on porcelain and bone china (such as New Hall and Spode). A flexible gelatinous sheet or bat took an impression in an oily medium from a prepared copper plate, usually stipple-etched and/or engraved, and conveyed it to the china. Colour applied in a glassy powder base adhered only to the oily print, to be fixed by firing. Not to be confused with the coarser stippled work printed with normal transfer papers.

Batswing fluting Ornament, especially of the late 18th century, on silver, each narrow channel ending in a dipping, concave arc; opposite of arch-ended petal fluting.

Battersea enamels Painted enamels made at Battersea, London, 1753—6. Notable for early and extremely delicate one-colour transfer-printed ornament on snuffboxes, wine labels, etc., but now mistakenly credited with many Birmingham and South Staffordshire enamels. *See* Enamels, painted.

Baxter print George Baxter (1804—67) patented (1836) a process for full-colour printing in oil colours from wood and soft-metal blocks over steel-engraved outlines in grey, brown or purple. Historical, sentimental, genre scenes, etc. Great collector-interest around 1900 led to over-pricing and many fakes. A few other print-makers used his process under licence and in 1868 Abraham Le Blond bought 69 sets of blocks to re-issue prints (now known as Le Blond-Baxters) of inferior finish.

Bay wood *See* Mahogany

Beadwork Wear-resistant trimming to gloves, book covers, etc., using English glass beads from the 17th century. Collectors seek mid 17th-century children's pictorial work such as Biblical scenes couched to fabric and mounted on cushions, caskets, mirror frames. Small bright beads popular in later 18th-century bags, purses. In the 19th century beads were stitched in rows and 'woven' into flat panels (for bracelets, etc.) on bead loom. Cheaper beads and better colours after 1845; jet, moonlight, 'rainbow' colours in the 1860s when big coarse beads and bugles, especially white and grey, were used for tasselled screens, etc.

Beaker Ancient style of drinking-vessel without handle, stem or cover. Usually straight, slightly tapering sides and plain base. In silver, pewter, horn, ceramics, glass.

Beauvais Important French tapestry centre from 1664. Popular tapestries including much for upholstery in the 18th and 19th centuries and knotted pile carpets.

Bed furniture The fabric curtains, bonegraces, vallances, bases, cantonnieres, coverlets and bedpost caps that draped the wooden bedstock around the mattresses, blankets, pillows, etc., that constituted the standing bed.

Bed wagon Hooped frame around a pan of charcoal, used for airing beds.

Beechwood Warm, light brown, close-grained with small satiny markings. Used for much cheap painted and upholstered furniture and for turnery, but subject to woodworm.

Beetham, Mrs Isabelle Silhouettist at work in London, *c.* 1760s–1809, the address on her labels being 27, Fleet Street. Delicate, fashion-conscious work usually painted in varying intensities of black, often on the inner side of slightly convex glass, sometimes with a decorative border. Also painted on card and plaster.

Beilby glass Decorated by William Beilby and his young sister, Mary, of Newcastle-upon-Tyne, at work *c.* 1762–78 – conspicuously fine armorial work, trophies, Rococo scrolls, in colours and dense white enamel fixed by firing which William had learned at Bilston. Occasional butterfly 'signatures', but many fakes.

Bellarmine German imports copied in brownish salt-glazed stoneware, 17th–19th centuries. Full-bellied, handled bottle with relief ornament of a mask so ugly that it acquired the name of the hated cardinal (1542–1621).

Belleek porcelain Made in County Fermanagh, Ireland, from 1858. Extremely thin parian porcelain with an iridescent glaze prompting marine motifs; also flower encrustations and delicate basket-work.

Bell flowers (Fig. 124) Repetitive ornament consisting of pendant three-petal flower-buds frequently introduced in succession as pendant swags, etc., in Neo-classical work. Also called husks.

Bells Silver including the 18th-century inkstand fitting; coloured glass, 19th century and modern, with clear clapper. *See* Nailsea; Horse bells; Horse brasses.

Bended-back chair. Fiddleback (Fig. 55) Comfortable early 18th-century chair with a baluster splat curved to fit the sitter's back below a centrally dipping crest-rail.

Bentwood furniture In beech wood usually black stained, curved by pressure and steam (like the hooped Windsor chair). Process perfected by Austrian Michael Thonet who labelled his work and displayed at the 1851 Great Exhibition; widely popular in England from the 1860s for cane-seated chairs, etc., by such makers as Hewett & Co.

Benoîton chain Jewellery worn 1865 to *c*.1870, an arrangement of chains hanging from the coiffure or bonnet down over the chest; a brief fashion inspired by a play, *La Famille Benoîton*.

Bergère French term for armchair. Developed in England as a deep, low-backed chair with horizontal arms often filled with upholstery or caning; by late 18th century sometimes a nursing chair. Bold Regency styles with massive arm rests, but a simple caned version was revived by the late Victorians.

Berlin cast-iron jewellery In 1813 given to patriotic Prussian women in return for their gold in the fight against Napoleon; in-scribed *'Gold gab ich für Eisen'*. But black lacquered iron jewellery had a much longer history before and after the war, some with a delicacy suggesting black lace; also buckles, watch-keys, fans. Also made at Frankfurt am Main, and, after the war, in Paris, Berlin iron jewellery in the Gothic manner persisted into the 1860s.

Berlin wool work Embroidery on squared-mesh canvas in soft merino wools mainly in cross-stitch and variants copied from squared paper patterns. German patterns available from *c.* 1805, but English work abundant, *c.* 1830s–80s, including many thousands of printed patterns, pictures of the royal family, Landseer paintings, Biblical themes; for framing, mounting on furniture, etc.; some incorporating beads. Aniline dyes facilitated crude bright colouring.

Berry spoon Victorian or later enrichment of a plain Georgian silver spoon-bowl embossed from below with fruit ornament.

Beryl Hard precious stone distinguished from emerald only by its colour – pale bluish seagreen in the aquamarine and yellowish in the chrysoberyl (including cat's eye).

Bestiary Medieval book describing and depicting animals.

Betty lamp *See* Lamps.

Bevel Slanting edge to a flat surface. Characteristic of mirror glass from the 17th century when it was hand-ground on thin glass, wide and too shallow to show prismatic colour.

Bezel Metal rim that secures a watch or clock glass in its frame, or a gemstone in its setting; hence the wide part of a finger ring.

Bianco-sopra-bianco Usual English term (from Italian maiolica) for white ornament in slight relief on near white (usually bluish or pale lavender) tin-enamelled earthenware (English delftware). Especially used at Bristol from the 1740s.

Bible box Small chest for family records, medieval or later, and much reproduced, black and heavily carved, by Victorians and Edwardians.

20 Billies and Charlies.

Bicker Shallow wooden drinking cup of staved pail construction.
Biedermeier style. Especially 1820s–30s, named from a character in the journal *Fliegende Blätter*. Exuberant bourgeois Austro-German caricature of French Empire Baroque with opulent carving and massive embossed metal mounts.
Biggin Traditional bag-shaped child's cap; hence coffee biggin (silver, Sheffield plate) from the 1780s: a squat, cylindrical, lidded jug containing a cap-shaped fabric filter, heated over a lamp. Silversmith George Biggin was a maker in 1800s.
Bijouterie Collective term for jewellery, but sometimes used to distinguish products of goldsmith and enameller from those of jeweller gem-setter and hence applied to trinkets which are carried (snuffbox, etui, etc.), as distinct from those worn.
Billies and Charlies Mainly poor quality copper and lead cheaply cast by William Smith and Charles Eaton as what they imagined ancient figurines, pendants, etc., to look like; they then 'discovered' them in the Thames mud, during the second quarter of the 19th century. Proved fakes in 1858, but still collected. Numbers still existing suggest that there were other makers also.
Billingsley, William (1760–1828) briefly made soft-paste porcelain at financially starved Pinxton, Nantgarw and Swansea, and was imaginative painter of delicately textured flowers at Derby and Coalport
Bilston (Staffordshire) enamels Now the usual name for painted enamels of the Bilston-Birmingham area, made through the 18th century from *c.*1740. More colourful than Battersea with much

gilded scrolling, although deteriorating in late work. *See* enamels.

Bin label Triangular tag for hanging on wine bin; some with rounded outline. From the early 17th century in thick ($c.\frac{3}{8}$ inch) flawy tin-enamelled earthenware, with wine name lettered in rich blue. Smaller in late 18th-century Wedgwood pearlware, part-glazed white with black lettering, leaving space at the top for pencil notes on unglazed biscuit. Spode made them with underglaze transfer-printed names. Made also by Minton and Davenport.

Birchwood White, turning pale pink or yellowish-brown, close grained, polishing well; sometimes used as a substitute for 18th-century satinwood in solid or veneer. Also from the later 19th century for plywood and mass-produced furniture.

Birdcage (Fig. 222) On an 18th-century pillar-and-claw table, the hinge device allowing the top to tilt or lift off when a wedge was withdrawn.

Birdcage clock *See* Lantern clock.

Bird's-eye maple wood Glowing yellowish brown with dark spots linked by wavy lines. Popular with Victorians for small frames, etc. *See* Oeil de perdrix.

Birmingham enamels An obvious source of the copper blanks and metal mounts and also many well-finished snuffboxes, etc., now attributed to Bilston. *See* Enamels.

Birmingham silver (Fig. 144) With the distinctive anchor mark of its own assay office from 1773.

Biscuit. Bisque In ceramics, once-fired unglazed ware. Might be left 'in the white' for delicately detailed (bisque) figures, in e.g.: 1. Derby soft porcelain (given satin sheen with a trace of smear glazing), and Bristol plaques. 2. Rockingham and other somewhat chalky white bone china ornaments. *See* Parian ware.

Blackbean wood Australian, golden-brown richly patterned with dark streaks and mottlings, taking a brilliant polish. Used for veneers, turnery, etc.

Blackjack Drinking-vessel with looped handle, entirely waterproofed with pitch, shaped in stitched leather. Jug in this style known as a bombard.

Black walnut wood 'Virginia walnut', darker than the European wood and straight-grained. American imports used through the 18th century until the 1770s (ending with the war) in solid for furniture, sometimes polished as a substitute for mahogany, and may be mistaken for faded mahogany. Fashionable in the US in the second quarter of the 19th century. *See* Walnut wood.

Blackwork embroidery Described by Chaucer (born *c.*1340) in his *Miller's Tale*, as already in fashion. Presumably derived from Arabic work in Spain, perhaps encouraged by Catherine of Aragon. Worked in black silk on white shirts, ruffs, hoods and household linen mainly in double-running stitch at first, but later showing a variety of stitch and texture in designs suggesting contemporary woodcuts from emblem books, furniture-lining papers, etc. Continued into the 17th century, sometimes spangled; in the 18th century's small print-like views, and in 18th- to 19th-century samplers and maps.

Blanket chest Storage chest for bedding typically over one or two drawers. Some of moth-defying cypress wood from the 16th century and many of sweet dry cedar wood from Holland. Plain handsome mahogany designs continued through the 18th century, some cedar-lined.

Blazes In glass, a series of parallel upright or slanting V-section cuts, their points forming a succession of crests and troughs around a vessel.

Bleeding bowl Now popular name for numerous 17th- to early 18th-century silver and pewter bowls, probably better defined as caudle cups and porringers.

Blister pearl Irregular swelling, often hollow, in the nacre of a pearl oyster. Popular in late 19th-century jewellery.

Bloodstone Opaque dark green form of chalcedony with red to crimson streaks or speckles, popular in high Victorian Scottish jewellery.

Bloomed gold In jewellery from *c*. 1840s, the gold surface treated chemically to remove its alloy leaving vulnerable but radiant pure gold.

Bloor, Robert Derby china factory proprietor, *c*. 1811–48 (but ill from 1828 and with economic problems). Term 'Bloor Derby' refers to his price-cutting decoration (including such colours as chromium green) on thickly glazed bone china, on some accumulations of earlier (Duesbury) porcelain and on figures taken from Duesbury moulds.

Blown glass *See* Free-blown glass.

Blown-moulded glass (Fig. 79) Vessel-shaped and relief-patterned on the glass-blower's blowpipe by inflating hot glass into a metal mould. Widely used from the 17th century onwards, mostly with one-piece moulds until 1800s, then two-piece and (1820s) three-piece. Small two-piece part-size moulds were in early use for patterning glass, e.g., with diamond shapes, before further inflation which enlarged but dimmed the pattern. Recognizable because the pattern undulations are discernible also inside the vessel, unlike pressed glass.

Blue and white In ceramics, a general term for white ware ornamented with zaffre. The term originally described imported Chinese Ming, imitated in English delftware, porcelain, bone china and earthenwares, painted and transfer-printed.

Blue-dash charger Modern term for often-reproduced work. Dutch ornament copied in England on 17th–18th century delftware, the plaque or wall-plate rim sponge-dabbed with slanting patches of blue to suggest rope-twist.

Blued steel Oxide colouring on steel heat treated against rust. Essential in the 18th century for such elegancies as snuff and nutmeg rasps.

Blue glass Made in Mesopotamia as early as 2000 BC. Made in Bristol through the 18th and 19th centuries and eventually also at Newcastle, Sunderland, Waterford, etc. Coloured with prepared cobalt oxide for vessels holding liquors that lacked clarity or colour-appeal, for protecting perfumes from light, and as a foil for gilding. Also for lining perforated silver sugars, salts, etc.

Blue john Gemstone variety of fluorspar with rich mottlings of deep purple-blue, amethyst and honey colours (*bleu-jaune*) mined in Derbyshire. Massive ornaments fashionable from the 1770s (brittle and sometimes strengthened with pine resin for clever turnery on water-driven lathes). Smaller souvenirs, tazze, 'eggs', costume jewellery, since exhaustion of the main seams.

Blue tint *See* Waterford glass.

Boarded chest Carpenter's work from the 13th century with flush surfaces front and back for iron straps. Of nailed planks (subject to shrinkage) with pegged strengthening bars.

Bobbin lace Made by intertwining a number of threads wound on bobbins, in contrast to single-thread needlepoint. Term often implies a coarse type of this pillow lace, with heavy threads on large bobbins.

Bobbin turning. Reel turning Repetitive turning in swell-and-ring outline suggesting a succession of small reels wound with thread, as distinct from still plainer ball turning. Popular in the second half of the 17th century.

Bocage In English porcelain from 1760s, a support behind a figure or group (to aid kiln firing), shaped as a leafy tree stump or flower-encrusted arbour. Simplified versions are to be found behind figures in early 19th-century earthenware (*See* Walton).

Body Basic potter's clay mix, in earthwares and stonewares; the equivalent term to porcelain and bone china paste.

Bog wood Black timber long buried (often deliberately) in Irish peat bogs. Some oak used in Tudor-Stuart inlay; bog yew fashionable with romantic-Gothic early Victorians, being ornately displayed at the 1851 Exhibition.

Bohemian glass From Central Europe, part of the Austrian empire; popular with Victorians. Long lacked the resonance and lustre of best English flint-glass, but was renowned for rich colours – bright red, yellow, etc. – and ornate engraving.

21 Bombé furniture outline (commode). **22** Bow outline (Shearer washstand). **23** Serpentine outline (Pembroke table).

Bois durci Hard non-flammable French-invented plastic composed of sawdust (ebony and rosewood) and albumen moulded under heat. Patented 1855 by Charles Lepage and made by Latry of Paris into clear, glossy plaques, picture frames, boxes, dominoes, jewellery, imitating carved ebony. Plaques usually marked BOIS DURCI in relief. Many unmarked French and English imitations.

Bolection moulding Covering the joint between two surfaces of different levels such as a panel and its framing.

Bombard *See* Blackjack.

Bombé French term for swelling outline in case furniture, seen in expertly veneered English 'French commodes', etc.

Bonbonnière Small box for comfits (lacking the patch-box's 'steel' mirror). Found in 18th-century silver, tortoiseshell, painted enamels, etc., including bird and other fancy shapes.

Bone Often found as a substitute for ivory, but brittle and of a splintery texture. *See* Prisoner-of-war work.

Bone china (Fig. 208) Made by Josiah Spode from 1794, becoming vastly important for attractive table-wares. Translucent but stronger and cheaper than soft porcelain. Typical formula consisted of hard porcelain ingredients with their combined weight in ground calcined bone, fired at *c.* 1250°C. Not to be confused with bone porcelain.

33

Bonegraces Pair of narrow curtains at the head of a fou[r] bed to prevent draughts between the main curtains; thos[e] bed foot being known as cantonieres (including short o[n] supplement the valances).

Bone lace 16th- to 17th-century term for lace worked on t[he] pillow around rust-free 'pins' of prepared fish or chicken bones[,] especially heavy metal-thread lace where the bobbins might be animal bones. *See* Pillow lace.

Bone porcelain Soft-paste porcelain strengthened with bone ash, from Bow, Chelsea, etc. *See* Bone china.

Bonheur du jour Lady's light, elegant writing-table with a low cabinet behind the writing area which might open forward over a fitted drawer. Introduced from France in the late 18th century and popular with Victorians.

Bottle glass Unrefined, cheaply taxed glass in green, amber and brownish tones popular with collectors in so-called Nailsea glass.

Bottle jack *See* Spitjack.

Bottles *See* Wine bottles.

Bottle ticket *See* Wine label.

Bouge Upward curve from the central area to the rim in a plate or dish.

Bougie box For a small, safe taper light, like a mouse-proof wax-jack. Silver, sometimes lined with blue glass, cylindrical, with a short tube in the lid holding the tip of a flexible wax taper kept coiled inside. Sometimes with a draught-shield. Mainly 1780s to 1840s.

Boule. Boulle. Buhl Delicate marquetry of tortoiseshell (or horn or ebony) inset with brass or silver, the two materials cut together to compose exactly interlacing patterns. Termed counter-boulle when left-over brass was inset with the pattern of left-over tortoiseshell. The brass might be engraved and the tortoiseshell laid over foil; intervening areas might be veneered with ebony and the edges protected with rich ormolu mounts. An Italian craft practised by Frenchman A. C. Boule (or Boulle) (1642–1732), superlative royal cabinet-maker, and widely since. Made in London from 1815.

Boulton, Matthew (1728–1809). At his important Soho factory in Birmingham he pioneered English ormolu, executing designs for the Adam brothers and contributing notably to the period's silver, Sheffield plate, cut-steel, etc.

Bourne pottery *See* Denby.

Bow (Fig. 247) Mid-1740s to 1776. Important London soft-paste porcelain factory making wares in Chinese mood, including very fine blue-painted practical table-wares as well as flowery-costumed figures comparable with those of Chelsea. *See* Duesbury; Frye; New Canton.

Bow front (Fig. 22) In furniture, the convex or smoothly rounded front of, e.g., a chest of drawers; a late 18th-century successor to the serpentine front.

Bow tongs *See* Sugar tongs.

Box iron 1. Smoothing iron with a lidded compartment for a fire-heated piece of metal to keep it hot. 2. Such a piece of iron for placing in the inner compartment of a tea or coffee urn, gravy argyle, etc. to keep contents hot during a meal; patented in 1774 and still popular with Victorians.

Box setting In jewellery, the metal pressed closely round the gemstone, keeping moisture from the coloured foil behind the jewel or paste. Improved as the collet setting.

Boxwood Hard, almost grainless pale brown, polishing to a silky lustre. Much used for inlay and marquetry; also for wood engravings.

Brace-back chair (Fig. 307) *See* Windsor chair.

Bracket Small shelf resting on a projection fixed to a wall. Popular from late in the 17th century, often gilded, in current furniture styles.

Bracket clock (Fig. 67) Modern term for a wooden table clock (spring driven, free of dangling weights).

Bracket foot Somewhat triangular in shape. Supporting case furniture by extending horizontally a few inches under the bottom front and side rails, the vertical corner line straight or swelling.

Braid Narrow band of fabric, hand-plaited or machine-made in a fancy weave. In the 17th century printed instructions were available for making it from as many as a dozen strands. Used for edging pelmets, upholstered furniture, etc., and popular with early Victorians for costume ornament. In metal thread (on uniforms, etc.) known as galloon.

Bramah lock Joseph Bramah (1748–1814) responsible for a wide range of important inventions, attracted great public interest in 1784 by patenting a lock with a rotating barrel: several differently notched sliders had to be brought into coincidence before the bolt was freed, each lock requiring its individually shaped (and conveniently small) key. His name is found on considerably later locks.

Brameld *See* Rockingham.

Brampton stoneware Brown salt-glazed with close, acid-resistant surface made near Chesterfield, Derbyshire, mainly in the 19th century, occasionally with an 18th-century date. Mugs, etc., with relief ornament, including a popular mask-spouted jug with a greyhound handle.

Brandreth Wrought-iron ring mounted on three legs and with a long horizontal handle for supporting a skillet, gridiron, etc., over the early down-hearth fire.

Brass (Figs 6, 172–4) Various alloys composed of copper and zinc, notably improved by James Emerson making a golden-toned brass, patented 1781, which became usual in the 19th century. Most English work was in imported brass until late in the 17th century. Collectors judge its date by composition, colour, manufacturing methods: small solid castings from the late 17th century; machine-rolled sheets for hand-hammered vessels from the 1730s; machine-stamped shape and ornament from the 1770s; spun hollowware from the 1790s; complex castings from the 1860s. *See* Latten.

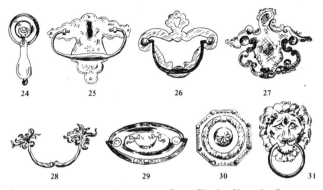

24   25   26   27

28   29   30   31

Brass drawer handles. In sequence from Charles II to the Regency. **24** Drop. **25** Early weak bail. **26** Early Georgian, stronger design. **27, 28** Rococo, 1750s, 1760s. **29** Neo-classical (stamped from thin brass). **30** 1800s. **31** Regency lion and ring.

Brazier Shallow metal pan for burning smokeless court charcoal for heating, cooking, pipe-lighting.

Brazil wood Orange-red colour with dark stripes, hard and polishing well. Conspicuous on Regency furniture; Sheraton noted its importance to dyers.

Break. Broken In furniture, any shaping that breaks the continuity of line or surface; hence 18th-century break-front case furniture with the central portion set slightly forward from the flanking sections.

In a *broken pediment* (Figs. 16, 19, 64) the line of the arch or gable interrupted for a bust or other ornament.

Bretby ware Earthenwares from Woodville, Derbyshire, established as an art pottery in 1883 by William Ault (later of Swadlincote) and Henry Tooth from Linthorpe; continued as Tooth & Co. from 1887, using flowing Linthorpe glazes. Much imitation of other materials from *c.*1890, the wares being called

Bretby and associated potteries (The two smaller vessels designed by C. Dresser). **32** Two by Linthorpe. **33** Bretby, imitating coopered wood. **34** Two by Adult.

'carved bamboo', 'copperette' (suggesting art metal work), 'cloisonné' (colours outlined in gold), etc., including unfired paintwork. A few early designs by Christopher Dresser; some figures and busts from *c.* 1890. Impressed design numbers may be mistaken for dates, but had reached 2000 by *c.* 1910.

Bright-cutting Silver ornament, especially 1780s–1800s. Tiny flakes cut away with bevelled gravers, giving a faceted light-catching brilliance.

Brilliant cut For diamonds from about 1700, a method of cutting more effective than the rose cut in exploiting the stone's refractive fire. Horizontal faces were cut on the upper and lower sides – the largest facet or table on the stone's crown and the smallest facet or culet on the base or pavilion. Thirty-two facets were cut above the stone's largest circumference or girdle and 24 between girdle and culet. This was a wasteful cut and only after the late Victorian South-African finds did the lapidaries obtain maximum splendour by reducing also the stone's thickness and cutting only a minimal culet. *See* Refractive brilliance.

Brins In a folding fan, the lower portion of the sticks that support the leaf or mount – displayed when the fan is opened and therefore a field for decoration; in carved ivory, mother-of-pearl, etc.

Briolet (Fig. 36) For gemstones, pear-shaped drop, cut all over with triangular facets.

Brisé fan (Fig. 107) In English use in the 18th century but associated especially with the tiny fans of the early 19th century. Composed of guards and sticks linked by ribbons round its outer edge, without a glued-on leaf. Often of painted and perforated

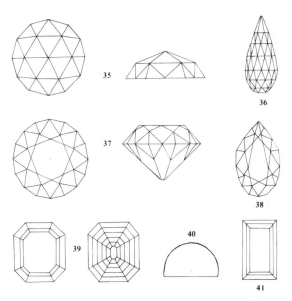

Brilliant and other jewel cutting. TOP ROW **35** (*left and centre*) Rose cut; **36** Briolet. CENTRE ROW: **37** (*left and centre*) Brilliant cut; **38** Pendeloque. BOTTOM ROW: **39** (*left and centre-left*) Step cut, top and bottom views; **40** Cabochon cut; **41** Baguette.

ivory or bone, tortoiseshell or paper-thin laburnum or sandalwood.

Bristlington and Bristol delft Important area for English delftware from about the mid 17th century until the late 18th century. Harder body than the Dutch and tending to have a thicker, harder, greyer white and softer colour than the London delft of Lambeth and Southwark. Punchbowls, tiles, etc., including bianco-sopra-bianco.

Bristol blue *See* Bristol glass.

Bristol diamonds. Bristol stones. Bristows Clear colourless quartz crystals, found in Clifton limestone.

In the early 18th century, these were rose-cut as *bristows* for jewellery. (Also a term mistakenly used for paste jewellery.) *See* Rock crystal.

Bristol glass Especially associated with clear blue, red and green glass, 1740s–1850s. But the term 'Bristol blue' derived from a Bristol dealer's brief monopoly, around 1760, of Saxony smalt blue for colouring glass, arising from Saxony's war with Prussia. Also renowned for densely white opaque enamel glass, painted like china.

Bristol glaze *See* Bristol pottery.

Bristol porcelain Some soft-paste soapstone porcelain, *c.*1748–51 under Benjamin Lund and William Miller. Hard-paste, 1770–81, made by William Cookworthy from Plymouth, followed in 1773 by Richard Champion, making table-wares and figures. Cookworthy's monopoly of Cornish china clay for translucent porcelain was extended for Champion to 1796, preventing the development of bone china until the 1790s.

Bristol pottery. Bristol glaze. Bristol ware 1. Good quality white-bodied earthenware with a cream-coloured glaze that gradually ousted delftware. 2. On stoneware (Bristol ware) the Temple Gate pottery in 1835 evolved their Bristol glaze, with vessels double-dipped to appear rich brown around the shoulders flowing into creamy yellow towards the base.

Britannia mark on silver (Fig. 143) Not to be confused with the figure of Hibernia (Fig. 155) with her harp on Irish silver. *See* Britannia standard silver; Drawback silver mark.

Britannia metal (Fig. 285) Widely successful leadless pewter (alloy of tin with a little antimony and copper) developed by John Vickers of Britannia Place, Sheffield. Important from the 1790s; by 1817 Sheffield had over 70 makers. Resembled silver when new. Long despised by collectors but now accepted as 'hard pewter', resembling best quality early pewter, but treated by current machine techniques of complex die-stamping, casting and spinning for all domestic metal-wares. Some electroplated: marked EPBM.

Britannia standard silver. High standard silver (Figs. 142, 143, 159) Compulsory 1697–1720 for silversmiths to prevent their use of scarce sterling silver coin. Has less copper alloy (4.16%) than sterling (7.5%). Recognized by punch marks: a seated Britannia figure; a lion's head erased (with a wavy neckline); a maker's mark composed of first two letters of his surname; a date letter (very important because this silver has continued in some use ever since though with its lion's-head erased mark omitted from 1975).

British plate Patented 1836. Variant of Sheffield plate with a core of whitish nickel alloy instead of copper. Often with marks suggesting silver hallmarks.

Broad glass Early window glass, cheaper and generally inferior to crown glass; heated, blown and shaped into cylinders, then cracked with a cold iron and opened into flat sheets. Ground and polished for earliest looking-glasses.

Broad sheet. Broadside Large sheet of paper; for cheapness printed on one side only; hence a term for innumerable crude advertisements, propaganda and woodcut-illustrated 'ballads' and lurid local news (often fictional) long hawked in the streets by 'flying stationers' at a fraction of the cost of taxed newspapers. Collectors enjoy, e.g., 1828 Maria Marten murder reports.

Dickens referred to the success of the early 19th-century London trade rivals, Catnach and Pitts.

Brocade Furnishing and costume fabric patterned in relief, originally with metal thread.

Broderie anglaise. Madeira work Minor white-on-white embroidery for baby-wear, etc., with simple patterns of stiletto holes, their edges overstitched.

Broken pediment *See* Break.

Bronze Ancient hard alloy of copper and tin, rendered more fluid with traces of lead and zinc, for finely detailed castings from moulds (statuary, medals etc.). Brassy tone mellowing to dark brown and acquiring a green patina. Bell metal and gun metal are types of bronze. *See* Ormolu.

Bronze powders Finely ground from copper, tin and other metals (including aluminium from the 1860s) and alloys in a wide range of colours applied over size for glittering ornament on japanned wares and especially on papier mâché using a method patented in 1812, popular from the 1820s and again in the 1840s. *See* Dutch metal; Wolverhampton style.

Brooks, John Dublin engraver working in London *c.* 1727–60, important in connection with the English development of transfer-printing on Bilston, Birmingham and Battersea painted enamels and on ceramics, which he attempted to patent in 1751 before going to Battersea.

Brown gold *See* Gilding.

Brussels lace In late 17th century became known as *point d'Angleterre*. Antique Brussels lace, needlepoint and pillow, was valued for the fineness of its thread. Brussels net was machine-made for Victorian shawls, etc.

Buckle Ancient easily detachable metal fastener for shoe-straps, belts, etc., with a hinged prong pressing on a D-shaped loop. Fashionable in the 17th to 19th centuries, with jewels and precious metals more widely copied in pastes, cut-steel, etc. Through the 18th century there were buckles for men's hats, cravats, knee-

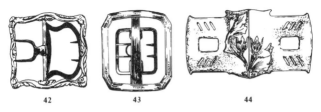

Buckles. 42 18th-century shoe buckle. **43** Eley's patent. **44** Liberty Cymric silver belt clasp.

breeches, etc., as well as for shoes where they were enormous in the 1770s–80s but soon began to be replaced by strings. Women wore them, jewelled, to fasten velvet bands at neck and wrist, at the waist and on their shoes. An improved, but heavy, shoe-buckle design was patented by William Eley, 1784, followed by an easily dislodged springy clip-on style. Art-jewellery 'buckles' were in fashion around 1900 (and machine-made imitations), but these were mainly two-part clasps.

Buffet 1. Term adopted from the 16th-century French for a tiered cupboard and the later court cupboard, forerunner of the sideboard. 2. From the 1690s also decorative shelving fixed in an alcove, a panelled forerunner of the double corner cupboard.

Buffet stool Probably early references meant the common joint stool, but to Victorians it was a padded footstool. *See* Hassock.

Buhl Victorians' usual spelling of boule.

Bulb Turned ornament on furniture (table-legs, etc.) from the later 16th century, the egg-shaped swelling often carved (cup-and-cover, acanthus, gadrooning, etc.).

Bullion In metal-enriched embroidery the heaviest style of purl.

Bull's eye Roughly shaped boss in the centre of a sheet of crown glass; generally any lens-shaped glass. In Victorian pressed glass, an oval hollow or printie.

Buncombe, John Isle of Wight silhouettist (*c.* 1745–1825) specialising in military portraits with costumes in full scarlet and only the faces black. These have been imitated.

Bun foot From the later 17th century in furniture a flattened sphere foot.

Bureau Mainly recent term for what the late 17th to 18th centuries knew specifically as a desk (sloping fronted), a secretary (vertical fronted) and a writing-table (flat topped).

The fitted *bureau dressing-table* had a folding mirror and other contents concealed so that guests could be received in their host's dressing-room.

Burmese glass *See* Queen's Burmese.

Burnishing To give a brilliant shine by friction with a hard smooth surface to mercury gilded ceramics, water gilded furniture, etc.

Burr or burl In wood, attractively marked grain for veneers from abnormal densely knotted growth, especially walnut, elm and yew.

Butler's tray. Supper tray Large rectangular wooden tray with hand holes in the vertical rim, sometimes with brass-hinged, folding sides. Intended for the butler's bottles and glasses, resting on a folding stand (X-shaped legs topped with strips of webbing), sometimes known as voider and voider stand. From 1720s but mainly the late 18th to early 19th centuries. *See* Coach table.

Butt hinge Sunk into the wood of a door, showing externally only the thin line of its knuckle.

Butterfly table Small 18th- to 19th-century table with hinged flaps supported by fly brackets instead of gate-legs.

Buttoning (Fig. 291) Strong method of securing upholstery on chairs, in coaches, etc., from the later 18th century, known as quilting, the buttons concealing stitches taken right through padding and covers. Emphatic contours on Victorian work.

Buttons Interesting to collect under many headings – jewelled, commemorative, livery, Art Nouveau, etc. Some silver hallmarked on their backs from *c.*1720. Cut-steel from the later 18th century; brass; Wedgwood and other ceramics; paste;

Victorian jet (and black glass); moulded glass; enamels; amber, ivory, tortoiseshell and their imitations, with changing styles of shank as some guide to their dating. *See* Dorset buttons.

Byzantine art Associated with Byzantium, when this important city became the seat of the eastern Roman empire, renamed Constantinople, AD 330. (Taken by the Turks 1453.) Elaborations of Oriental detail grafted onto classical forms.

Cabaret set In ceramics from the later 18th century onwards. Teaset for one or two people, including a matching tray usually of porcelain or bone china.

Cabinet-makers Craftsmen trained to make, e.g., veneer patterns and perfectly fitting details of small cupboards and dovetailed drawers, as required in later 17th-century display furniture, beyond the scope of the joiner.

Cable moulding *See* Trafalgar fashion.

Cabochon (Fig. 40) In jewellery, the oldest form of cutting (still used for opaque stones and star-stones) with rounded, unfaceted top. In furniture, from the 16th century in strapwork; in the 18th century popular in acanthus-leaf scrolling, e.g., for the knee of a cabriole leg.

Cabriole leg (Fig. 118) Derived from Oriental and classical design, but having lost much resemblance to a capering animal's leg. Out-curving at the knee, tapering and incurving above the projecting foot (hoof, paw, club, etc.). Fashionable *c*. 1690s–1750s, when modified to gentler curves (Fig. 123) but continuing much later on country furniture. The term cabriole lost definable meaning in the late 18th century.

Cabriolet fan (Fig. 106) From France, *c*. 1755, named after a dashing two-wheel carriage, the wheel-suggesting mount consisting of two or three narrow arc-shaped bands on simple spoke-like sticks and painted with light-hearted cabriolet scenes.

Cadogan teapot (Fig. 282) Puzzle pot with handle and spout, but no lid opening. Filled when upside down, with strained tea, through a tube spiralling inside the body from the base. First

45

made at Rockingham copying an Oriental wine pot lent by the Hon. Mrs Cadogan; then by other potters such as Spode. In pearl-ware from the 1790s, brown 'Rockingham glaze' from the 1800s, some green from the 1830s.

Caduceus Winged staff of Mercury entwined with snakes – a frequent decorative motif, symbol of peace, healing, happiness and riches; Mars was often portrayed carrying spear and caduceus to suggest peace succeeding war.

Cairngorm Yellowish variety of smoky quartz, popular in Scottish jewellery.

Calamander wood *See* Coromandel.

Calico. Calicut Cotton cloth originally from Calicut (coast of Malabar), imported from the 16th century; popular in the 18th century for painted and printed furnishings despite import bans 1701, 1720 ('any callicoe stitched or flowered in foreign parts'). *See* Chintz.

Calotype. Talbotype A negative-positive photographic process invented by W. H. Fox Talbot, 1839, somewhat resembling the daguerreotype.

Camaieu Method of painting in varying tones of one basic colour.

The term *en camaieu* is frequently applied to such ornament on porcelain.

Cameo In jewellery, etc., ornament such as a mythological figure or scene carved to stand out in partial relief (opposite to intaglio), frequently arranged so that its colours would contrast with its background tone by using the natural strata of the stone (onyx, cornelian, etc.) shell or coral.

Cameo glass Using a colour contrast contrived by casing white glass over dark and removing unwanted white with carving tools and/or acid so that the ornament appears in varying intensities of white against the dark ground. A highly skilled classical craft revived by John Northwood and others in the late 19th century. Not to be confused with pâte de verre. By use of acid and etching tools cameo effects were made on a considerable scale by major

46

glass manufacturers including Webb & Sons (some marked), Stevens & Williams and the Richardsons of Wordsley.

Cameo parian Domestic parian ware with colour introduced as a flat background to white ornament moulded in relief. Colour might be bright blue or sage green, with an 'orange skin' surface.

Campaign furniture Modern term for small, portable furniture such as the Wellington chest and folding washstand, associated especially with the Peninsular and Crimean wars.

Camphine lamp *See* Lamps.

Candlebeam Medieval term outmoded by the 17th century for a form of chandelier composed of two to six flat horizontal strips of wood centrally crossing each other, with candle sockets or prickets and metal cups at their ends; or a similar design in latten or brass.

Candle box For storing candles, laid flat and safe from mice. Rectangular or cylindrical, of wood from the Middle ages; usually metal from the 17th century – brass, japanned tin-plate, etc.

Candle douter. Extinguisher (Fig. 253) Cone shape in silver, Sheffield plate, brass, etc., often with a hook at the side to attach to a saucer-shaped chamber candlestick. Sometimes with a long handle from the cone tip for reaching a candle inside a glass draught-shield. An alternative design has a scissor action like snuffers, but ending in flat discs to pinch out the flame.

Candle screen 1. Half-cylinder of wood placed vertically behind the candle as a draught-shield. 2. An adjustable miniature table pole-screen to stand between the candle and its user's face.

Candle slide In 18th-century bureau bookcase, etc., a small rimless tray, often slightly dished, to pull out like a drawer for resting a candlestick. Often a pair to minimise shadow problems.

Candle-snuffers (Fig. 253) From the Middle Ages to the 1840s when outmoded by candles with improved inward-curling wicks. Trimmed the wick with a scissor action, acquiring increasingly reliable attachments for quenching and holding the charred wick (basically a small box fixed to one blade). Mechanical devices

Candlesticks. 45–49 chronological sequence (*left to right*): 1680s, *c.*1715, 1760s, 1770s, *c.*1820.

from 1749, some patented. In silver, Sheffield plate, brass, iron. Because they were laid flat in candle-snuffer trays Georgian snuffers might have three tiny feet (under the finger loops and lower blade) for easy lifting.

Candle-snuffer stand From *c.*1690s to hold the snuffers upright, finger-loops upward. Georgians preferred snuffer trays.

Candle-snuffer tray From 1660s to early Victorian days, to hold snuffers and charred wick, offering scope for decoration in silver, japanned tin plate, papier mâché, etc. Shape at first in snuffer outline or as a rectangle. Georgian designs had deeper rims, some with handles; some in waisted outline, followed by the late 18th-century ellipse and 1800s' four-lobed shape to include a douter, becoming ornate from the 1820s.

Candlestick Made as a pricket in iron or latten followed from the 16th century by the usual socket style in metals, glass, painted enamels, ceramics, including ornate figure groups and flower encrustations in porcelain and bone china. Many with loose nozzles for easy cleaning.

The *save-all* had spikes for burning candle ends. *See* Chamber candlestick; Pricket; Taperstick; Telescopic candlestick; Wax-jack.

Cane Slender glass rod drawn out from a small cylinder built up in concentric layers of different colours, varied with such details as ribbing, all fused by heating. While hot, the rod could be extended, reducing its thickness without altering the pattern. Thin slices from different canes could then be used as 'flowers' in millefiori work such as paperweights. Twisted rods encased in smooth-surfaced clear glass were used for twist stems in drinking glasses (Figs 102, 103). *See* Air twist glass.

Cane ware Fine cane-coloured stoneware evolved by Josiah Wedgwood *c*.1770 and widely imitated. *See* Piecrust ware.

Cane work Split canes of Malayan rattans (species of climbing palm) woven into open mesh for comfortable chair seats, etc., from the 1660s. Finer mesh by the 1700s. In fashion again from the late 18th century and with Victorians and Edwardians.

Cannal coal Very hard clean coal from some northern coalfields carved and polished like jet; found occasionally as ornaments, from garden seats to coal-and-alabaster chess sets.

Cannetille jewellery setting Soft lacy effect as a foil for massive amethysts and other semi-precious stones in England from *c*.1800, using filigree scrolls, flowers and granules of gold on a matted gold ground.

Canted With a slanting face, cutting off a right-angled corner as, e.g., to the sides of the drawers or cupboards in much early Georgian case furniture.

Canterbury 1. A small stand on castors with a vertical gallery and divisions to hold sheet music, from the late 18th century. 2. Victorians eventually extended the term to the box music stool. 3. Sheraton gave this name to the Georgian supper-tray or trolley, also on castors, with a gallery and divisions for self-service supper plates and cutlery.

Canton enamel Enamel-covered trays, kettles, etc., exported from Canton, often with extremely detailed painting in opaque *famille rose* colours, of European subjects then popular at the Chinese court. Attractive 18th-century work by skilled porcelain decorators, greatly deteriorating later.

49

Cantonieres *See* Bonegraces.

Capital Decorative head of a column or pilaster supporting the entablature. Distinguished by its order of architecture (Figs. 209–213).

Capodimonte Delicate soft-paste porcelain made near Naples from 1743 under Charles, King of Naples, who took the factory to Madrid when he became King of Spain in 1759, where it continued to 1808. Notable for a room in the royal villa at Portici entirely covered with porcelain, including chinoiseries in high relief, 1757–9, and later two rooms in Madrid.

Capuchin Drinking-vessel which, inverted, suggested a Capuchin friar's pointed hood, made, e.g., in Nottingham stoneware.

Caqueteuse Gossip chair, French 16th- to 17th-century design with a triangular seat, narrow raked back and curved arms to accommodate wide skirts.

Carat 1. Standard of weight used for gemstones, 200 milligrams. 2. The measure of fineness of gold alloys, pure gold being 24 carat. Hallmarked like silver until 1844. Until 1798 the standard was 22 carat (2 parts alloy). From 1798, 18 carat allowed, marked with a crown and *18*. From 1854, 15, 12 and 9 carat allowed, with figures in hallmarks and decimal values: ·625, ·5, ·375. In 1931, 14 carat replaced 15 and 12. Continental equivalents to 22, 18 and 14 carat are ·916, ·75, ·585; Russian 84, 72 and 56.

Carbuncle Intensely blood red garnet, cabochon-cut, often hollowed on the underside to improve its colour.

Carcase In furniture the basic box-like structure.

Carcel lamp, French lamp *See* Lamps.

Card case For carrying engraved visiting cards when paying calls. Mainly 19th century. Usually *c.* 4 x 3 x $\frac{7}{16}$ ins., with a deep lid sliding off or hinged on one narrow side; some book-shaped. Delightful to collect in silver (embossed, engraved, etc.), tortoiseshell, papier mâché, Tunbridge ware, lacquered or painted wood, leather, etc. Many of wood covered with small pieces of lustrous mother-of-pearl; others with embroidery, porcupine quills, etc.

Card-cut work 1. In furniture, lattice ornament carved in low relief or more easily made as thin strip pierced and applied as a blind fret, especially on mid 18th-century 'Chinese' chairs, etc. 2. In silver, especially the 1670s to the early 18th century, silver sheet cut in ornamental outline soldered onto a vessel around its handle, spout-base and other vulnerable areas, useful in Britannia standard silver, but developed by refugee Huguenot silversmiths into elaborate relief ornament, occasionally pierced.

Carlton House writing-table Late 18th-century design for the centre of a less formally furnished room, its finely veneered back curved so that the table-top is D-shaped, the curve emphasised by a low superstructure of small drawers and cupboards behind and flanking the writing area. So-named by the Gillow firm, 1796, after the Prince of Wales's residence. Frequently reproduced.

Carnations Traditional term for flesh colours in painting. Fleeting in 18th-century miniatures.

Carnelian. Cornelian *See* Chalcedony.

Carpet bowls Earthenware balls *c.* 4 ins diameter, patterned and

50, 51 Carlton House writing-table and late Georgian davenport.

51

in plain colours, widely made for the early Victorian indoor game.

Caroline Applied to styles current during the reigns of Charles I (1625–49) and, more frequently Charles II (1660–85).

Carrara 1. Italian marble; hence the Wedgwood firm's name for early Victorian parian porcelain. 2. From *c.* 1885, a Doulton name for a dense white matt-glazed stoneware sometimes with coloured and gilded patterns and lustre effects. 3. A Doulton corrosion-resistant facing to buildings.

Carriage clock (Fig. 65) Portable, with an escapement platform at the top and characteristic ball-jointed bail handle. Usually of brass, framing panels of glass. Popular through the 19th century.

Carrickmacross appliqué From the 1840s, a long popular substitute for lace: muslin embroidery cut out and mounted on machine-made net, sometimes enriched with needlepoint fillings.

Carte de visite Portrait photograph, *c.* $2\frac{1}{4}$ x $3\frac{1}{2}$ ins, card-mounted, with the photographer's name, etc., on the back. Cost cut by use of multiple lens. Collected (friends, celebrities, etc.), for albums; not used as visiting cards. Mainly 1860s, but the fashion was revived in the 1890s with a larger 'cabinet' card.

Cartel clock (Fig. 70) Ornate wall clock following flamboyant French Louis XV–Louis XVI styles, English frames usually being of carved and gilded wood instead of ormolu.

Carton pierre Paper pulp mixed with whiting and glue for moulded architectural ornament, lighter and harder than plaster of Paris. French process made in London by Jackson & Sons who also made papier mâché, from *c.* 1830s.

Cartouche Decorative motif suggesting an unrolled scroll or an inscription tablet revealed by rolled back parchment, lending itself to elegant flourishes on furniture, clock dials, presentation silver.

Caryatid *See* Atlantes.

Cased glass. Overlay glass From two to *c.* five layers of glass in different colours, often including clear glass and opaque white, fused one inside the other while hot. Blown into decanters, etc., decorated by the glass-cutter who ground away parts of each layer down to the innermost clear glass, creating geometrical facets or such motifs as fruiting vine, obliquely edged in colour-stripes, all brilliantly polished. Made in England mainly after 1845. Birmingham glass firm of Bacchus & Sons made a series of fine vases in the 1850s. Rice, Harris & Son cased some in black and white enriched with gilding. Collectors must avoid coarsely cut shallow ornament imported from the Continent in the 1920s and later. *See* Acid etching.

Case furniture Storage furniture as distinct from tables, chairs, etc.

Cassolets 'Fumitories' from the 16th century, cassolets from the 1690s, continuing in wealthy homes through the 18th century to burn cone-shaped scented pastilles (finely powdered wood charcoal, benzoin, gum arabic and suitable perfume oils). Now rare in 17th-century slipware and delftware. As 'essence vases', urn shaped, they were made in the later 18th century in silver, bronze, marble, ceramics, some on Neo-classical tripod stands. *See* Pastille burner.

Casting, ceramics *See* Slip casting.

Casting, metal To shape silver, bronze, brass, pewter, etc., by pouring while molten into a sand (marl) mould prepared from a wooden or other model. By the 19th century many metal domestic wares could be shaped instead by die-stamping in thinly rolled metal.

In the ancient *cire perdue* method for casting intricate shapes the model used to shape the mould was of wax, melted and poured away (lost) before the metal was poured in.

Cast Iron (Fig. 99) Ancient technique of foundry work. Iron with high carbon content, much cheaper than wrought iron, but of less tensile strength. Used for, e.g., firebacks, 15th to 19th centuries (and 20th-century copies). From the later 18th century it relegated wrought iron to a secondary place as a supporting framework for cast-iron ornament. Architectural work included railings, etc., designed by the Adam brothers, associated with

Carron Co., Falkirk (founded 1759). Period 1851–1900 is often called the Foundry Age, products ranging from buildings, church windows and shop fronts to mirror frames, umbrella stands, pub tables, letter racks, often in flamboyant Victorian-Elizabethan style and much originally painted to resemble stone, wood or marble. *See* Coalbrookdale Co.; Darby; Wrought iron.

Castleford, Yorkshire Closely associated with the Leeds Pottery. Under D. Dunderdale made creamware, black basaltes, etc. Noted for relief-moulded teapots with sliding or hinged lids (made also elsewhere) *c.* 1795–1821. *See* Chessmen.

Castle Hedingham, Essex Idiosyncratic 'primitive' wall plates, etc., some with 17th-century dates, showing potter Edward Bingham's enthusiasm for Essex history, such as his Essex jug bearing historical scenes and the arms of Essex boroughs, etc. At work 1864 to 1901, continuing as the Essex Art Pottery Company to 1905.

Castor, Caster Vessel with a perforated top for sprinkling sugar, pepper, pounce, etc. In silver from the 1660s.

Castors, casters Small solid wheels for furniture. Hard wood from the end of the 17th century; from *c.* 1750 leather discs held by brass arms. The rollers also brass from *c.* 1760s. Brass socket castors and projecting swivel horns from around the 1800s. Some with glazed earthenware wheels from the 1850s.

Cat Plate- or muffin-warmer, of turned wood or metal. Double tripod shape with six rods projecting in different directions from a central ball. Would stand steady on uneven hearth stones.

Cat's eye, Chatoyant Cabochon-cut gem showing a changeable undulating lustre suggesting a cat's eye in the dark. Honey-coloured cat's eye chrysoberyl was popular with late Victorians.

Caudle cup In 18th century richly enamelled porcelain, silver, etc., and in 19th-century bone china. Two-handled cup with lid and saucer, sold in pairs as presentation pieces, especially in celebration of a birth, caudle being a nourishing, richly flavoured drink for the mother and her visitor (compare posset – hot spiced milk curdled with ale). To Victorians it was known merely as a cabinet cup for display.

Caughley, Shropshire Earthenware factory from 1750s. Salopian China Manufactory established *c*.1775 by Thomas Turner from Worcester, followed, 1799, by John Rose of Coalport; the plant transferred to Coalport in 1814. Made soft-paste soapstone porcelain much like Worcester, lavishly glazed. Much transfer-printed ornament, some in vivid violet blue, including pseudo-Oriental patterns such as the 'Fisherman' (again like Worcester but with a smaller fish.) Collectors sometimes confuse Caughley and Worcester marks.

Cauldron Round metal cooking-vessel with a loop handle to hang over the primitive down-hearth; sometimes with three short legs. Still made in the 19th century.

Cauliflower ware Cream-coloured earthenware teapots, etc., relief-moulded and glaze-coloured to suggest cauliflowers, sweetcorn, pineapples. Made by the Wedgwood-Whieldon partnership from 1755 and much reproduced by Victorians.

Cedarwood Warm light brown. Dry aromatic and insect-repellant and from the mid 18th century used for drawer linings, etc.

Ceiler *See* Selour.

Celadon ware Chinese, dating from late in the Sung dynasty onwards (960–1280). High-fired porcellaneous ware with whitish body and hard feldspathic glaze in restrained green tones (Chinese 'colour of nature') sometimes touched with brown from iron oxide in the body clay imitating precious jade. Widely copied in Near East and Europe.

Cellaret. Gardevin Georgian compartmented container, lidded and locked (unlike the wine cooler) to keep wine in the dining-room, standing under the sideboard when this lacked adequate cupboards or pedestals. Became taller late in the century to suit changing bottle shape. Some in the Regency were elaborately fitted for glasses, etc.

Celluloid Early transparent coloured plastic, highly inflammable, but in wide use by the 1870s.

Ceramics General term covering all fire-baked clay vessels from stonewares and porcelains to terracotta.

Chaffers, Richard Liverpool potter making delftware from *c.*1752 and soapstone porcelain from 1756. Remembered for high-spouted jugs and barrel-shape mugs. Died 1765; his pottery continued by Philip Christian until the 1770s.

Chafing dish 1. Medieval name for portable grate holding smokeless charcoal; hence the food-warming vessel placed upon it. 2. In the late 18th to 19th centuries, a lidded dish (silver, etc.) for heating food, with a hot-water compartment as its non-stick base, resting on a spirit lamp stand.

Chair bed *See* Day-bed.

Chair table Now sometimes called a monk's table. An occasional find in 17th- to 18th-century oak, but often reproduced. Dual-purpose chair (or settle) with a solid vertical back that tilted forward to rest on the chair's horizontal arms when required as a table.

Chaise longue *See* Day-bed.

Chalcedony Mineral mixture of quartz and opal, with a watery lustre, including cornelian (dull red or reddish white, for seals etc.) plasma, sardonyx, chrysoprase, agate, bloodstones, onyx.

Chamber candlestick (Fig. 253) For carrying, e.g., to the bedroom, with a low stem and wide saucer to catch drips. Frequently fitted with snuffers slotted through the stem and a cone extinguisher hooked to the rim handle. In metal from the 1700s; some in late 18th- and 19th-century porcelain and bone china. An

Chairs. 52 Glastonbury, *c.* 1600. **53** 'Cockfighting', *c.* 1700s. **54** Compass chair. **55** 'Hogarth' bended-back armchair. **56** Corner chair, early Georgian. **57** Hall chair, late 18th century. **58** Two-person sociable, Victorian.

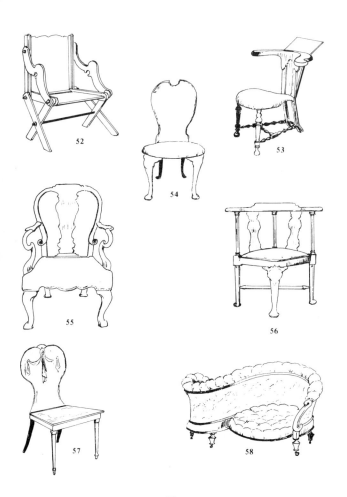

52

53

54

55

56

57

58

alternative form for carrying had a pierced cylindrical base supporting a glass shade and a long-handled extinguisher.

Chamber horse Georgian seat with leather-covered springs to exercise the user in his bedroom as if on horseback.

Chamberlain, Robert Worcester-trained, independent porcelain decorator from c. 1783 (mainly of Caughley ware). Died 1798 but his sons Humphrey and Robert continued the Chamberlain Worcester factory, making and richly decorating bone china (and costly Regent china from 1811). The firm acquired the older Worcester factory in 1840.

Chamfered *See* Canted.

Champagne glass (Fig. 103) From the late 1670s, usually a flute, as was customary for strong ale. But also some early Georgian use of a tazza shape from Hanover, almost hemispherical on a silesian stem. Improved champagne from the late 1820s prompted a return to a wide-rimmed hemispherical bowl then called a coupe, occasionally hollow-stemmed for any sediment. From the late 1850s usually a tulip shape.

Champagne decanter Evolved in the 1750s with a silver-lidded pocket for ice extending into the body from the shoulder.

Champion, Richard *See* Bristol.

Champlevé enamel Ornament made by Etruscans, Greeks and Celts at least 300 years BC. Enamel colours separated into tiny hollows cast or cut in bronze or other base metal, the edges of the hollows showing as narrow outlines level with the flat-surfaced enamels and often gilded. Largely restricted to opaque enamels because bronze contained tin.

Chandelier Sixteenth-century development from the candle beam. Silver, brass, bronze or carved and gilded wood, combined with glass as a hanging frame for candles. Many magnificent designs through the 17th to 19th centuries.

Chantilly lace Source near Paris of earliest black silk lace industry, using a grenadine, not a shining silk. Victorians' so-called Chantilly shawls were made mainly at Bayeux.

Chantilly ware From 1725. Soft-paste porcelain with an opaque milky white tin glaze, with distinctive colouring and graceful designs much influenced by Japanese porcelain until the 1750s; thereafter lead-glazed and under Meissen and Sèvres influence. Dainty Chantilly flower-sprig ornament was copied on late 18th-century English porcelain, especially the cornflower.

Chapbook Popular small booklet of tracts or ballads, hawked by chapman.

Chapter ring. Hour circle In a clock dial, the graduated circle showing the hours. This was a separate ring attached to the dial until *c*. 1750s.

Character jugs and mugs Especially popular from the late 18th to early 19th centuries. Mainly commemorative such as Doulton stoneware heads of Nelson, Napoleon, etc.; long-popular Derby porcelain Rodney mementoes; earthenware with brightly coloured topical figures and scenes moulded in low relief.

Charger Large serving-dish. In pewter until the 17th century in four sizes weighing 7, 5, $3\frac{1}{4}$ and $2\frac{3}{4}$ lbs. From late in the 17th century dishes were recorded in eighteen sizes from 28 inches in diameter downwards. Oval shapes only from 1770s. *See* Blue dash chargers.

Charles, A Georgian silhouettist of Bath and London who claimed the invention of silhouettes painted on the inner side of convex glass using intense black with translucent detail. He also painted on card.

Chasing. Flat chasing Decoration of silver or other metal using punches tapped with a hammer to compress the surface into patterns without removing any metal (and thus differing from engraving or piercing). *See* Embossing.

Chatelaine Medieval waist-chain, becoming important daytime jewellery for women through the 18th century in gold, pinchbeck, painted enamels, steel, etc., as an ornamental arrangement of hook and chain, at its finest suspending a matching watch and key. Early Georgians favoured elaborate chains suspending also

59 Chatelaine, 18th-century Rococo. 60 Chinoiserie expressed in detail from Chippendale design for china shelves.

or alternatively such details as etui, smelling bottle, etc. Popular again around 1850. *See* Macaroni.

Chatoyant *See* Cat's eye.

Cheese scoop Spoon shape in silver, etc., with a half-cylinder bowl for serving Stilton cheese. Late 18th to 19th centuries.

Cheese toaster (Fig. 257) Rectangular dish in silver or Sheffield plate, containing six small trays for bread spread with cheese. With a handle at the back for holding it in front of a fire with the hinged lid tilted open (on an adjustable chain) to reflect heat onto the cheese while the trays remained flat. Often with a compartment underneath for hot water (filled through a hole in the handle).

Chelsea Most valued English soft-paste porcelain, under the influence of Chinese wares, Meissen and then Sèvres, *c.* 1745–56 and 1758–69. Collectors distinguished the periods by their marks despite innumerable fakes. *Incised triangle mark* until 1749 when output was mainly table-wares, including silver shapes decorated in relief. *Raised anchor mark*, 1749–53, better paste with creamy glaze for table-wares and some figures. *Red anchor*, 1753–56, more translucent paste with smooth glaze, the products including delicately modelled figures in pastel colouring. *Gold anchor*, 1758–69, brilliant colours, ornate figures, great use of tooled gilding. *See* Sprimont; Girl-in-a-swing porcelain.

Chelsea-Derby (1770–84) Chelsea productions on a limited scale under Derby proprietor William Duesbury after he acquired the factory. These included table-wares and Sèvres-type figures in smooth waxy porcelain, some marked with an anchor in gold across a cursive D.

Chenille (French for hairy caterpillar) Cord with velvet pile used in embroideries and trimmings in the late 18th and 19th centuries; the soft silk or wool fibres standing out round a core of thread, or occasionally wire.

Cherry wood Pinkish, darkening to brown and could be stained to suggest mahogany. Used in the 17th to 18th centuries for country furniture, especially turnery and popular around the end of the 19th century for Arts and Crafts work.

Cherubim In Christian literature a higher order of angels. *See* Amorini.

Chessmen Distinctive graded pieces from the 12th century. Ivory, bone, hardwood supplemented by gold, silver and jewelled sets from the 17th century; also amber, hardstones, etc., and cheaper bronze and pewter. In ceramics by Doulton and Wedgwood; so-called Castleford stoneware sets unmarked and much reproduced. *See* Staunton.

Chesterfield Late 19th-century name for double-ended over-stuffed couch.

Chestnut roaster From the 18th century, but mainly Victorian and later, a small metal box (sheet iron rather than the cast brass of modern imitations) with perforated lid and sides, both box and lid having long horizontal wrought iron handles, held together when the box was closed and thrust into the fire embers.

Chestnut wood Horse and Spanish or sweet, both light-toned, but the latter whiter, less yellow. Some turned work and occasional use as a late 18th-century substitute for satinwood.

Cheval glass To the late 18th century this was a 'horse dressing-glass'. Full-length mirror swinging between tall supports on extensive claw feet.

The *cheval firescreen* had a similar design, its rectangular frame flanked by vertical supports on forward and backward projecting feet.

Cheveret *See* Sheveret.

Chevron Heraldic device in the shape of an inverted V, used as ornament in paint and inlay on some 16th-century English furniture.

Chiaroscuro (Italian for light-dark) Applied to pictorial work such as a print in varying tones based on a single sombre colour, such as black or sepia.

Chicken skin Finest lambskin vellum used for costliest painted fan mounts.

Ch'ien Lung (1736–95) The last emperor of China's great artistic period which was associated with technical skills in ceramics (including *famille rose* and self-colour glazes), red stoneware teapots, Canton copper enamels, ivory and rhinoceros horn carvings, brilliant embroideries, the first so-called Spanish shawls, so-called Coromandel lacquer, carved glass and jade.

Chiffonier (Fig. 135) From the end of the 18th century a low cupboard often with serpentine shaping and space for books above. In the Regency, the doors were often filled with silk-lined brass lattice; Victorians preferred wood or glass-fronted doors with greater elaboration above, the piece often serving as a small mirror-backed sideboard.

Chimera Greek mythological monster, symbol of cunning, killed by Bellerophon. With a lion's head, goat's body and dragon's tail. Romans added eagle's wings and other variants, copied in early and late Georgian furniture.

Chimney crane Wrought-iron wall bracket for hanging pots over the fire on pot-hooks. Often with both horizontal and vertical movement to make best use of the fire.

Chimney ornaments 19th-century name for popular celebrity figures, miniature furniture, shoes and other cheap 'toys' for the mantel shelf in earthenware, brass, coloured glass, etc. *See* Flatback ornaments.

China Originally Chinese hard-paste porcelain. Now applied indiscriminately to glazed ceramics from bone china to stone china.

China clay and china stone Basic ingredients of hard-paste porcelain including its glaze (almost entirely china stone): white refractory clay (Chinese kaolin) and fusible pulverised feldspathic stone (Chinese petuntse), both derived from feldspar rock at different stages of decomposition.

Chiné ware Doulton stoneware with a textured surface achieved by pressing lace, etc., into its unfired surface; sometimes finally gilded. 1886–1914.

Chinese Chippendale (Fig. 119) Mid 18th-century furniture with distinctive square outlines and Chinese frets, illustrated by Thomas Chippendale and contemporaries. A modern term.

Chinese Lowestoft *See* Lowestoft.

Ch'ing dynasty, China (AD 1644–1912) Dominated by long prosperous reigns of emperors K'ang Hsi (1662–1722) and Ch'ien Lung (1736–95). *See* Ch'ien Lung, *Famille rose*; Jade. In the 19th century a more limited artistic output included Cantonese carved ivory balls, sandalwood boxes, chess sets, tortoiseshell, painted fans, etc.

Chinoiserie (Fig. 60) Recurring fashion (especially *c.* 1680s, 1750s and 1820s) for European notions of Oriental designs (Chinamen, pagodas, etc.), stimulated by spectacular imports from the 17th century onwards prompting japanned and carved-and-gilded furniture, embossed silver such as tea caddies, and blue-painted and printed ceramics.

Chintz Indian dye-patterned white cotton cloths. Imported from the 17th century, but use restricted to protect English woollens. Important English imitations from the late 17th century.

63

61, 62 Chippendale dressing-commode (V. & A. Museum) and design for basin-stand. **63** Comparable Ince & Mayhew design for 'commode dressing table'.

Smoothed under pressure and sometimes starch-glazed from the 1850s. *See* Printed fabrics.

Chippendale style (Figs 60, 248) Now describes furniture resembling designs by Thomas Chippendale (1718–79) and his contemporaries and recorded in his design book *The Gentleman and Cabinet Maker's Director*, 1754, 1755, 1762. Known work by Chippendale's firm is in subsequent contrasting Neo-classical style. Son Thomas (1749–1822) continued the business until his death (Chippendale, Haig & Co., until 1796). Issued his own rare *Book of Designs*.

Chocolate pot Especially 1680s–1750s, in silver, etc., distinguished from a coffee pot by a small lidded aperture in the cover for inserting a boxwood swizzle stick (with a notched knob on the end of a long handle, to froth up the liquid).

Chopin. Chopine 1. Lady's high-soled overshoe for muddy paths. 2. A liquid measure: *See* Tappit hen.

Christmas card A few on sale in the 1840s, but mostly from the 1860s; including three-dimensional and other surprise designs from the 1880s, also folding booklet shapes.

Chromium green Used in ceramics from early in the 19th century prepared from chromium oxide. With a distinctively yellower tone than the earlier copper oxide green enamels.

Chromolithograph Lithograph printed in full colour by using a succession of stones (later often zinc or aluminium). Costly in the 1840s, but by the 1870s machines produced much cheap commercial work.

Chronometer 1. Historically a timepiece of great accuracy for determining longitude at sea. 2. Now also applied to a certificated precision watch.

Chrysoberyl *See* Beryl.

Chrysoprase Translucent apple-green variety of chalcedony.

Cire perdue *See* Casting.

Citrine Clear yellow crystalline quartz. Popular in Victorian jewellery, but not to be confused with topaz.

Classical Belonging to ancient Greek and Roman times. *See* Neoclassical.

Clan tartan ware *See* Mauchline ware.

Clap table *See* Console table.

Clavichord Medieval development from the dulcimer. A stringed keyboard instrument, simple forerunner of the pianoforte.

Claw setting In jewellery tiny claws to hold the crown facets of a gemstone.

Claw table *See* Pillar-and-claw.

Clay's paper ware. Clay ware Glossy, heat-varnished, hand-polished paper ware, patented 1772 by Henry Clay for trays, etc. Many sheets of linen-rag paper, soaked in flour-and-glue paste, were overlaid and shaped over moulds and stove-dried, layer by layer. Stronger than pulp papier mâché; could be planed, filed, etc. Clay's business was taken over by Jennens & Bettridge of Birmingham, 1816–64.

Cliché Electrotype duplicate of a woodcut or wood engraving.

Clobbering Overglaze colour and gilding added to enhance the value of blue transfer-printed ware, as distinct from normal hand-colouring over transfer-printed outlines in the course of manufacture.

Cloisonné enamel Medieval ornament inspired by Byzantine work. Enamel colours separated into compartments by vertical gold strip edge-soldered to the gold base; jeweller's use of gold meant that the enamels stayed translucent. The craft was continued in the Orient and then revived in Victorian England, notably by the Elkington firm and later by such artist craftsmen as Alexander Fisher.

Close plating Improvement on ancient attempts to silver-coat base metals, such as flavour-tainting steel; also to resilver Sheffield plate. English patent, 1779, improved 1809, using silver foil with a trace of tin, and heat and pressure. *See* French plating.

Club foot. Pad foot (Fig. 274) Sometimes called snake's head: a rounded projection at the base of a leg, frequent on cabriole and turned legs for chairs and tables, especially 1700s–1760s.

Cluster-column (Fig. 120) Three or four shafts with a common top and base, popular in 'Gothic' furniture. As a furniture leg, associated with imitations of 'Chinese' bamboo.

Clutha glass (Fig. 9) Patented by James Couper & Son, Glasgow, *c.* 1890. Reputedly named after the 'cloudy' river Clyde, being clouded with streaks and bubbles in green, brown, etc., some sparkling with aventurine. Included designs by C. Dresser and George Walton.

Coaching horn Slender copper tube several feet long with a silver or plated mouthpiece. Liable to be a reproduction.

Coaching-inn clock (Fig. 68) Weight-driven, short-bodied wall timepiece (no strike) with a large clear unglazed face. Often called an Act-of-Parliament clock from the notion that they were introduced into inns for the use of those who had sold their clocks and watches following William Pitt's extremely brief tax of 1797. But this tax was repealed in 1798 and the clock's popularity was much more probably due to the linking of clock and coach times nationwide.

Coach table So-called. Top with central hinges, to close up like a book, on X-shaped legs. A variant of the webbing-topped stand for a butler's tray.

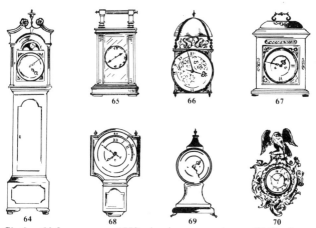

Clocks. **64** Longcase, *c.* 1770, showing moon phases. **65** Carriage.
66 Lantern. **67** Bracket or table. **68** Coaching-inn. **69** Balloon (popular
late 18th century). **70** Cartel.

Coade stone Artificial stone (named from the owner of the
process, Mrs Eleanor Coade, 1732–1821) made in Lambeth,
1769 to the 1830s. Frost-resistant and used, plain or painted, for
sculptered plaques, church and garden ornament, etc.
Coal Early references (in silver braziers, etc.) are to charcoal,
especially smokeless court charcoal, when mined coal was seacoal.
Coalbrookdale Generic term for flower-encrusted china
occasionally so marked (or *C. D.* or *C. Dale* or *Coalport*).
Coalbrookdale Company Founded 1708 by Abraham Darby,
making cast-iron cooking pots for those who could not afford
brass, but associated with items ranging from the original Crystal

Palace gates (then bronzed) now between Hyde Park and Kensington Gardens, to ornamental door-knockers and porters. Had a terracotta department from 1861.

Coalport (Fig. 74) Shropshire. Ceramics factory c. 1795–1841 under John Rose who acquired the Caughley factory. Mainly bone china and feldspar porcelain. Lustrous leadless glaze from 1820. Rich enamelling on table-wares, etc., and gilded Rococo ornaments, especially from the 1830s, their flower encrustations often confused with those of Minton, Derby, Spode, Grainger and Rockingham. Date AD 1750 (Caughley's supposed founding date) was used with the Coalport mark from 1875.

Coaster *See* Wine coaster.

Cobalt blue *See* Zaffre-blue; Smalt.

Cockade fan With a central rivet allowing the folding mount to open to a full circle. Early 19th century. *See* Quizzing fan.

Cock beading Small projecting mould round the edge of a drawer front, used from c. 1730.

'Cockfighting chair' (Fig. 53) Modern name for a reading or conversation chair for a man to sit astride, back to front (with uncreased coat tails) on a narrow padded seat, resting his arms on a specially designed crest-rail. From c. 1730s.

Cockshead cupboard hinge (Fig. 169) Ornate 16th- to 17th-century version of the hinge, each arm S-shaped, usually of wrought iron, thinning towards its extremities and with a bevelled edge. Coarsely copied in many reproductions.

Coffer. Trussing coffer. Sumpter chest Chest with handles and without feet, for the traveller, often round-topped and hide-covered to throw off the rain. In the early 18th century this trunk shape was used for decorative lacquer and japanned storage-chests (which thus escaped damage from table-use).

Coffered panel Sunk panel as distinct from a projecting or a fielded panel.

Coffin Small pie dish, in pewter, etc.

Coif Cap, close-fitting over the head and ears, long worn by men and women. Notable when showing fine late Tudor or early Stuart embroidery in silks and metal threads on linen; these assumed to be women's, comparable with men's embroidered round 'night caps' (for informal daywear).

Cole, Henry *See* Summerlys Art Manufactures.

Collet Costume neckband; hence a metal ferrule and, in jewellery, a setting around a gemstone, like a box setting, but filed down to allow more light to the stone.

Collotype Process from the 1870s to print clear colour pictures without the dotted effect of the screen associated with half-tone work.

Colonette In furniture a miniature column, usually with a plain shaft, *e.g.*, supporting a Regency bookshelf.

Colophon In a book the details of the printer, etc., formerly found at the end; now the publisher's distinctive emblem on the book's spine.

Colour twist glass *See* Air twist glass.

Column Vertical support in classical architecture. *See* Orders of architecture.

Comb-back chair (Fig. 305) Early style of Windsor.

Combing Earthenware covered with stripes of thick slip, in contrasting tones worked into parallel wavy lines with a notched tool. *See* Marbling, paper.

Comfit holder For tiny strong-scented breath-sweetening comfits (popular from the 15th century) – aniseed balls, etc. Including shallow glass vessels and porcelain figures holding open baskets available to guests at social gatherings. *See* Bonbonnière.

Commemorative wares (Figs. 111, 227) Attractive to many collectors in silver, glass, ceramics. Caution needed, e.g. with Shakespeare's birthday items, frequently dating to celebrations in 1864; Nelson commemorated in 1905; Columbus 1906. *See* Flasks; Flatback ornaments; Horse brasses; Pressed glass; Princess Charlotte souvenirs; Rodney mementoes; Toby jugs; Trafalgar fashion.

Commode (Figs. 21, 61, 63) 1. From the early 1700s, a French chest of drawers for the salon. 2. In England from the 1740s, an elegant low cupboard with or without drawers. Earlier styles were revived in the 19th century.

Compass chair (Fig. 54) Round-seated with a narrow base to its 'spoon back' to accommodate men's fashionable coats. Popular early in the 18th century. In the 1720s the back had a cupped recess for a wig queue.

Compendium Fitted box or casket, a compact container for toiletries, sewing equipment, etc., styled for men as well as women. Many fine specimens remain from the early 19th century.

Composite order *See* Orders of architecture.

Composition. Compo. Gesso duro (Fig. 205) Composed of whiting, resin and size, especially popular through the later 18th century with, e.g., Robert Adam, for moulded and carved ornaments, some with wire cores.

Concertina card-table Modern term for design (first half of the 18th century) with half its under-framing triple-hinged to close by folding in on itself when the top was folded over.

Confidante Late 18th-century upholstered settee with an additional corner seat at each end; in Hepplewhite design these were removable.

Console table (Fig. 273) From the architectural term for a scrolled bracket: a table supported at the back as a wall fixture, its front legs often shaped as in-curving scrolls or a more ornate spread-eagle, etc. French origin, early 18th century.

Consulate period From 1799 to 1804 when Napoleon was Consul of France.

Conversation chair *See* Caqueteuse; Cockfighting chair; Sociable.

Coopered Barrel construction of staves and hoops. *See* Quaich. Or imitating this. *See* Barrel designs.

Copeland china From 1829 when W. T. Copeland, son of sales manager William Copeland, became proprietor of the Spode factory, Stoke, on the death of Josiah Spode III. Traded as Copeland & Garrett (1833–47); thereafter the Copeland family continued in control, with the Spode name in some marks. Conspicuous success with bone china, parian ware, jewelled ware, stone china.

Copper lustre *See* Lustrewares.

Copper ware Warming pans, from *c.*1730s; some urns and kitchen wares, machine-stamped from the late 18th century. But mainly 19th- to 20th-century articles such as bedroom jugs, pans, jelly moulds, etc., (requiring frequent interior tinning) and notable late Victorian-Edwardian art wares.

Copper plate Basis for etching and engraving to make prints.

Coptic art Work of Egyptian Christians.

Copyright Concerns the right to control literary, musical or artistic works for a certain number of years. The words 'Published according to the Act' under a print refer to the Engraving Copyright Act. The first (Hogarth's in 1735) gave 14 years' protection from copying, followed by improvements in 1767, 1777, 1836, etc.

Coral A kind of hard shell (skeleton remains of sea creatures). Deep red, white, pink (including pale 'angel skin'); occasionally black or blue. Popular for secondary jewellery, easily carved cameos, etc., through Victoria's reign and long given to children to ward off evil.

Corbel Projecting bracket found on the frieze of cabinet furniture.

Cordial glass. Flowered glass (Fig. 101) For strong aromatic alcoholic drinks (equivalent of French liqueurs) served in the 18th century with evening tea; hence a decorative small-bowled drinking-glass often flower-engraved and with a colour-twist or facet-cut stem to suit the porcelain tea ware.

Corinthian order *See* Orders of architecture.

Cork pictures Late 19th century, inspired by Japanese and Spanish work. Three-dimensional effects achieved by carving thin strips of dried tree-bark and assembling them in layers.

Corkscrew Wimble (auger style) from the 16th century; pointed helix from the mid 17th century. Sheathed for the pocket from *c*.1750. 'King's screw' with a socket for the bottle top patented 1794, other patents following, many with additional gadgets.

Cornelian Red form of chalcedony valued for a rare translucence.

Corner chair (Fig. 56) Early Georgian, for card-playing, etc., in the centre of room because of its attractive back view. With a horizontally rounded crest-rail and two short splats; the four equidistant legs including an imposing cabriole at the centre front.

Corner cupboard To fit the corner of a room, hanging (single) or free-standing (two-tier) derived from the built-in buffet. Some early to mid Georgian (pedimented, with chamfered panels flanking the door); more late 18th century and later, often bow-fronted.

Cornice Projecting moulding at the top of a bookcase, bed, etc. *See* Orders of architecture.

Cornucopia Horn of plenty: widely used decorative motif associated with the classical goddess Ceres. Found as a porcelain wall pocket, silver posy-holder, etc.

Coromandel wood. Calamander wood Very dark with yellowish stripes or brown mottling. Used for bandings, etc., in the late 18th century and Regency.

Coster Medieval term for a cloth wall-hanging.

Costrel (Fig. 114) 1. Ancient pilgrim bottle, a flattened globe shape with loops for a carrying strap. 2. Popular Victorian ornament ('moon vase') in ceramics, glass, etc.

Cosy corner Late 19th-century high-backed angle-settle, sometimes with small book-shelves, etc., forming an alcove set apart from the rest of room, the wooden framework sometimes in elaborate fretted 'Turkish' patterns. *See* Turkish style.

Cotswold group Architect furniture-designers. *See* Ernest Gimson.

Cottages, ceramic (Fig. 208) 1. Many early 19th-century bone-china pastille burners. 2. From late in the 19th century souvenir cottages (First and Last House in England, etc.,) were made by W. H. Goss following the success of his armorial ware.

Couch Georgian descendant of the Stuart day-bed, becoming an attractive scrolling shape on scimitar legs in the Regency. *See* Méridienne. The single-ended form continued into the 1830s as the Adelaide couch. *See also* Duchesse; Settee; Sofa.

Couching Embroidery in which thick or costly thread or braid forms a continuous pattern by being held to the surface of the fabric with inconspicuous self-colour overstitching.

Counterfeit Pewter bowl with a flat handle pierced to suggest silverwork – now more often called a porringer.

Counterpane. Counterpoint Quilted or more generally embroidered bed coverlet.

Court cupboard 16th- to 17th-century ornate side-table for silver plate, etc., shortened (court) into two or three tiers linked by heavy corner pillars. Revived in the 19th century.

Cove Large concave moulding, e.g. on cornice furniture, deeper than a cavetto.

Coventry ribbons *See* Picture ribbons.

Cow jug With an open mouth for pouring, a lid in the centre of the back, and a raised tail as a handle. Silver from *c.*1755; cheap earthenware from early in the 19th century, sometimes with a tiny milkmaid.

Crabstock Shaped like a gnarled crab-apple branch; frequent as a handle or spout in ceramic table-wares.

Crabwood Tropical American wood for furniture, etc., reddish brown, straight-grained, tough.

Crackle *See* Crazing.

Cranberry glass Now popular name for Victorians' blown-moulded clear glass tinted a cherry red as distinct from better quality English and imported-Bohemian ruby glass. Sparingly coloured to mask imperfections in the cheap glass itself and often combined with uncoloured glass (stems, handles, etc.) to avoid difficult colour matching.

Cravat-stand Small turned pillar with projecting arms for hanging a man's neckcloths.

Crayon etching Suggests a chalk drawing on rough paper, being taken from a copper plate stippled with a roulette. Sometimes confused with a soft-ground etching or a lithograph.

Crazing 1. Ceramics marred by hair-line cracks due to the effect of atmospheric changes on ill-matched ware and glaze. Rare on hard-paste porcelain. Sometimes coarsely faked; also on japanned furniture. 2. Known as *crackle* when used as deliberate ornament.

Crazy quilt Late 19th-century coverlet of irregularly shaped patchwork.

Creamware An important widely made English development: refined cream-coloured earthenware dipped in liquid glaze, evolved in the 1740s. *See* Queen's ware; Leeds pottery.

Creepers Small firedogs on the down-hearth, for use not show.

Cresset Open-topped iron basket to hold an oil lamp or other light, with a socket base for a carrying pole. Improved in the 16th century as a horn-paned lantern on a pole, known as a moon.

Cresting Carved ornament surmounting furniture.

Crest-rail Top rail of a chair back.

Crewel embroidery. Crewel work Originally worked with cheap ends of worsted cut from the weaver's loom. Especially popular in the late 17th century for magnificent linen-hangings in foliage patterns using many different stitches. Renewed late Victorian popularity as 'art needlework'.

Cricket stool. Cricket table With three turned legs to stand steady on hearth stones, haunt of noisy insects called crickets.

Crime pieces Cheap earthenware models of buildings associated with notorious 19th-century murders, such as Stanfield Hall (1848).

Crinoline Originally springy cotton or linen fabric woven with horsehair; hence the early Victorian's stiffened or hooped petticoat.

74

Crizzling Defect in the earliest flint-glass which gradually became opaque.

Crochet work Ancient craft popular with Victorians. Worked with a hook and a single continuous thread basically in chain stitch.

Croft Small table for travellers, etc., with D-shaped flaps, a secretary drawer and, below, small drawers secured by a single wide door.

Cross banding *See* Banding.

Cross stitch. Gros-point embroidery Pairs of stitches making regular Xs to cover meshed fabric. *See* Berlin wool work; Tent stitch.

Crouch ware Late 17th-century name for Staffordshire's drab salt-glazed stoneware.

Crown Upper part of cut gemstone. *See* Brilliant cut.

Crown Derby (Figs. 71, 72) Popular but confusing name for the original Derby porcelain, which was marked with a crown from *c.*1773; also for china from the Old Crown Derby China Works *c.*1860–1935 (*See* Hancock, Sampson); and for wares from the Royal Crown Derby Porcelain Co. Many other potteries used crown marks.

Crown glass Used in furniture, etc., made by the early process of blowing then flattening by spinning into a huge circular sheet. Thinner from the 1740s; hence lighter cabinet glazing. *See* Broad glass; Bull's eye; Plate glass.

Crown ware Heavy Royal Worcester earthenware for hotels etc., 1870–1930.

Crusie. Chill *See* Lamps.

Crystal. Lead crystal Modern term for flint-glass.

Crystal cameo Patented in England 1819, as crystallo-ceramie. French technique importantly developed at the Falcon Glassworks, Southwark, by Apsley Pellatt, MP (1791–1863); copied less perfectly by others. Tiny bas relief portraits, etc., (sulphides) cast in china clay were wholly embedded in

COALPORT
A.D.1750
74

OLD HALL
1790
75

Royal Chelsea
ENGLAND
76

Crown Derby (and other ceramic marks which may puzzle beginners). **71** Typical Derby mark, *c.* 1782–1820. **72** Mark of the Old Crown Derby China Works, *c.* 1860–1935. **73** Wedgwood & Co. of Tunstall (not Josiah Wedgwood & Sons). **74** Coalport, late 19th century including founding date of predecessor Caughley. **75** Old Hall mark used from the 1880s including founding date (by Job Meigh). **76** Twentieth-century New Chelsea Porcelain Co., having no association with 18th-century Chelsea porcelain which used tiny anchor marks.

exceptionally clear flint-glass. The Falcon Glassworks continued to 1895.

Crystallised ware *See* Moiré.

Cucumber glass Victorian. Like a slender bottle without a base, 12–13 inches long, to make a cucumber grow straight.

Culet Horizontal facet at the base of a brilliant-cut diamond. Extremely small from late in the 19th century. In paste, usually marked by a black spot to aid refraction. *See* Brilliant cut.

Cullet Broken glass, added during glass-making. (Cost-cutting when glass materials were taxed.)

Curfew Cover to keep a fire alight safely through the night; a quarter-sphere of iron or brass fitting closely against the fireback.

Curule Most usual stool or chair of antiquity, camp-stool style with ornate X-shaped legs. Sometimes with a back.

Cusp Architectural term for the point projecting between two curves in Gothic tracery. Found, e.g., in Neo-Gothic furniture and some facet-cut drinking-glass stems.

Custard glass (Fig. 96) Dessert glass in a cup shape with or without a handle.

Cut-card work *See* Card-cut work.

Cut-glass (Figs. 88, 89, 91–93, 175) Ornament ground into the glass surface with revolving wheels to enhance its refractive brilliance. Improvements in glass annealing increased the glass cutter's scope early and late in the 18th century.

Cut-steel Used as a stronger alternative to marcasite for jewellery, sometimes with jet, enamels, jasper plaques, etc.; also for decorating buttons, shoe buckles, chatelaines, where a hard-wearing,

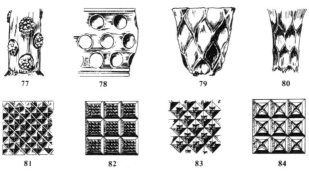

Cut glass. **77** Hollow stem of early roemer with raspberry prunts. **78** Printies on Regency tumbler. **79** Blown-moulded diamond pattern on 18th-century jelly glass. **80** Shallow-cut hexagonal diamonds on 18th-century wineglass stem. **81** Deep-cut diamonds. **82** Strawberry diamonds. **83** Cross-cut diamonds. **84** Hobnail diamonds.

rust-resistant glitter was required, the steel studs individually faceted and polished for riveting on to steel mounts. In inferior, late work, the facets were stamped *en bloc*. Important from the later 18th century with closely faceted studs; more plentiful 1800s to 1860s.

Cymric silver (Figs. 44, 268) Made by W. H. Haseler of Birmingham for Liberty & Co. from 1900, designed by Archibald Knox, Rex Silver, etc., with strong leanings to Art Nouveau. 'Craft' effects largely achieved by mechanised processes. *See* Tudric pewter.

Cypress Reddish, very hard, close-grained aromatic wood, used from the 16th century for chests, etc.

Dado In architecture, the part of a pedestal between cornice and base; hence the lower part of an interior wall distinctively treated.

Daguerreotype From the late 1830s, named after its French inventor Louis Daguerre (1789–1851). A direct–positive photographic process by which only one photo results. Superseded in the 1850s by a negative–positive process by which any number of copies could be made. Fragile, costly, with tiresome metallic glare. *See* Calotype.

Damascening Gold, silver or copper wire hammered into grooves undercut into steel or bronze in arabesque patterns.

Damask Fabric woven with an elaborately figured weft to produce surface contrasts, glossy and matt.

Dan Day chair *See* Mendlesham chair.

Dangle spit *See* Spit.

Danske or Danzig chest Spruce-wood chest imported from Danzig, especially in the 16th to 17th centuries.

Darby, Abraham (1677–1717) British ironmaster, founded Coalbrookdale Co. 1708 and was immensely important to the whole history of domestic and architectural ironwork. Originated smelting of iron ore by coke from seacoal as distinct from wood charcoal. Patented an improved casting method 1707, widening the range of possible products and prompted widespread substitution of cast iron for cast brass. Son, also Abraham (1711–63), continued his father's work.

Darby and Joan 1. Two-seated settee. 2. A pair of cottage chimney ornaments. From the song (*Gentleman's Magazine*, March 1735) about an aging couple who were 'ever uneasy asunder'.

Date letter (Fig. 158) On English silver, a punch-mark indicating the year of hallmarking. Each assay office used its own series of letters in changing types and punch outlines. London changed its style each May. *See* Assay; Hallmarks. Some leading potteries have used date letters or symbols in the 19th and 20th centuries. *See* Marks.

Dates in ceramic marks (Figs. 74, 75) Usually refer to a factory's establishment. *See* Coalport.

Dates on furniture Most usual on Victorian imitations of 16th- to 17th-century work.

Davenport desk (Figs. 51, 294) Introduced during the fashion for compact campaign furniture. A small slant-topped desk mounted on a stack of side-faced drawers and (on the other side) sham drawers. Probably from 1789, first made by the Gillow firm for 'Captain Davenport'. By 1833 had become a lady's writing-table with a forward-sliding desk section; later with a fixed projecting desk section resting on pillars or cabriole legs.

Davenport wares Ceramics made by the Davenport family, Longport, Staffs, 1793–*c*.1885. Ornate Derby-style bone china, moulded stonewares and fine quality earthenwares; also some glass.

Day-bed Style of couch with one end in chairback form; sometimes adjustable. Established by the late 17th century and continuing for about 100 years.

Deal Pine or other coniferous softwood in plank form shipped in huge quantities from the 1660s onwards from the Baltic coast where cold conditions produced close grain, to meet increasing demand for furniture carcase work, drawer-linings, etc.

Decalcomania From the 1860s, a process for transferring pictures from prepared paper on to furniture, porcelain, glass, etc., using a photographic process.

Decanters. 85 Labelled (in white enamel). **86** Neo-classical liqueur vessel. **87** Ship's decanter with target stopper. **88** Prussian with deep-cut diamonds and mushroom stopper. **89** Early Victorian. **90** Late 19th-century (Whitefriars, H. Powell design). **91** Edwardian claret jug cut and engraved, with silver rim. **92** Edwardian spirit square.

Decanter Glass vessel with an ornamental stopper for tabling decanted wine. Can be dated from the 1670s onwards by changing shapes and by ornament such as wheel engraving (from *c.*1750), deep cutting (from *c.*1790), 'rock crystal' engraving (from the 1880s). *See* Labelled decanters; Squares.

Deckle edge Rough untrimmed edge to a sheet of hand-made paper.

Del. Delin., etc *See* Inscriptions.

Delftware. Tin-enamelled ware. Tin-glazed ware (Fig. 234) English earthenware in the style associated with Delft, Holland, but traceable through Italy to the Moorish invasion of Spain. Once-fired earthenware dipped in lead glaze opacified with costly tin oxide, to give it a fine white surface for painting, all fixed by a second kiln firing. Sometimes given an additional lead glaze (third firing) for extra gloss. Notable as the first British ware white enough for ornament in blue or polychrome (in high temperature colours) imitating Chinese porcelain. Made briefly in the 1560s; mainly in Southwark from the 1620s; Brislington from *c.* the 1640s; Lambeth from the 1660s; Bristol from the 1680s; also Liverpool – all accessible by sea for supplies of Cornish tin. *See* Engobe; Faience; Hispano-Moresque ware; Maiolica.

Della Robbia Henry Rathbone's art pottery, Birkenhead (1894–1906). Architectural panels and plaques shaped in deep relief, also wall plates, vases, etc. (based on maiolica work of the renowned Florentine Renaissance Della Robbia family). Opaque white grounds used as a basis for decoration in flowing colours controlled by incised lines, often the work of two artists and initialled by both.

Demantoid garnet *See* Garnet.

Demijohn Large bottle with a narrow neck and swelling body, frequently encased in wicker.

De Morgan, William (1839–1917) Inventive artist, friend of William Morris who turned from stained glass to pottery, evolving vivid 'Persian' colours (blues, greens, turquoise) and lustres for his rich two-dimensional designs of mythological creatures, etc., on tiles and vases. His most notable pottery was Sands End, Fulham, with Halsey Ricardo. Retired through ill-health, 1905, becoming a successful novelist.

Dempsey, John Silhouettist, at work in Liverpool through the second quarter of the 19th century when cheap cut silhouettes were popular with emigrants; he charged 3d and 6d for memento likenesses and also made silhouettes for jewellery.

Denaby Pottery Near Mexborough, Yorks, at work 1864–70 making cheap sponged and printed earthenware, granite ware.

Denby Pottery Derbyshire. Established 1809 by Joseph Bourne, making stonewares, notably spirit flasks from the 1820s to 40s.

Dentelle Bookbinder's tooled pattern suggesting lace.

Dentils Classical architectural feature used in Georgian furniture cornice mouldings: a series of small rectangular blocks protruding downwards like teeth.

Derby porcelain (Fig. 71) Soft-paste porcelain from *c.*1749; bone china from *c.*1810. Derby Porcelain Company under William Duesbury from 1755 and under his son William Duesbury II, to 1796, made notable figures including white bisque, ornaments and table-wares. Under Robert Bloor (*c.*1815–48), who became mentally ill, work deteriorated despite use of old Chelsea and Derby moulds and colouring of old stock. *See* Duesbury; Chelsea-Derby; Crown Derby; Old Crown Derby China Works; Royal Crown Derby Porcelain Co.

Derbyshire chair (Fig. 316) Modern term. *See* Yorkshire chair.

Derbyshire spar. Fluorite *See* Blue john.

Dessert glasses Sweetmeat glasses for the 18th century's informal parties when guests were offered rich sweets and fruits in individual glasses closely arranged on pyramids of glass salvers. 'Dry' sweetmeats (candied fruits, etc.) filled tall-stemmed shallow glasses with fancy rims; 'wet' sweetmeats were served in glasses separately described as jelly glasses, custard cups, syllabub glasses.

Dessert glasses. 93–95 For dry sweetmeats (95 still with original cover).
96 Custard cup. **97** Syllabub glass.

Devonia lace Honiton products of the 1870s with flower petals raised in relief by tension on the threads.

Diagonal barometer *See* Yard-arm barometer.

Dial barometer *See* Wheel barometer.

Diamond (Figs. 35–41) Hardest of all minerals, rare, valuable, with high refractive and dispersive levels; hence its brilliant fire when skilfully cut. Usually clear white, sometimes tinged blue, yellow, etc. Important in jewellery from the 17th century, with Brazilian discoveries in the 1720s when Indian supplies were faltering, but becoming much more plentiful with the development of the South-African mines from the 1870s. Facet-cutting was aided by the stone's tendency to split along planes related to its crystalline form, known as cleavages. *See* Brilliant cut; Refractive brilliance; Rock crystal; Rose cut.

Diamond cutting (Figs. 80–84, 101) Glassware patterned in diamond shapes by cutting on variously edged revolving wheels. Shallow facet cutting from *c.*1720s; diamond shaped projections separated by deep mitre-cuts from the 1790s, these often further cross-cut in 'hobnail' or 'strawberry' pattern. A skilled specialist craft, imitated in pressed glass.

Diamond-point engraving on glass Using a diamond-topped hand tool as distinct from more usual wheel-engraving. Some

83

armorials, etc., from the 1720s; scenes, etc., on Victorian glass. *See* Engraved glass.

Diamond-shaped mark *See* Registration marks.

Diaper (Fig. 104) Reticulated pattern of lines crossing diamond-wise, the spaces filled with dots, on ceramics, etc.; or cloth, especially linen, woven with such a pattern.

Die Engraved metal stamp (often one of two) for striking metals, etc.

Dimity Cotton cloth woven with two threads to make raised stripes, for curtains, etc., from the late 17th century and for early 19th-century dress.

Dipped seat Chair seat curving slightly upwards to the sides, associated with the low back and sabre legs of the Regency period.

Diptych Anything folded so as to have two leaves, e.g., a pair of paintings closing on a hinge.

Similarly *triptych*, having three leaves folding over each other.

Directoire French fashion style named from the executive body in France (1795–9) showing classical severity, reflected in English early Regency styles.

Dish-cross In silver, Sheffield plate, for keeping dishes warm, adjustable to their size and shape. Pivoting arms in X-shape radiating from a central spirit lamp, each arm with a sliding bracket and foot. In a late model, the lamp had a disc to spread the heat. From the 1750s to the 1800s.

Dished (Fig. 221) Shaped with a depression, as on a card-table for counters or on a slide for a candlestick.

Dish ring Not always Irish. Hollow-waisted cylinder of silver, pewter etc., with the same purpose as the dish-cross through the late 17th and 18th centuries, and to protect the table from a hot dish. As a potato-ring it was placed on a dish to support a napkin containing jacket-baked potatoes.

Distaff Cleft stick to hold combed wool or flax for woman's work of hand-spinning.

84

Distressed Furniture dealers' term for a damaged surface, not necessarily old. Originally described badly cut veneer.

Divan Associated with the mid to late 19th-century 'Turkish' or 'Moorish' furnishing style, mainly for smoking-rooms. A long low cushioned seat against a wall. Turkish divan became a term for a cigar shop. *See* Ottoman.

Dog grate Iron or steel. 18th-century development of the basket grate with fireback and four legs to stand in the living-room hearth. With flat-topped hobs to the sides of the bars holding the fire it was known as a duck's nest or hob grate.

Dogs, ceramic 18th-century specimens (porcelain, agate ware) now rare. Poodles etc., in 19th-century bone china, but mainly early Victorian earthenware: sporting dogs and lapdogs for cottage ornaments, in full colour, gold on black or with lustre patches. Many reproductions.

Dogwood Contrasting yellow and yellowish tones in sap and heartwood. Hard but of small girth. Some early inlay, lace bobbins, etc.

Dole cupboard Recent name for early hanging cupboard with ventilated door, e.g., for a church to supply bread to the poor.

Dolls Dated by style. Early, mainly wooden heads. In the 19th-century heads of wax, moulded papier mâché, some bone china and 1850s parian ware. Biscuit porcelain from the 1860s. Sleeping, walking, talking from the 1820s. Blue eyes usual from the 1840s. *See* Pedlar dolls.

Don Pottery Yorkshire, *c.* 1790–1893. Associated with the Leeds Pottery 1800–20. Made earthenwares, fine stonewares, etc., in large quantities for home and export, but lacked the finish of Leeds work.

Door knocker In wrought iron, 16th–19th centuries; cast iron or brass from the early 19th century when the rapper was fixed more strongly. Some castings marked Coalbrookdale. Indoor knocker from the later 19th century might be in cast brass, as local souvenirs, Dickens' characters, etc.

Door porter. Door stop (Fig. 99) In demand after the 1775 introduction of a patent door-closing hinge. Many of cast iron, some bronzed, some brass or steel. Flat-backed from *c*.1790. Celebrity and other figures, such as Coalbrookdale knight in Gothic setting, registered 1841, Mr Punch, Jumbo, etc. Others in Derbyshire marble, Minton terracotta, glass (*See* Dumps), etc.

Dorcer. (And other spellings) Medieval hanging on the wall behind the customary backless bench seats.

Dorset buttons Stitched through the 18th and early 19th centuries in linen thread on a metal ring, either flat, in cartwheel patterns, or as solid little domes, size ranging from *c*.$\frac{1}{8}$ inch to 1 inch. Associated especially with Blandford.

Doric *See* Orders of architecture.

Dos-à-dos Back to back, especially in bookbinding as in some conjoined Bibles and prayer books.

Doubler Pewter, frequently mentioned in 17th- and early 18th-century records until outmoded by Georgian soup plates. Deep plate with a sloping rim for semi-liquid 'spoon meats'.

Double scent bottle Victorian, usually *c*.3–6 inches long, made as a glass tube from two bottles welded together, base to base; some glass-lined silver or base metal, some china. With a different metal lid at each end, one springing open for access to crystals of smelling salts, the other unscrewing over a glass stopper securing a 'handkerchief scent'.

Doublet 1. In costume, man's sleeved jacket worn under an outer cloak or coat (originally under his breastplate). 2. In jewellery, the effect of a large precious stone achieved by cementing together either two thinner stones or a stone backed with paste (opal, garnet, etc.). In a triplet both crown and base are genuine with a central layer of glass.

Double-spouted teapot With a second spout near the top of the vessel used only for pouring away any dust from the tea-leaves that might accumulate on top of the freshly made tea. Mainly 1840s–80s.

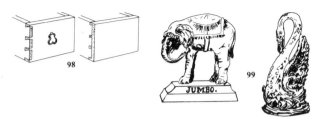

98 Dovetails on drawer fronts: through (*left*), and lapped (ready for fronting of veneer). **99** Door porters, cast iron: Jumbo and swan.

Doughty birds Limited editions of life-size bird models in Worcester porcelain designed by Dorothy Doughty, 1930s–60s.

Doulton wares (Figs. 13, 111, 112, 281) Lambeth, London, from 1815. Some early celebrity figures, but art wares mainly important from the 1860s, especially artist-decorated (and initialled) stonewares. Became Royal Doulton in 1901. Included silicon ware, Lambeth faience, majolica, marqueterie ware, chiné ware, terracotta, etc. Doulton & Co., established in Burslem in 1882, made bone china, etc.

Douter Candle extinguisher from the late 17th century. Scissor-shaped with flat disc ends or a simple cone shape. *See* Chamber candlestick.

Dovetail In furniture, for joining end-grain wood as in drawer corners. Fan-shaped projections fitting corresponding slots. Crude *through dovetails* from *c*.1600. *Lap dovetails* from the late 17th century do not penetrate the drawer front where their end-grain might affect subsequent veneering (which adheres poorly to end-grain wood).

Dowel Wood peg securing a mortise-and-tenon joint.

Down-hearth Primitive stone slab with andirons under the smoke hole in the roof or a wall chimney.

Dram glass. Joey Small, for holding *c*.2 oz. of spirits with a short thick stem (or none) and heavy foot.

Drawback silver mark Britannia figure incuse (hollow) used December 1, 1784 to July 1795, showing that a duty refund had been made on export gold and silver.

Drawing table *See* Architect's table.

Drawn stem, Straw-shank (Fig. 100) Drinking-glass stem drawn out from the bowl as distinct from the stuck-shank or three-piece glass.

Drawn-thread embroidery. Drawn-and-cut work Some horizontal fabric threads were removed and the remaining (vertical) threads grouped into patterns by stitching. Elaborated by cutting some vertical fabric threads and filling the spaces with needlepoint lace stitches. *See* Pulled-thread embroidery.

Draw table (Fig. 271) Extending table with two leaves under a central section supported by slanting bearers so that, with either or both drawn out, they present a level table surface. Made in England from the 16th century. Many modern (popular in the 1930s).

Dredger Castor with a loop handle at the side – 'kitchen pepper'.

Dresden Pattern name found on 19th-century English ceramics. *See* Meissen porcelain.

Dresser Medieval-Tudor side-table for displaying plate. With a rack of shelves fixed above it from *c.*1700 as a single piece of furniture and elaborated in the 18th century. *See* Welsh dresser; Yorkshire dresser.

Dresser, Christopher (Figs. 32, 34, 287) (1834–1904). Botanist and freelance designer of silver, electroplate (including such firms as Elkingtons and James Dixon), base metals, carpets, furniture, glass and ceramics, reflecting his wide-ranging interest in Chinese, Islamic, Peruvian and Italian artefacts. Visited Japan in 1877 and became a leading enthusiast for Japonaiserie. A pioneer of modern design, delighting in the machine age, he approved severely functional forms, accepting the need for factory processes and cheaply prepared materials. *See* Clutha glass; Linthorpe.

Drinking glasses. 100 For strong ale, engraved with hop and barley, drawn stem. **101** Cordial glass, flowered ogee bowl, cusped, diamond-cut stem, *c.* 1770. **102** Cider flute, apple engraving, air-twist stem, *c.* 1760s. **103** Champagne coupe with Venetian-influenced fancy colour-twist stem, mid 19th century.

Drinking table *See* Horseshoe table.

Drizzling bag or box Containing scissors, pins and small boxes supposedly for the late 18th-century women's French-inspired pastime of drizzling – unpicking gold and silver embroideries and braids in order to sell the metal for pin money.

Drop front *See* Secretary.

Drop handle (Fig. 24) For furniture drawers, etc. Metal drop or acorn shape hanging loosely from its backplate. Popular in late 17th-century brass, and in modern use.

Drop Small glass pendant or lustre. From around 1730; more from the 1760s. Simple faceted, flattened pear shapes changing to the 19th-century's long icicles and early Victorian sharp-cornered prisms. On épergnes, girandoles.

Drum table Modern name for a round-topped four-footed pillar-and-claw table with drawers in the frieze, often including shams, from late in the 18th century.

Drunkard's chair Victorian name for Georgian elbow chair with a spindle back and wide low seat, sometimes saddle-shaped.

Dry-edge figures In soft-paste porcelain, figures glaze-dipped by hand, head downwards so that the glaze might fail to reach the base, leaving paste uncovered. No glaze 'shrinkage', but the base might be wiped.

Drypoint engraving Print with textured effect from the burr left by drawing a pointed tool across a copper plate. Often used to improve etchings and widely on steel-faced copper plates.

Dry stonewares *See* Fine-stonewares.

Duchesse French couch formed of two tub-shaped easy chairs linked by a stool, illustrated by Hepplewhite, etc. From *c.* 1760s.

Duck-egg porcelain Swansea porcelain with greenish translucency only briefly made by William Billingsley, 1816, but reproduced.

Dudson, James Hanley potter at work 1838–88 making ornaments, etc., in earthenwares and, notably, in fine stonewares with relief decoration, many registered. Mosaic work from 1856.

Duesbury, William (1725?–86) China decorator. Directed Derby Porcelain Co. from 1756; also acquired Chelsea, 1769, Bow 1776. Followed by son, same name (d. 1796) and grandson.

Dulcimer Popular Medieval musical instrument with horizontal wire strings, vibrated with hammers.

Dumb waiter (Fig. 221) For self-service at supper, etc. Elaboration of the claw table with two or three circular tiers on a central pillar. Georgian and later.

Dummy board From Holland. A flat board cut in the silhouette of a human or animal figure, flower group, etc., made more realistic by having the edges thinned from the back, painted in full colour as a house or garden decoration, especially to fill a summer fireplace. Soldiers and maidservants were especially popular. In England from the 17th century, but more from the late 18th century onwards, perhaps painted by out-of-work sign painters.

Dump Door-stop or large paperweight shaped as a tall dome in cheap greenish bottle glass containing long air bubbles. Victorian.

Du Paquier porcelain Important early 18th-century Viennese factory making hard-paste porcelain under C. I. Du Paquier from 1719, aided at first by two workmen from Meissen. Sold to the Austrian state in 1744, continuing with intermittent success, mainly around the 1800s to 1805, but declining thereafter until it closed in 1864.

Dust boards Introduced between drawers as part of the chest of drawers carcase, customary in antique specimens.

Dutch metal. Dutch gold Alloy of about 11 parts copper to 2 parts zinc. A substitute for gold leaf, but needed protecting with varnish. In powder form it was used for papier mâché ornament, etc. *See* Bronze powders.

Dutch oven Rectangular box shape on short legs, to stand with its open back against the fire grate, its contents accessible by a door in the front. Some of copper or handsomely japanned.

Duty ace Decorative ace of spades in a pack of cards, showing duty paid from 1712 (the amount and monarch's initials). From 1765 part of the duty was shown on the wrapper. From 1862 the whole payment (3d) was shown on the wrapper, but the ace was still decorated. *See* Playing cards.

Duty mark, silver *See* Monarch's-head duty mark.

Dwight, John (d. 1703) Founded Fulham Pottery, 1671, noted for brown, white, red and mottled 'agate' stonewares, including notable figures. The pottery was continued by the family to 1862.

Eagle table *See* Console table.

Early Georgian General term usually applied to products of the reigns of George I and George II (1714–60).

Earthenware General term for opaque clay wares porous after kiln firing so that for most purposes they require glazing. Thus it includes, e.g., slipware and ironstone china, but not stonewares.

Eastlake, C. L. (Fig. 296) (1836–1906) Author of influential *Hints on Household Taste in Furniture, etc.*, 1868 (several editions). Offered soundly constructed, but massive rectilinear, 'early English' furniture designs in contrast to the high Victorians' niggling curves, glued on mouldings and 'gouty table legs'. Inspired American fashion for plain furniture in so-called 'Eastlake style'.

Eaton Hall chair In use from the 1840s, but so named from 1867 when supplied to the Duke of Westminster. Padded arms and back forming a continuous bow shape following a nearly circular seat-line and supported on turned spindles. Short front legs, turned; back legs swept back for rigidity. *See* Smoker's bow chair.

Ebéniste French equivalent of the British cabinet-maker.

Ebonite *See* Vulcanite.

Ebony Lustrous black wood, hard, heavy, reintroduced to Europe early in the 17th century. Its brittleness may have prompted the development of veneering. Much imitated in black stained ebonised furniture, especially by the Victorians.

Echinus *See* Egg-and-dart.

Ecuelle Saucer-shaped bowl or porringer with a lid and frequently two horizontal handles. Of French origin, a few English-made in silver in the early 18th century and in porcelain later in the century.

Edkins, Michael Bristol-based decorator of ceramics and glass including opaque white enamel glass and Bristol blue (1760–1780s).

Edouart, Augustin (1789–1861) Silhouettist. French refugee in England from 1814. Extremely prolific freehand cutter, 1826–38, some full-length groups being set against washed in or lithographed backgrounds. Published his now rare *Treatise* in 1835 and was much copied.

Edwards, George Remembered for line engravings of 'uncommon birds', etc., 1740s–60s.

Egg-and-dart. Egg-and-tongue. Egg-and-anchor Classical architectural ornament used as carved moulding on English furniture from the 16th century. Series of alternate ovals and points sometimes called echinus from mouldings often so carved above a Doric column. *See* Orders of architecture.

Egg boiler. Egg frame Silver, etc., for the late Georgian and Victorian breakfast-table. The boiler with a spirit lamp and, often, an egg timer; the frame, like a cruet set, but holding egg cups, gilded spoons and sometimes a salt cellar.

Eggshell porcelain Imitating Chinese ware in its extreme thinness, made by Coalport, Minton, Belleek, etc.

Eglomisé *See* Verre églomisé.

Egyptian black Black fine-stoneware from the 1720s, improved by Wedgwood in the 1770s, but inferior to his basaltes.

Egyptian ornament (Fig. 126) Egyptian heads carved on pilasters, chimera monopods, sphinxes, scarabs, lotus, etc., introduced in English furnishings through much of the 18th century, becoming more widely popular around 1800 due to Napoleon's campaign and Denon's illustrated *Voyage*, 1802.

Electro-gilding *See* Gilding.

Electroplate Sometimes, confusingly, called plated or electroplated silver. Base metal wares thinly coated with a frosting of pure gold, silver or other metal by electro-chemical galvanic action. Patent taken out 1840 by G. R. Elkington of Birmingham in association with John Wright. When the silver has been electroplated over copper there is a possibility of confusion with the entirely different process of Sheffield plate. *See* Electrotype.

Electrotype. Galvano Patented 1841. Rare original models (antiquities, etc.) made available to the public by being copied in wax or wax-saturated plaster and exactly reproduced in electroplate. Replicas of engraved wood blocks were made in this way for printing many Victorian 'wood engravings'.

Elers red ware Fine stoneware made by Dutchmen J. P. and D. Elers, in England from 1688 using a formula from Dwight of Fulham to make, e.g., Chinese-style teapots, lathe-trimmed and with die-shaped decoration.

Elevators In sets of four to raise plinth-based furniture two—three inches above the floor. Earthenware, brown or brightly coloured in imaginative shapes such as celebrity heads, lions, fruit, etc., as well as plain bun shapes. 19th century.

Elizabethan (1558–1603, reign of Elizabeth I) expressing Italian Renaissance influence with ostentatious carving, inlays and ironwork, but confused by Victorians who applied the term to their imitations of 17th-century styles.

Elm Tough, light brown, coarse-grained wood, hard-wearing, much used for seats (e.g. on Windsor chairs, and in railway locomotive engines). Wych elm, pinkish brown for similar uses.

Elton ware Made by self-taught Sir Edmund Elton at the Sunflower Pottery, Clevedon, (c. 1880–1920), who devised his own kilns, wheel, metallic glazes, coloured slips, etc., winning many exhibition awards.

Email ombrant Developed by the French from the lithophane, but in reverse: when flooded with translucent glaze colour (usually green) the irregular surface presented a pattern in varying intensities, with the thinnest areas, where glaze was deepest, showing darkest. Process acquired by the Wedgwood firm 1873.

Embossing. Repoussé chasing 1. In metal, raised ornament pressed or beaten outward from the back usually with hammer and punches, without removing any metal, the detail often sharpened by chasing. 2. Decorating with applied bosses or rounded knobs.

Embroidery (Figs. 270, 303) Ornament in needlework stitches.

Embroidery frame Rectangular or round (tambour) frame to hold fabric taut for embroidery. *See* Tambour embroidery.

Emerald cut *See* Step cut.

Empire style Associated with Napoleon's first empire (1799–1815), its heavy Neo-classical features continuing into the 1820s; more ornate than the austere Directoire, with much ormolu, dark red mahogany, military motifs.

Enamel Basically glass, opacified or/and coloured using pigments derived from metallic oxides which combined with the lead oxide glaze for heat-fusing on to metal, ceramics, glassware. *See* below.

Enamel glass Vases, candlesticks, etc. of glass opacified with tin oxide to look like translucent white porcelain, similarly decorated with enamel colours or transfer prints. From the 1750s. Imitated in inferior 'sunset glow' glass.

Enamelled glass (Fig. 85) Clear glass with enamelled ornament. Developed in 12th-century Aleppo. *See* Beilby; Mary Gregory.

Enamelled metals *See* Cloisonné; Champlevé; Plique-à-jour.

Enamelling, ceramic Coloured enamels fused to glazed surface by kiln firing, the colours brush-painted and fired in succession beginning with those requiring the greatest kiln heat. Improved muffle kiln invented 1812, widespread by 1820 giving more brilliant results.

Enamels, painted Successful minor English manufacture from the 1740s; deteriorating towards 1800. Opaque white enamel fused over the entire surface of thin copper as a basis for hand-painting and/or monochrome transfer-printing in enamel colours and black. At first small wine labels, snuffboxes, étuis, scent bottles, etc.; later also tea caddies, candlesticks, pierced counter trays, etc. Associated with London, including the notable Battersea factory, 1753–6, and with Birmingham, Bilston and Wednesbury where bright ornament included gilded Rococo

104 Enamels, painted: scent bottle and snuffbox. **105** Engraved glass (Jacobite symbols).

95

scrolling in low relief, coloured diapered backgrounds, pastoral scenes, etc., probably finest in the 1760s–70s. *See* Battersea enamels; Limoges enamels.

Enamel twist Stem ornament in drinking-glasses; spirals of colour and opaque white, mainly 1760–80. *See* Air twist glass.

Encaustic ornament Colours burnt-in to decorate ceramics, as in ancient application of colour over chalk-coated wax. Wedgwood, 1769, patented a method of painting in encaustic colours including gold bronze 'in imitation of ancient Etruscan and Roman earthenware'. *See* Basaltes. In encaustic tiles the pattern in coloured clay was set into mould-shaped cavities in the tile and fused by firing, a Medieval method revived by Samuel Wright (patent 1830) and Herbert Minton. *See* Tiles.

End grain Wood surface revealed by cross-cutting.

Endive marquetry *See* Marquetry.

End-of-day glass. Slag glass (Fig. 228) Names prompted by the inclusion of purplish glassy blast-furnace waste or slag from the molten metal taken at the end of the working day. This cheap, strong ingredient was mixed with clear glass and pressed into a wide range of minor items such as spill jars, cream jugs, basket vases, candlesticks and so on, in opaque purplish marble effects. These are often found with registration marks or with makers' marks (*see* Pressed glass), the same moulds being used over a very long period which may prompt over-early dating. The same moulds also might be used to press other opaque glass – white, turquoise, etc. – made by the same firms, but this is not slag glass; it is also incorrect to regard end-of-day glass as a mixture of glassworks waste. *See* Queen's-ware glass; Vitro-porcelain.

Engine turning. Rose engine turning Close repetitive line patterns engraved on metal by a lathe with an eccentric motion, first evolved by wood-turners for shaping the rim outlines of piecrust tables, etc.; applied by Josiah Wedgwood in 1763 to incise fine-stonewares. (It obviated finger marks on Victorian silver card cases and Edwardian cigarette cases.)

ENGLAND as a ceramic mark Applied only from 1891 which is helpful in dating much late Victorian ware. Then the McKinley Tariff Act required the mark on exports to the United States so that it came into widespread use. This century more usually MADE IN ENGLAND.

English plate *See* British plate.

Engobe Whitish clay, mixed to a creamy consistency, applied over a rough earthenware body as a basis for glaze and ornament. Not to be confused with delftware's costlier tin-enamelled surface.

Engraved glass (Figs. 91, 100–102, 105) Pattern cut into the glass surface by holding it against a revolving wheel with abrasive. From *c.* 1730. *See* Diamond-point engraving.

Engraved metal 1. To ornament silver, etc. 2. To prepare a copper plate for the printing of engravings. Linear designs using sharp-pointed gravers or burins to cut away tiny fragments of metal, leaving tapering hollows.

Engraving. Line engraving Print taken by applying damped paper to an engraved and inked copper plate. Requiring considerable pressure, leaving a slight depression (plate mark) over the area of paper that the copper plate has covered and also a very slight projection of the ink above the level of the paper. *See* Etching; Wood engraving.

Enseigne Man's hat ornament, 16th century, frequently of enamelled gold.

Entablature *See* Orders of architecture.

Entrée dish For made-up foods in contrast to joints. Mainly from the 1740s in silver, Sheffield plate, ceramics – round, oblong, etc., often kept hot by a matching hot-water stand and with a close-fitting lid, sometimes flat with an unscrewing handle, to serve as a second dish.

Envelope table Square topped, with hinged triangular leaves folding over to the centre.

EPBM mark Electroplated silver ware with a base of Britannia metal, instead of the more usual nickel alloy. From the 1840s.

Epergne Dining-table centrepiece hung with detachable dishes around a central bowl. From *c.*1760, often very ornate in silver, Sheffield plate, glass.

EPNS mark. Indicates silver electroplated on to an article constructed of nickel alloy. *See* Nickel silver.

E Pluribus Unum One from many: United States motto associated with American-eagle marks on English export ceramics.

Escapement To control the power from the spring or weight that drives a clock or watch mechanism. Many types.

Escallop shell (Figs. 118, 310) 1. Badge of many Medieval pilgrims. 2. As a vessel, found, e.g., in 17th-century silver spice boxes, 18th-century ceramics. 3. Ornamental motif carved on much early 18th-century furniture and later worked in marquetry.

Escalloped or scalloped In embroidery, glass, etc., a series of convex curves.

Escritoire *See* Secretary.

Escutcheon 1. Shield shape for an armorial device. 2. Ornamental plate round a keyhole.

Etagère *See* Whatnot.

Etched glass Cheap shallow substitute for hand-cutting, e.g., on Victorian cased glass. Hydrofluoric acid applied to patterns scratched through acid-resistant wax or, from the 1890s, around protected areas printed in acid-resistant ink.

Etching, print Lines cut with pointed tools through wax varnish on a copper plate so that aqua fortis (nitric acid) could bite away the metal, forming hollows that would hold printing ink, to be applied under pressure to paper. Freer, less delicately tapering lines than those of an engraving.

Eternity ring Finger ring with a continuous jewel mounting.

Etruria Ceramics factory, hall and village founded by Josiah Wedgwood in 1769 with his partner Thomas Bentley, following European interest in ancient Etruria, Italy. The firm moved to Barlaston in 1940.

Etruscan style in ceramics Part of the Neo-classical vogue from the 1760s, showing confused admiration for Etruscan, Greek and Roman ornament, revived by early Victorians, with Neo-classical figures and other motifs in contrasting black, white and terracotta colouring. *See* Encaustic ornament.

Etui. Tweezer-case Flattened, slightly tapering cylinder with a deep hinged lid, to carry or hang on the chatelaine, slotted to hold personal trifles such as scissors and memo slip. Delightfully decorative in jewelled precious metals, painted enamels, porcelain, ivory, etc. *See* Nécessaire.

Ewer Large water jug with accompanying basin. Ornate in early silver for dinner guests. On the wash-basin stand it replaced the customary small bottle, late in the 18th century, gradually becoming larger.

Exercising chair *See* Chamber horse.

Eye portraits Ancient fashion, revived in the late 18th century by Richard Cosway and other miniaturists, for jewellery and snuffboxes. Less attractive stock designs painted in enamels were available by the 1830s; Victorians liked them pearl-framed as mantelshelf ornament. Minor revival among Edwardians.

Fabergé, Peter Carl (1846–1920) Russian silversmith and jeweller of French Huguenot descent, who opened his London shop in 1903 to sell the creations of his St Petersburg master-craftsmen.

Face-piece Horse brass for a horse's forehead.

Facet One of the small cut and polished faces of a gemstone.

Facet cutting (Figs. 80, 101) In glass, the grinding of shallow hollows to make a pattern of diamond or triangular shapes on, e.g., a candlestick or a wineglass stem or a pendant drop. Very shallow in the 1720s–40s; elaborate in the late 18th century until overtaken by deep diamond cutting in the 1790s.

Façon de Venise *See* Venetian glass; Verzelini.

Facsimile Exact reproduction such as copy of an original print. Not usually of collector interest.

Faience Originally the French name for tin-enamelled ware, probably from Faenza, important Italian maiolica centre, but its meaning has been lost through indiscriminate use. *See* Delftware. The ware was important throughout France, especially in the 18th century until largely ousted by porcelain and, especially, by English cream-coloured earthenware from Leeds, Wedgwood, etc.

Fairings Cheap novelties sold at fairs, of glass and especially ceramics such as the late 19th century's poorly finished figure groups of 'comic postcard' humour, German-made for the English market, with English inscriptions.

Fairy lights *See* Night-lights.

Fake Article made or in some way altered with the deliberate intention of deception so as to increase its value.

Faldstool Medieval stool with a folding X-frame.

Fall-front. Drop-front *See* Secretary.

Famille rose Chinese porcelain classified for its enamel decoration in soft delicate colours dominated by a range of opaque pink tones (derived from gold-and-tin purple of Cassius) introduced from Europe, *c.* 1720. Terms with similar application include *famille verte* (translucent green used mainly with strong rust red, restrained purple, yellow and blue), and *familles jaune* and *noire* (yellow and black backgrounds combined with famille verte ornament): yellow and black being of the K'ang Hsi period (1662–1722) preceded the more familiar opaque enamels of *famille rose*.

Fan Ancient device for cooling and screening the face, folding designs gradually becoming predominant in England in the late 16th century. With a folding leaf or mount of vellum or paper painted in pliant gouache, or of silk, lace, etc., mounted on sticks which are held together at the base by a rivet, all folding between more substantial sticks known as guards. *See* Brins; Brisé fan; Cabriolet fan; Chicken skin; Cockade fan; Medallion; Pompadour; Quizzing fan.

Farthingale Woman's skirt expanded at the hips over metal

Fans. 106 Cabriolet with painted leaf. **107** Brisé, pierced ivory.
108 Cockade, painted silk.

hoops, worn in the late 16th and early 17th centuries; hence contemporaneous 'embroiderer's chair' with broad upholstered seat and back panel, without arms, now known as a *farthingale chair.*

Favrile glass From the American Long Island glass-works of L. C. Tiffany, established 1893. Extremely wide range of brilliantly coloured, iridescent and variously textures glass-wares, probably invented by Englishman Arthur Nash.

Feather edge 1. From late in the 18th century on silver spoon and fork handles: an edge pattern of small slanting lines. 2. A cabinet-maker's term for planing down to a fine edge.

Feathers Popular in 18th- and 19th-century hobbies, gummed into pictures, stitched into embroideries, cut and curled into flower posies, etc., Victorians often bleaching and spray-dyeing them.

Fecit. Fecerunt *See* Inscriptions.

Fede ring (Fig. 178) Finger ring with central motif of two clasped hands.

Feldspar (felspar) porcelain Evolved by Josiah Spode II, *c.*1800 and continued to the 1830s, modifying the firm's successful bone china formula to include pure feldspar, fired at a high temperature to produce extremely hard, translucent, brilliantly white ware. Other makers included Coalport, Worcester (Chamberlain) and Derby.

Fender Metal guard to the hearth from late in the 17th century with a bottom plate from late in the 18th century and becoming more ornate in the 19th.

Ferronière. Ferronnière Forehead chain with a central dangling jewel – a brief fashion around 1835 imitating Francis I's mistress (blacksmith's wife) in the Leonardo da Vinci portrait, *La Belle Ferronnière*.

Festoon *See Swag.*

Fibula Clasp for draped garments worn from the Bronze Age to the Middle Ages.

Fiddle back Applied to an early 18th-century chair, describing either its pierced splat or, in the bended-back chair, its waisted outline.

Field bed. Slope bed Quickly assembled for the traveller, with essential curtains hung on the space-saving arched or slanting frame of the field bedstead. No implication of campaign rigours; 16th to 19th centuries. *See* Tent bed.

Fielded panel With a flat central field above sunken bevelled edges.

Figure flask *See* Flask.

Filigree metal work Curled and twisted openwork ornament in gold or silver wire giving lace-like effect. Imitated in 19th-century stamped gilt-metal.

Filigree paper work. Quillwork For ornamental panels, etc., in the late 17th century, but mainly from the late 18th century, for decorating screens, tea caddies, etc. Paper strips $\frac{1}{8}$ inch wide were rolled and curled into patterns and edge-glued to paper, silk, occasionally metal foil or mother-of-pearl. The paper's projecting edge was often coloured or gilded to suggest stained ivory or gold wire.

Fillet 1. Flat narrow band, e.g., between pillar flutes. 2. Ledge supporting a shelf.

Filter Important through the 19th century, but often unrecognised today, containing a filter-stone for purifying water.

Cylindrical stoneware five-gallon vessel often decorated in low relief, with cover, handles and tap. Made by Doulton (improved design 1870), Lipscombe, Stiff, etc. (20 makers exhibited at 1851 exhibition).

Fin de siècle Implies the end of the 19th century, often suggesting decadence.

Fine stonewares. Dry stonewares Like common stonewares these were vitrified by high-temperature firing, needing no glaze, but finer-grained and in a range of colours – including black basaltes, Egyptian black, cane ware, jasper ware.

Finger bowl For rinsing finger tips at dinner. Provided from *c*.1760 as a 'wash hand glass' and by *c*.1780 as a 'finger cup', usually in clear blue glass with low, nearly vertical sides. In many colours from *c*.1845. Not to be confused with the individual wine-glass cooler.

Finial Topmost ornament whether on furniture pediment, teapot lid or spoon handle, e.g., the flambeau or flaming torch on a longcase clock.

Fireback Cast-iron slab with relief ornament at the back of a fire to protect the walls and reflect heat into the room. In the 15th century was a wide rectangle; by the late 17th century, an arch-topped, tombstone shape.

Fireclay ware Cheap Victorian substitute for basaltes, used for wine coolers, conservatory ornaments, etc., in classical styles made by J & M. P. Bell and others.

Firedogs *See* Andirons.

Fire gilding *See* Gilding.

Fire plate. Fire mark (Fig. 110) Symbol such as an insurance company's trademark (phoenix, sun, etc.) mounted on the wall of an insured house, to guide the company's firemen. Of lead in the 18th century; later might be of iron, tin or copper. Many fakes.

Fire polishing In glass, reheating at the furnace mouth to remove mould marks, etc., so that a moulded or pressed piece may suggest free-blown, hand-cut work.

109 Food warmer or veilleuse showing typical vessels and their stand.
110 Fire plates: Sun office, founded 1710 and Westminster, founded 1717.

Firescreen *See* Cheval glass; Pole screen.
Firing glass To signify approval of toasts by a 'volley' of rapping on the table; hence a stumpy dram glass with a short thick stem and heavy disc foot. From *c.*1760 onwards.
Fishley earthenware From a Fremington, Devon potter family from late in the 18th century. Marked wares are associated with Edwin Beer Fishley, in charge 1861–1911, including primitive shapes with 18th-century dates.
Fish server. Fish slice Silver, Sheffield plate, electroplate. Pierced or engraved triangular trowel blades from the 1750s, fish shapes, and some diamond shapes, *c.*1780–1820; asymmetrical with the blunt edge in a cyma curve from *c.*1800. With a serving fork from *c.*1820.
Fitzroy barometer (Fig. 17) First inexpensive mercury barometer. In a glazed rectangular frame, the tube flanked by 'remarks' and other weather lore (several variants are known) by Admiral Fitzroy, director of the Meteorological Office. He died in 1865 but his design was registered against copying in 1881.
Flagon Metal, for serving wine. With hinged lid and tankard-type handle, but usually taller; some with beaked lips from

104

c. 1720. The Oxford flagon with urn-shaped body, double-dome lid, came early in the 19th century.

Flambé glazes. Transmutation glazes. *See* Glazes.

Flame stitch *See* Bargello embroidery.

Flanders chest Not always Flemish. A 15th- to 16th-century chest with low relief 'church window' arcadings. These might be glued on; the term was applied also to 17th-century chests with other applied ornament (mitred mouldings, split turnings, etc.).

Flashed glass Cheap substitute for cased glass. With tinted molten glass briefly skimmed over clear blown glass before being reheated and blown into shape. Victorian.

Flasks Flattened bottles for travellers, in silver, pewter, etc., such as the collectable spirit flasks in brown and buff stoneware made in Derbyshire, Lambeth, etc., especially in the 1820s to 1840s. Shapes of these included popular head-and-shoulders models of political figures and other celebrities, especially those associated with the Reform Bill; also mermaids, jolly sailors, powder horns, fish, etc.

Flat-back ornaments Victorian Staffordshire figures for the mantelshelf, mould-shaped, with relief detail and colour on the front and sides only. Much collected, especially celebrity and

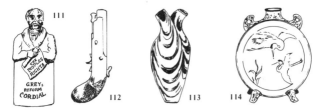

Flasks. 111, 112 Spirit flasks by Doulton: political (1832) and pistol shape. **113** Gemel flask in Nailsea glass. **114** Costrel or moon flask, late 19th century.

topical figures, but old moulds were used for reproductions until the 1960s.

Flat chasing *See* Chasing.

Flatware 1. In ceramics, plates, dishes, etc., as distinct from hollow-ware vessels. 2. In metal, spoons, forks, etc., lacking cutlery's cutting edges.

Flemish scrolls Sharply opposed curves forming S-shapes in late 17th-century chair legs, etc.

Fleur-de-lys Heraldic stylised lily motif associated with the French Bourbon family, probably derived from the ancient Egyptian stylised lotus.

Flight porcelain Worcester porcelain mark (and thus able to be dated) with the initials, etc. of the following: Thomas Flight, 1783–93; Flight & Barr, 1793–1807; Barr, Flight and Barr, 1807–13; Flight, Barr & Barr, 1813–40. Bone china from *c.*1800. *See* Worcester.

Flint-glass Now called lead crystal. For table glass, chandeliers, etc. World-renowned English development (rather than discovery) by George Ravenscroft (1618–81). This contained lead oxide from 1675 instead of lime, the name flint-glass long being retained although the silica was obtained from sand rather than from crushed flints after *c.*1730. (Typical modern formula contains sand, red lead, potash and saltpetre, with borax for greater strength and a little arsenic.) Much finer refractive fire than lime-soda glass and heavy, with a resonant ring. *See* Glass; Lehr.

Flounce *See* Ruching.

Flowered glass *See* Cordial glass.

Flower-encrusted china (Fig. 208) Flowers fashioned petal by petal and applied to ornaments in soft-paste porcelain from the 1750s including white biscuit, but mainly in bone china from the 1820s – Minton, Coalport, Rockingham, etc. – and a little parian ware from the 1850s.

Flown blue Delicate blurred effect of colour flowing slightly into the surrounding glaze. By the Wedgwood firm from *c*.1820 followed by others; sometimes other colours from the 1830s.

Fluorspar *See* Blue john.

Flute (Figs. 100, 102) Drinking-glass from the 1680s with a deep conical bowl to allow for the sediment usual in cider, etc. From the 1740s often attractively wheel-engraved with apples or fruiting vine (for champagne), but most usually for strongly alcoholic strong-ale, (as distinct from frothy nappy ale or beer). *See* Ale glass; Champagne glass.

Fluting (Fig. 125) Close-set semi-circular grooves or channels, as on many pillars. The opposite of convex reeding. *See* Batswing fluting.

Fly bracket (Fig. 276) Hinged rail swinging out horizontally to support a light table-flap.

Fly catcher From the 1780s–90s to the 1860s. Resembled a wide-based decanter on three small feet, but with an open base, its lower rim curved in and upward, forming a two-inch gutter to hold sweetened strong-ale. Insects were attracted, stupefied and drowned.

Fly terret *See* Horse bells.

Fob *See* Watch fob.

Folded foot. Welted foot Wine-glass foot folded back on itself (upward or downward) to make a strong rim. Especially from the late 17th century to the 1750s, and in reproductions.

Foliate Leafy.

Folio Describes an approximate size of book, being composed of paper sheets folded once to make two leaves (four pages) Twice folded for *quarto size*; folded into eight leaves for *octavo size*. Exact measurement depends on size of unfolded sheet; usually *c*.8 inches high.

Food warmer. Veilleuse (Fig. 109) Early Georgian to late Victorian bedside gadget. Tall, hollow, cylindrical stand containing a lamp heater and with its open top supporting a lidded vessel for hot caudle or other drink, fitted closely over a hot-water bowl.

Found in delftware, stoneware, bone china, etc. May be spouted.

Footman Four-footed variant of the trivet.

Fore-edge painting On the edges of book pages, visible when the book is closed, making the words of a title (from the Middle Ages) or a picture from *c.* 1520. Developed as an English craft from the mid 17th century with disappearing fore-edge paintings which became visible only when the leaves were fanned or slanted by opening the book at its title page. Book-binder William Edwards of Halifax revived the fashion in the 1780s with paintings of tiny landscapes, etc., including the rare double-paintings revealed by slanting the pages in opposite directions. Sometimes the paintings were more completely concealed by gilding on the closed page edges. Many date to the 19th century and some are still being produced, on old volumes.

Forgery Anything made deliberately as a fraudulent imitation.

Fork Considerable use from the 17th century, dated by comparing with knife and spoon handles. Number of tines, or prongs, is no guide to its age. Collectors must avoid forks made from less valuable old spoons.

Form watch From the 17th century, a watch in the form of a miniature violin, a shell or any other unlikely item.

Fortune doll With folded paper slips giving brief 'prophecies' under her skirts to be pulled out at random, replacements being available. Mainly Victorian.

Foster, Edward (1761–1864) of Derby. Practised as a silhouettist after retiring from the army in 1805, painting on card, frequently in reddish brown with occasional touches of other colours and considerable bronzing.

Four-poster Differentiated in the 18th century from a standing bedstead by having a low head-board and so requiring four posts to support the tester.

Fox head *See* Stirrup cup.

Fox marks Rusty brown stains on paper, usually due to damp affecting traces of iron.

Free-blown glass Shaped by glassblower without moulds, by 2000-year-old technique, implying high quality work. A 'gather' of hot glass was inflated into a bubble by blowing down a metal tube, for tooling into the required hollow-ware shape.

Freedom box Ornate container for a key or document conveying the freedom of a city. Popular with Victorians.

Fremington pottery *See* Fishley.

French foot Bracket foot with a simple concave outward curve, fashionable in late 18th-century chest furniture.

French plating Attempt to protect base metals from corrosion by covering in layers of thinly beaten silver leaf. Improved as close plating.

French polish Shellac, gum copal and gum arabic applied to furniture as a hard glossy protection against damp, but easily spoilt by heat. Widely used from *c.* 1820.

Fresco Ancient technique of painting on damp plaster.

Fret. Greek key. Labyrinth (Fig. 206) Strictly geometrical running pattern of parallel horizontal and vertical straight lines, intermingled without intersecting, for furniture friezes, etc.

Fretwork (Figs. 60, 119) Thin wood delicately sawn into openwork patterns. In a blind fret the pattern is cut into the face of the wood without piercing it.

Frieze In furniture, the horizontal member below the cabinet cornice or table top. *See* Orders of architecture.

Frigger In glass, an original piece made by a glassworker, but a term now applied to all cheap Victorian–Edwardian commercial novelties including 'Nailsea'.

Frit Glass maker's basic mixture (sand and alkalis). Mixed with clays to give translucence to imitations of Chinese hard-porcelain, making soft-paste or frit porcelain.

Frith, Frederick Silhouettist at work in the early 19th century who frequently placed his cut full-length figures (in black touched with bronze) against sepia-wash backgrounds – sometimes against elaborate detailed drawings.

Frog 1. Ornamental button-and-loop fastening for a military coat. 2. Waistbelt attachment for a sword or bayonet.

Frog mug From the late 18th century in lightweight earthenware, but mostly found now in heavy Victorian granite ware. With a modelled frog or toad attached inside, revealed near the startled drinker's mouth when he drained his murky beer.

Frosting 1. In silver, a matt white surface produced by acid fumes or scratch-brushing, popular with early Victorians as a contrast to polished modelling. 2. In silvered glass, achieved by grinding.

Frye, Thomas (1710–62) Irish painter and mezzotint engraver, partner and manager of Bow porcelain factory, patenting, 1749, the firm's use of a formula containing bone ash.

Fuddling cups Three or more earthenware mugs so conjoined that the contents flows between them.

Fulham pottery *See* Dwight; Elers.

Fumed oak From the 1890s, wood rendered greyish (fading yellowish) with ammonia fumes. *See* Limed oak.

Fusee 1. Early match for cigar lighting. 2. In a *fusee watch or clock*, a conical pulley for equalising the power of the mainspring.

Fustian In 16th to 19th centuries, coarse twill cotton-and-linen or cotton cloth for embroidered bed furnishings, etc.

Fustic Yellow wood, soon turning brown; for inlay and dyeing.

Gable Triangular shaping at the end of a ridged roof; hence this shape in clock-case, etc.

Gadrooning, Knurling. Nulling (Fig. 47) Series of convex knobs, upright or slanting, to edge furniture, silver, etc. suggesting the knuckles of a clenched fist. Hence the late 17th-century Spanish foot and 18th-century knurled foot − inward-curling reeded scrolls or formalised paws.

Galena *See* Lead glaze.

Gallé, Emile (1846–1904) Imaginative, nature-loving French designer of glass, furniture, jewellery, etc. in *Art Nouveau* manner (employing *c.*300 craftsmen in 1900). Signed work from his Nancy factories continued to 1914.

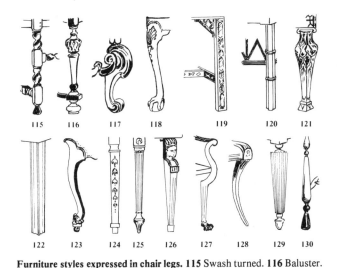

Furniture styles expressed in chair legs. 115 Swash turned. **116** Baluster. **117** Scroll. All later 17th century. **118** Cabriole with ball-and-claw foot; **119** 'Chinese'. **120, 121** 'Gothic'. All early and mid 18th century. **122** Wave moulded. **123** 'French'. **124** Square taper (marlboro'). **125** Fluted round taper. All later 18th century. **126** Egyptian. **127** Spavin. **128** Sabre. **129** 'Greek'. All Regency and late Georgian. **130** Turned shaping timelessly popular on country chairs.

Gallery Raised border or miniature railing, in wood or metal on furniture.

Galon. Galloon Decorative braid for upholstery or dress.

Galvanised *See* Electroplate. A term inexactly applied to the coating of iron with zinc for rust prevention.

Games-table (Figs. 277, 278) With reversible top or flap marked on one side for chess or draughts; often elaborated with provision for backgammon, etc. Mainly from the 1750s onwards, including many pouch tables and sofa tables.

Gardevin *See* Cellaret.

Gardner porcelain factory Established 1765 near Moscow by Staffordshire-born Francis Gardner who emigrated in 1746. Eventually became the second largest in Russia making table-wares, figures, etc., in hard-paste with magnificent colouring.

Garnet Hard minor gemstone popular for day-wear from early in the 18th century, mainly in rich red tones but some green with flashes of red (demantoid) from the 1860s. *See* Carbuncle; Almandine.

Garnish Set of pewter table-ware – twelve each of plates, etc.

Gasolier Frame for multiple gas lights, from the 1840s.

Gate-leg table (Fig. 272) With falling flaps hinged to a central fixed top: raised, these rest on additional legs which are hinged top and bottom to swing out from the table framing. From 17th to 20th centuries.

Gate table (Fig. 274) In strong mahogany (early Georgian onwards), requiring no stretchers. Instead of gate-legs, the opened flaps rest on two of the table's four legs, vertically hinged to swing out with parts of the underframing.

Gather Glassblower's blob of hot molten glass taken on to the end of the blow pipe for inflating into a vessel.

Gem Precious or semi-precious stone, especially when cut or polished for display.

Gemel. Gimmal (Figs. 113, 179) 1. Twin items joined together as in popular 'Nailsea' surface-fused flasks. 2. Double finger rings.

Genre Style or sort; in painting implies scenes of everyday life.

Georgian period Generally divided into *early Georgian* (George I and George II) 1714–60 (Figs 26, 56); *George III*, 1760–1820, including Regency, 1811–20; *late Georgian* (George IV and William IV) 1820–37 (Fig. 51).

German silver Another name for nickel silver.

Gesso Composition of whiting and parchment size skilfully tooled in low relief for water-gilded or painted ornament on furniture. Medieval use revived especially 1660s–1730s.

Gibbons, Grinling (1648–1721) Fine carver especially in lime wood, but very many flower festoons, cherubs etc., ascribed to him are merely of his style. Unfashionable and forgotten by 1720 but widely copied by early Victorians.

Gilding Gold used to protect silver and other metals from tarnish or to decorate ceramics, glass or furniture, various techniques being applied in an attempt to achieve permanent adhesion and brilliance.

Acid gilding On china plates, etc., invented 1862 by J. L. Hughes for Mintons. The surface patterned in a resist substance, then briefly immersed in hydrofluoric acid to remove the exposed glaze background, leaving ornament in low relief. Then all-over gilding and burnishing to emphasise the raised detail. Alternative from 1810 was gilding applied over a raised pattern painted on in white.

Brown gilding For stone china, patented 1853, using gold chloride. Could be burnished to great brilliance.

Electro gilding From 1840. *See* Electroplate. Less health-hazardous than mercury gilding.

Fire or mercury gilding On ceramics, glass, brass furniture mounts, silver from the 1780s. Gold applied in a mercurial amalgam, its mercury content removed as a dangerous vapour by heating over fire, leaving a hard, permanent film of pure gold that required laborious burnishing. *See* Ormolu.

Honey gilding For low-temperature kiln firing on ceramics, enduring, but never brilliant, used from *c.* 1755. Powdered gold leaf was mixed with honey and oil of lavender.

Liquid gold gilding Brilliant but easily worn, on cheap ceramics and glass mainly from the 1850s.

Oil gilding On furniture, etc., from the Middle Ages, an alternative to water gilding, cheaper, less brilliant, but more damp-resistant. Gold leaf was attached by a sticky linseed 'fat oil' size.

Transfer-printed gilding On ceramics, patented 1810, improved 1835 and 1853. *See* Transfer-printing.

Water gilding On furniture, required the preparation of a smooth gesso base under gold leaf which was attached by a wetted 'burnish size'; could be double-gilded and burnished for greater brilliance. *See* Oil gilding.

Giles, James (1718–80) London-based independent decorator of porcelain (Bow, Worcester, etc.) in enamels and gold; also of glass.

Gillow firm Founded in Lancaster, 1695, with London showrooms from the 1760s. Important furniture-makers who might mark work from the 1790s and customarily did so from 1820.

Gilt metal Brassy alloys (mainly copper with a little zinc) that could be protected against tarnish by gilding; cheaper than rolled gold. Used for a wide range of little boxes, buttons, posy-holders and other adult 'toys' through the 18th and 19th centuries.

Gimp Ornamental tape for edgings, usually strengthened with cord or wire running through it.

Gimson, Ernest (Fig. 132) (1864–1918) Architect and designer of high quality furniture and metalwork in simple outlines finely enriched. With Ernest and Sidney Barnsley he established the Daneway Workshops in 1902 (with manager Peter Waals).

131 Sideboard designed by Ambrose Heal. **132** Cabinet designed by Ernest Gimson (Leicester Museum).

Gingham Cotton or linen cloth woven with colour stripes or checks.

Gipsy setting (Fig. 186) In jewellery, to make the most of a small gemstone by setting it at the centre of a radiating star cut deeply into the gold around it.

Girandole (Fig. 248) 1. Revolving fountain or firework; hence a wall candlesconce or branching candlestick ornately carved and gilded, often with mirror backing and hung with cascades of glass lustres. Mainly from around the 1750s onwards in Rococo and Neo-classical designs. 2. Simple lustre-hung girandole-candlestick from the 1780s.

Girandole jewellery Brooches and earrings in ribbon-bow or similar symmetrical horizontal outline suspending three – or sometimes five – pear-shaped drops. From the 17th century onwards.

Girl-in-a-swing porcelain Name taken from figure at London's Victoria and Albert Museum for a group of glassy, soft-paste porcelain figures ascribed to a nebulous second Chelsea factory, *c.*1749–54.

Glasgow style in design (furniture, embroidery, etc.) *See* Mackintosh, C. R.

Glass Basically mixture of sand and carbonate of lime with an alkali flux (to lower its melting point) – soda or potash. Made by Syrians over 4000 years ago. European luxury manufacture centred in Venice through the Middle Ages, including fairly clear, colourless glass from the 14th century (see Venetian glass). Some Roman and Medieval manufacture in England, but demand continued for fragile table-ware from Venice until the development of English flint-glass. *See* Broad glass; Cased glass; Crown glass; Flint glass; Looking glass; Plate glass; Rock crystal glass.

Glass prints 1. Mezzotint print fixed (with varnish) face downward on a sheet of glass so that the paper could be wetted and removed leaving print outlines for hand-colouring in opaque colours from behind. Most popular late in the 18th century; often

often poor later. Not to be confused with verre églomisé. 2. Print on light-sensitive paper taken from lines scratched by the artist through a light-resistant covering on a sheet of glass.

Glastonbury chair (Fig. 52) Victorian name for an early folding chair with legs crossing in X-shape below pivoting arms, all members being flat rails fastened by wooden pins, a style associated with church use from late in the 16th century. Victorians probably invented the legend that such a chair was owned by the last Abbot of Glastonbury, executed 1539.

Glaze Glassy substances kiln-fired on to a ceramic ware to make it watertight, scratch-resistant, smooth, etc. *See* Cauliflower ware; Lustres.

  Bristol glaze *See* Bristol pottery.

  Flambé glazes. Transmutation glazes Imitating Chinese Sung, Ming and Ching wares in a wide range of brilliant flowing glaze colours, blended, striped and mottled including most familiar rouge flambé and sang de boeuf (ox blood), using metallic compounds high-fired and dependent on the effect of an oxygen-reduced atmosphere in the kiln. An important contribution to English ceramics around the beginning of the 20th century involving Bernard Moore and the Doulton firm, the Ruskin Pottery, the Royal Lancastrian Pottery, etc.

  Granite glaze Grey and bluish mottled slip glaze used by Wedgwood from c.1770.

  Green glaze Deep green (copper oxide) lustrous liquid glaze used for successful Wedgwood table-ware, such as Cauliflower ware, from 1759, in leaf shapes from 1764; with a lighter, harder body from 1775. More varied green tones including yellowish chromium green from c.1800. Widely used by other potters through the 19th century.

  Lead glaze Simplest was powdered lead ore (galena) sprinkled on the ware, clear but turning yellow in the kiln firing from contact with the ware. Clear colourless liquid lead oxide glazes were applied by dipping from about 1750; leadless glaze, to avoid the health hazard, was introduced to a limited extent in the 19th century. *See* Coalport.

Mother-of-pearl glaze Based on resin with gold chloride, patented in England in 1858, by Frenchman J. J. Brianchon, when it was introduced as a nacreous lustre on Belleek porcelain. In modified use by Worcester, Goss, Minton, Copeland, etc., but much work unmarked.

Rockingham glaze Lead glaze stained rich purple-brown with manganese oxide; usually on red earthenware after 1825. Evolved *c.*1790 at Rockingham, but the name is applied to all such wares, from Sunderland, Alloa, Swansea, etc. Name introduced *c.*1830.

Salt glaze On stoneware, a thin, hard, non-poisonous film of glass, translucent, but slightly rough textured (unsuitable for drinking-vessels, but *see* Nottingham ware). Created by the fumes of volatilised salt, shovelled into the kiln at greatest heat (*c.*1200°c).

Smear glaze Applied to domestic parian ware as an almost invisible trace. A vessel containing glaze was placed in the kiln and melted into a vapour which settled on the ware.

Globes celestial (sky) and terrestrial (earth) from antiquity. Handsome English specimens from the 16th century; widely made from the 18th century. Dated by paper surfaces, remembering the long-continued use made of the copper plates that printed these. 19th-century globes included information about physical geography; some of papier mâché were shaped in relief.

Globe inkstand. Globe writing-table Inkstand, globe-shape on claw feet or plinth made in 1770 by John Wakelin and from *c.*1787 by John Robins and others in silver and Sheffield plate. Pressure on the globe's quadrant finial released upper quarter spheres which then disappeared into the lower half, revealing ink and pen holders. A writing-table on the same principle called Pitt's cabinet globe writing-table was produced by the furniture-makers Morgan & Sanders, who acquired the patent from George Remington, dated 1806, immediately after the death of Prime Minister William Pitt. Compare Nelson souvenirs.

Gobelins tapestry Named after the Gobelin family of Belgian dyers whose Parisian workshops were acquired with others for Louis XIV in 1662, making notable tapestries (favoured by Robert Adam) until late in the 18th century, and upholstery also. Revived after the French Revolution, adding carpets to their output.

Goblet Handsome, deep-bowled, stemmed drinking-vessel: silver or glass, at its finest with a tall cover; occasionally in ceramics such as lustreware.

Godwin, E. W. (Fig. 297) (1833–86) Architect and designer of furniture strongly influenced by Japanese work. Designed also wallpaper, textiles and theatrical sets.

Goffered 1. Fluted or crimped dress frills, etc., pressed between heated goffering irons. 2. Ornamental shaping of book page edges.

Gold Precious metal, heavy, non-tarnishing, for jewellery etc. May be tinged red with copper, green with silver, blue with iron, white with nickel or palladium. *See* Carat; Gilding; Gilt metal; Rolled gold; Verre églomisé.

Gold leaf Gold hand-hammered into filmy thin sheets applied by 'breathing' on to prepared adhesive.

Gold, liquid *See* Gilding.

Gold lustre *See* Lustre wares.

Goss, W. H. (1833–1906) Potter of Falcon Pottery, Stoke-on-Trent who from 1858 made fine parian-ware busts, etc., biscuit-porcelain jewellery, ivory-porcelain ornaments. *See* Armorial ware; Cottages; Mother-of-pearl ware.

Gothic taste, Neo-Gothic (Fig. 309) To collectors implies successive fashions for romanticised revivals of the style in architecture, etc., associated with the Germanic tribes from the Baltic that plundered Rome in AD 410 and eventually dominated Medieval Europe; hence an escape from Greek and Roman classical influences that re-emerged in the Renaissance. Revivals around the mid 18th century and through the early to mid 19th

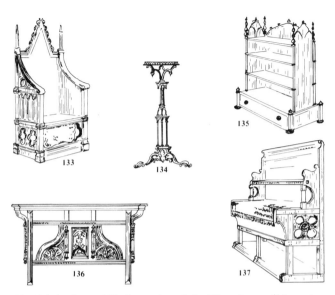

'Gothic' furniture. **133** Coronation chair, Westminster Abbey: the pinnacles once supported leopard ornaments. End of 13th century. **134** Chippendale *Director* candlestand design. **135** George Smith chiffonier design, 1808. **136** Table designed by A. W. Pugin from his *Gothic Furniture*, 1835 **137** Dresser designed by Bruce Talbert from his *Gothic Forms Applied to Furniture*, 1867–8.

century. As popular ornament it was expressed in pointed arch and pinnacle, 'church window' quatrefoils, and galleries and rims composed of concave-sided cusps surmounted by flower heads. Acknowledged in some Chippendale design, Horace Walpole's light-hearted Strawberry Hill Gothic villa, 1753 and in much 19th-century work when serious Gothic-revivalist

119

architects included Gilbert Scott (1811–78) and A. W. N. Pugin (1812–52) who designed furniture and silver. *See* Talbert, Bruce.

Go-to-bed matchbox Early matchbox with a holder for a burning match to light the user to bed after extinguishing his candle. Figures and other decorative shapes.

Gouache For substantial opaque painting, e.g., on fans, in water-colours fixed with gum and honey.

Graham, George (1673–1731) Important maker of clocks and astronomical instruments. Improved clock accuracy with, e.g., his dead-beat escapement and mercurial pendulum.

Grainger, Thomas Worcester porcelain-decorator under Chamberlain. From 1812 made bone china (Grainger Lee & Co.). From 1839 his son traded as George Grainger & Co., making semi-porcelain, parian, etc. Absorbed into the Royal Worcester Porcelain Co. in 1902.

Graining On furniture, from the Middle Ages and popular with Victorians – variously painting cheap woods to imitate costlier ones.

Grande sonnerie Clock or watch striking both the hour and quarter every quarter-hour.

Grandfather clock. Grandmother clock *See* Longcase clock.

Granite glaze *See* Glaze.

Granite ware. Flint ware Popular name from the 1840s for tough feldspathic earthenware with a faintly yellowish tinge.

Granulations In jewellery, a lost ancient Etruscan art using minute gold granules to form surface ornament. A successful imitation introduced by Italian F. P. Castellani (1791–1865) became popular with Victorian jewellers.

Grave slabs and plaques Made in earthenware and terracotta as churchyard memorials, especially in Staffordshire in the 17th to 19th centuries.

Grecian style (Fig. 237) Attempting more accurate imitation of ancient Grecian form and ornament than the mainly Roman imitations of the 1760s' Neo-classical style. Important through the Regency period, expressed, e.g., in the klismos chair, stimulated by new excavations, by the writings of, e.g., Thomas Hope and by the Greek revolt against the Turks, 1821.

Greek key pattern *See* Fret.

Greek leg (Fig. 129) For tables and as the heavy, straight front legs of chairs from *c*.1800 to the 1830s. Wide below a turned knee and tapering quickly to a bun or thimble foot. Circular on plan, frequently heavily fluted or reeded.

Green glass Flint-glass in deep green from about the 1750s onwards; in a wider colour range in the 19th century. Cheap dark bottle glass was cleared to a pale green by the 1800s for, e.g., 'Nailsea' curios.

Green-glaze ware *See* Glaze.

Grille In furniture, brass wire lattice for doors of cabinets, etc., popular instead of glass around 1800.

Grisaille Painting restricted to shades of grey, suggesting relief work.

Grooved drawer In the earliest chests of drawers (17th century) the drawer sides being grooved to fit bearers attached inside the carcase.

Gros-point embroidery *See* Cross-stitch.

Grotesque Ancient Roman ornament revived by Raphael, incorporating fabulous human and animal creatures among scrolling arabesques. In strapwork panels this was popular in 16th to 17th-century England and among late Victorians.

Ground laying In ceramics, dry powdered colour dusted over an oiled surface for a smoother effect than brush-painting.

Guards The end-sticks of a folding fan of wood, mother-of-pearl, tortoiseshell, etc., giving it strength and often richly decorated.

Gueridon Small table or stand for a candlestick or lamp, introduced from France in the 17th century when it consisted most popularly of a negro figure (Moor or blackamoor) holding a tray.

Guild and School of Handicraft Founded 1888 by C. R. Ashbee

(1863–1942) an architect much influenced by William Morris and concerned for the well-being of his craftsmen, moving his Guild workshops from London's East End to Chipping Campden in 1902. He was mainly responsible for the design of furniture, silver and most especially jewellery, made and marked by the Guild, but was forced out of business in 1909 by competitors using factory methods to copy his fine Art-Nouveau designs. Founded the Essex House Press in 1896, his publications including one on the private press, which he described as *A Study in Idealism*. Honorary member of Munich Academy of Arts.

Guilloche Running ornament of counter-changed ogee curves producing an effect of interlaced circles, derived from classical architecture. In English carving, etc., from the 16th century.

Guipure Lace motifs linked by bars or brides instead of a net ground. Originally a form of lace with raised patterns of silk or metal thread twisted round strips of parchment – probably the work implied by the term 'parchment lace' in early English inventories. Later more widely applied to include, e.g., *tape guipure* with patterns outlined in braid. Victorian *Honiton guipure* (praised in Mrs Palliser's *History of Lace*) had pillow-lace sprigs, some partly detached and with embroidered reliefs, linked by bars in a range of lace stitches. Victorian *guipure d'art* consisted of patterns darned in coarse linen thread on squares of hand- or machine-made net. *See* Maltese lace.

Gutta foot In Neo-classical chairs, etc., at the base of a square-section leg, the foot swelling slightly and vertically incised to make four or more small wedge-shaped drops (guttae).

Gypsum Hydrous calcium sulphate, a chalky mineral used to make plaster of Paris. In crystal form (selenite) it can be split into thin sheets, used for some early window glazing. *See* Alabaster.

Hadley, James (1837–1903) Important ceramic-modeller for the Royal Worcester Porcelain Co. With three sons he launched his own art pottery in 1896; this was absorbed by the Company in 1905 but 'Hadley ware' continued through Edwardian days.

Hair work 1. In human hair, mementoes shaped into plumes, etc. for lockets, rings and pendants, especially popular from the 1780s to the 1840s. Some embroidered into watch discs, but other print-like pictorial 'hair embroidery' often proves to consist mainly of springy unravelled piece silk. 2. In horsehair, delicate, lightweight bracelets, muff-chains, rings, etc., woven or worked in crochet, in the hair's natural colours or dyed.

Half-head bedstead With head-board, but no tester.

Half-hunter. Napoleon Like a hunter watch (with a spring-controlled metal cover over the face), but with a hole cut in the centre for viewing the hands without opening it. An idea attributed to Napoleon I.

Half-tester bed *See* Angel bed.

Halifax clocks. Halifax moons (Fig. 64) 18th-century longcase clocks with arched dials, the arch disclosing part of a circular revolving disc painted with two full moons to reveal in turn the moon's phases – important to the night traveller. By the 1750s Thomas Ogden (1692–1769) of Halifax had made such a reputation for his rotating moons that they acquired this name.

Hall chair (Fig. 57) Found in successive period shapes through the later 18th and 19th centuries. Intended for messengers, etc., in rough clothes, so of plain polished wood, its solid seat often slightly dished and the flat back often painted with an impressive crest or cypher.

Hallifax barometers (Fig. 14) Made by John Hallifax, clockmaker of Barnsley (1694–1750). Wheel barometers, but in cases resembling those of longcase clocks.

Hallmarks (Figs. 138–61) Small marks punched on gold or silver plate from 1300, indicating the hall where it was assayed (*see* Leopard's-head mark). The term is now applied more generally to all the punch-marks found on plate including the maker's mark, date letter, Britannia or sterling quality mark and monarch's-head duty mark.

Hallmarks on gold *See* Carat.

Hallmarks, silver. TOP ROW: **138, 139** Leopard's head before and after 1820. **140, 141** Sterling lion before and after 1820. **142, 143** Lion's head erased and Britannia figure used on Britannia standard silver. SECOND ROW: Town marks. **144** Birmingham. **145** Sheffield. **146** Chester. **147** Exeter. **148** Newcastle. **149** York. THIRD ROW: Town and quality marks. **150, 151** Edinburgh. **152, 153** Glasgow. **154, 155** Dublin. BOTTOM ROW: **156, 157** Monarch's-head duty marks (George III and Victoria). **158** Date letter. **159, 160** Maker's marks of Paul de Lamerie, conforming with rules for marking Britannia standard and sterling silver. **161** One of several used by Hester Bateman firm.

Hambone holder With an adjustable split tube extending into a handle to aid the carver. From the early 19th century onwards.

Hamlet, William Painter of silhouettes on flat and convex glass, at Bath c.1780–1815. His son Thomas worked at Bath and Weymouth.

Hancock, Robert (1729–1815) Engraver for early transfer-printing of the 1750s on painted enamels and on Worcester porcelain in the early 1760s. Went to Caughley in 1775.

Hancock, Sampson (Fig. 72) Joined Stevenson at the Old Crown Derby China Works in 1861, becoming proprietor in 1866, followed by other members of his family; continuing the old Derby patterns, figures, etc. Collectors should note that the firm's mark greatly resembled the early Derby mark of a jewelled crown, but with swords instead of batons and flanked by his initials SH. The firm was absorbed by the Royal Crown Derby Porcelain Co. in 1935.

Hand cooler Egg shape for overdressed Victorian ladies, in glass, ceramics (some with bird's-egg markings), blue john, etc.

Handkerchief *See* Snuff handkerchief.

Hand raising Shaping of flat silver plate into a rounded vessel by row after row of hammer blows interspersed with annealing. *See* Planishing.

Hard-paste porcelain Chinese or 'true' porcelain, first made in England (Plymouth) in 1768. Harder (fired at a higher temperature), with a colder brilliance than soft-paste porcelain, resonant and breaking with a clean smooth fracture. *See* Bristol; China clay; Meissen; New Hall; Plymouth; Sèvres; Soft-paste porcelain.

Hardwood From broad-leaved trees – mahogany, oak, beech, etc. – irrespective of hardness, as distinct from pine, fir and other conifers.

Harewood 'Aierwood' to 17th-century tree authority John Evelyn. Usually sycamore or maple veneer stained greyish with oxide of iron for marquetry, etc. Popular in the late 18th century when known as silverwood.

Harlequin Character in Italian comedy (*Commedia dell' Arte*) in diamond-patterned costume; found as a ceramic figure paired with the female figure of Columbine, along with Pierrot, Pantaloon, etc., by Meissen, Bow and Chelsea (and later in Staffordshire earthenware) their source being a history of the Italian theatre by L. Riccoboni, 1728.

Harlequin table (Fig. 166) Variant of the Pembroke,with a small super-structure of drawers and pigeonholes rising at a touch from the table top by means of weights and springs. Named after the pantomime character who was supposed to be invisible to the clown and Pantaloon. Described by furniture designers Sheraton, Shearer, George Smith, etc.

Harlequin table-ware Tea or dinner-ware with each piece in a different colour.

Harpsichord Stringed instrument shaped like a recumbent harp with one or more keyboards causing its strings to be plucked by a plectrum of quill or leather. From the 16th century or earlier.

Harrington, Mrs Sarah Profilist to George II who usually cut her silhouettes in the centre of white paper, backing the hole with black paper or silk. In the 1770s she patented a 'machine' to aid her work.

Hasp Hinged metal clasp or strap secured by a lock to fasten a door, chest-lid, etc.

Hassock Early name for a strong upholstered cushion used for kneeling or as a footrest.

Hausmalerei General term for ceramic ornament in enamel colours by outside or freelance decorators.

Haviland, Limoges Mark frequently noted on imported Victorian table-wares, sometimes beside the name of the importer, e.g., 'made for Oetzmann & Co., London'. From 1797 onwards the firm made hard-paste porcelain under different members of the Haviland family.

Heal, Sir Ambrose (Fig. 131) (1872–1959) Furniture designer with cabinet-making experience, influenced by William Morris, Ernest Gimson and the Arts and Crafts movement. He was successful alike with exhibition pieces and with well-proportioned unobtrusive work, especially in light oak and chestnut, for the progressive middle-class market.

126

Henri deux (Henry II) ware 1. Earthenware with difficult inlaid ornament in coloured clays, originally made at St Porchaire, France, 1525–60; 2. Victorian reproductions made at Tours and by Mintons and Worcester.

Hepplewhite, George Owner of a small London cabinet-making business. Remembered for influential furniture designs in *The Cabinet-Maker and Upholsterer's Guide*, published 1788, two years after his death; with new designs in a revised third edition, 1794, reflecting current taste for pleasantly modified Neo-classicism, quietly delicate and graceful.

Herculaneum Pottery, Liverpool (1790s–1841) Name prompted by excavations of Roman classical art. With Staffordshire labour, made cream-coloured earthenware, some bat-printed and, from 1801, bone china.

Herringbone banding *See* Banding.

Hibernia figure (Fig. 155) *See* Britannia silver mark.

High relief. Alto relievo Carving or casting with ornament standing out boldly.

High standard silver *See* Britannia standard.

High temperature colours For ceramic decoration, able to endure the heat of the glazing kiln – important for table-wares where glaze protected the pattern from wear. Included most popular cobalt blue, antimony yellow, manganese purple, iron red, brownish orange and a drab olive green. *See* Pratt ware. Wider colour range by the mid-19th century including chromium green, brown, grey, black. But in the great kiln heat required for hard-paste porcelain the potters could use only cobalt blue and (rare) copper red. Other colours had to be applied overglaze, fixed by a lesser kiln heat.

Hipped leg Cabriole leg that rises above the level of the chair's seat-rail.

Hispano-Moresque wares General term applied to Near Eastern ceramic techniques introduced into Spain by the Moors between their invasion in 711 AD and expulsion in 1492. Especially the

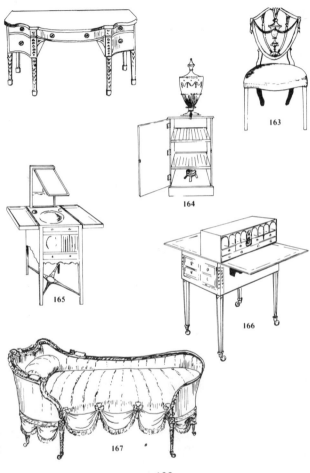

163

164

165

166

167

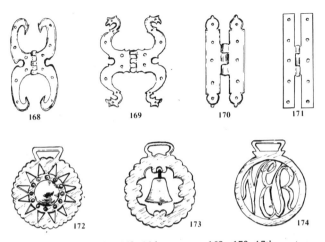

Hinges for cupboards. 168 16th century. 169, 170 17th century.
171 18th century. Horse brasses. 172 Sunflash. 173 Bell. 174 North
Eastern Railway.

technique of covering coarse earthenware with opaque tin-white
enamel as a base for painting in metallic lustres, which
eventually incorporated Christian as well as Islamic motifs;
finest in the early 15th century, deteriorating by the end of the
16th century. *See* Delftware; Maiolica.

Hobby horse Child's toy with a horse's head on a long stick.

Hob grate *See* Dog grate.

Hobnail cutting (Fig. 84) In deep-cut glass, each projecting

Hepplewhite, Shearer and Sheraton furniture designs. 162–164
Sideboard, chair and dining-room vase-and-pedestal by Hepplewhite.
165 Shaving-stand by Shearer. **166, 167** Harlequin table and chaise
longue by Sheraton.

diamond shape cross-cut and the four resultant points further cut into eight-pointed stars.

Hob-nobs Sturdily constructed glass goblets used for hob-nobbing – companionable fireside drinking of mulled ale or other hot drink from about the 1770s onwards.

Hock leg Form of cabriole leg with a broken curve under the knee.

Hogarth chair (Fig. 55) Victorian name for the early Georgian bended-back elbow chair appearing in a self-portrait by the artist William Hogarth.

Holbeinesque jewellery Victorian pendants influenced by Renaissance designs drawn by the artist Hans Holbein after he came to England, 1526. With a large central stone framed in an oval of enamels and minor jewels and with a drop hanging below.

Hollie work Simple needlepoint for filling holes and bands cut in, e.g., 17th- to 18th-century baby caps. Rows of a twisted button-hole stitch were worked so as to leave holes forming simple patterns, sometimes including initials (and providing ventilation).

Hollow stem In a wine glass a stem drawn from the bowl, to retain sediment. In use *c*.1760s–70s; revived 1830s–40s for champagne glasses.

Hollow ware In table-ware, hollow vessels as distinct from flat-ware plates, etc.

Holly wood Hard, white, fine-grained, slightly flecked. Used for inlays and marquetry, sometimes stained.

Honeysuckle ornament *See* Anthemion.

Honiton lace Flourishing Devonshire pillow-lace trade by the late 16th century, imitating the Flemish, at first with a net back-ground worked around sprigs; later with sprigs applied to a plain net ground – renowned for its fine quality, especially *c*.1790–1820. Deteriorated when applied to machine-made net, but revived by the development of guipure. Cheap trolly lace was also made using English thread.

Hope, Thomas (fig. 235) (1768–1831) Connoisseur whose books such as *Household Furniture and Interior Decoration*,

1807, encouraged a revival of extreme-looking Grecian and Egyptian furnishings.

Horn Of cattle, rams etc., silver-mounted as beakers and snuff-mulls. Was carved, turned, heat-softened for shaping in moulds, flattened and split into pliant plates for non-burning lantern windows, table-wares. Used also as a cheap substitute for tortoiseshell in brisé fans, snuffboxes, combs.

Hornbook Page of reading for a child in a handled frame protected with a sheet of transparent horn. Genuine medieval specimens now rare.

Horse bells Harness detail for driven horses in country lanes. Included, e.g., rumblers with several rows under leather hoods above the horse's collar, and the fly terret with a cockade of coloured horsehair among bells on the animal's head. Bell shapes are also found among harness brasses described below. *See* Horse brasses.

Horse brasses Ornamental discs derived from amulets with shoulder loops to hang on the harness of driven horses, especially along the martingale strap linking the horse's girth to its head harness. Some finely finished early Victorian castings; more flat stampings from about the 1870s; many datable souvenirs; innumerable poor quality modern pieces.

Horse furniture *See* Cheval glass.

Horsehair Mane and tail hair woven with linen or cotton warp for furniture coverings, popular from *c.*1775. Also crimped and combined with wool waste for stuffing. *See* Hairwork.

Horseshoe tables 1. Small kidney-shaped writing-table with a concave-fronted drawer. 2. Social table for men to drink at around the fire, sometimes with a brass rail on the inner side controlling the movements of a pair of japanned coasters for bottles or decanters that could thus be passed safely from end to end of the table. 3. Dining-table with flaps unfolding to make a semi-circle: a waiter on the concave side could serve diners around the outer side; late 18th to 19th centuries.

Hour-glass. Sand-glass Ancient time-measurer. An open frame holding a vertical glass vessel with a narrow waist that allows sand or marble dust to trickle from upper to lower section in one hour (or other specific period). The glass blown as a single unit from *c.* 1760 (previously in two parts welded).

Hubard, William (1807–62) skilful freehand cutter of silhouettes as a boy prodigy, his 'Hubard gallery' travelling widely, including New York. He cut many scenes such as Epsom races (with over 200 tiny figures) for scrapbooks. Eventually he settled in America as a portrait painter.

Huguenot work Attributed to notable French Protestant silk-weavers established in Spitalfields, London, in the early 17th century: also silversmiths and other craftsmen and their descendants who fled from French religious persecution, particularly after the revocation of the Edict of Nantes, 1685. In silver, typical detail included ornate handles, profile heads, card-cut foliate strapwork, by such men as Pierre Harache, David Willaume, Paul de Lamerie, Augustin Courtauld.

Hunter watch *See* Half-hunter.

Hull pottery Belle Vue pottery, familiar in marks on blue- and brown-patterned table-wares, 1802–41.

Husks *See* Bell flowers.

Hutch From Medieval days, a cupboard for food, usually on legs or hanging, and with ventilation holes or a panel of spindles, cloth-backed, in the door.

Hyacinth Name applied to transparent reddish-orange varieties of the gemstones zircon, garnet and topaz.

Hygrometer Instrument to measure humidity, a popular addition to the wheel barometer.

Ice pail Mainly from the 1780s onwards and typically found in massive Regency and Victorian Neo-classical urn and low-waisted thistle shapes in silver, Sheffield plate and ceramics. Originally made in pairs, or sets, each holding a single bottle of wine at table, becoming taller and narrower, to suit changing bottle proportions. An inner compartment kept the bottle from contact with the ice.

Icon Representation of sacred figures associated with the Eastern church, painted on a wood panel or created in enamels, metal etc., including modern work.

Illumination Manuscript, given colour and ornamental detail with gold leaf and paint.

Image toys 18th-century name for early ceramic figures.

Imari ware. Brocaded Imari English name for 18th-century export Japanese porcelain (distasteful to the Japanese) with patterns taken from brocaded textiles; in underglaze blue and overglaze enamels and gilding. Made at Arita, shipped from Imari. Much copied in English 'japans' of Worcester, Derby, Davenport, etc.

Imperial dining table Patented by the Gillow firm, 1800. A telescopic dining-table extended by inserting loose leaves on a movable underframe, but lacking the later screw action.

Impression Print taken from a prepared metal plate, wood block or stone.

Ince, William and John Mayhew (Fig. 63) Remembered for their furniture designs in the *Universal System of Household Furniture* issued 1759–62, illustrating (like Chippendale) current Rococo and Neo-Gothic styles. Their important London cabinet-making business continued to 1803.

Incised ornament Cut or engraved, as on rough early 'scratched' furniture; on lacquer such as 17th-century Bantam work; in the sgraffito technique on ceramics; on glassware including 'incised twist' stems, *c.* 1740–1820, surface-incised and twisted while hot in cable effects.

Incunabula Books and wood-block prints printed before 1500 when printing was in its infancy.

Incuse Decoration stamped in intaglio into the surface of, e.g., a medal or coin.

Indian In the 17th-18th centuries, implying an import from the

East, especially by the East India Company. Sometimes emphasised as 'Right Indian' (or 'Right Japan') to distinguish from European imitations.

India paper In the later 19th century, tough, thin paper used for intaglio printing. Used for Victorian etchings with backing.

Inescutcheon In heraldic devices, a small shield as a detail in a large one: an aid in dating some 19th-century china marks as this was omitted from the royal arms from 1837.

Inglenook Fireplace corner, 'chimney corner' popular, e.g., in late Victorian and Edwardian cottage-style homes.

Inkstand *See* Standish.

Inlay. Setwork Small hollows cut in solid wood filled with similarly shaped pieces in contrasting wood, metal, ivory, etc. Not to be confused with marquetry. *See also* Champlevé enamels; Damascening.

Inro Decorative small box serving as a pocket in Japanese costume, attached to the belt by a netsuke.

Inscriptions Latin words or abbreviations frequently found with a name, on or under a print, etc., defining the contribution he or she made to it. These include: *Ad vivam*, taken from life; *Composuit* ('he designed it') for the designer; *Delin* (*eavit*), draughtsman; *Exc* (*udit*) or *Divulgavit*, or *Formis*, publisher; *F* (*ecit*), ('he made it'), usually the etcher, but sometimes on silver, etc.; *Figuravit*, maker of a drawing for engraving from another artist's composition; *Imp.*, printer; *Inven*(*it*), designer; *Lith.* may mean actual artist who drew on lithographic stone, or merely that the print is a lithograph; *Lith by*, lithographer reproducing another man's design; *Original engraving*, print in which etcher or engraver has himself created the design, regardless of the number of these prints issued; *P.* or *Pinx* (*it*), painter; *Published according to Act of Parliament* refers to copyright acts passed 1735 onwards (usually with date of most recent act); *S* or *Sculp*(*sit*). or *Caelavit*, or *Incidit*, engraver, carver; *Del. et sc.* or *Del et lith.* designer who also prepared the plate or stone. *See* Copyright; Proofs.

175 Irish glass 'kettledrum' fruit bowl with vesica pattern and diamond cutting. 176 Kakiemon style ornament on porcelain.

Intaglio In jewellery, etc., a design cut into a hard surface as a hollow; opposite to the cameo; hence a copper plate prepared for making etched or engraved prints, a stone cut for a seal matrix, etc. *See* Plate mark.

Intarsia Italian elaboration of inlay, forming pictorial wood mosaics applied to furniture. *See* Tunbridge ware.

Ionic *See* Orders of architecture.

Iridescent Reflecting light in interchanging colours as in some gemstones, mother-of-pearl, glass and ceramic lustres-wares.

Irish Chippendale Modern term for ornate, boldly carved versions (not always of high quality) of furniture fashionable in the 1750s—60s illustrated by Chippendale and his contemporaries.

Irish glass Exported to England, especially 1784—1825 when it escaped the English glass tax-by-weight; hence heavy decanters, kettledrum and canoe-shaped bowls, etc. Rarely distinguishable from English glass except when showing the vesica pattern or the rare marks of makers and wholesalers, which include; Edwards, Belfast; Collins, Dublin; Carter, Dublin; Penrose, Waterford; Waterloo, Cork; Cork Glass Co. *See* Vesica pattern; Waterford glass.

Irish yew *See* Bog wood.

Iron *See* Cast iron; Wrought iron.

Ironstone china Like stone china, etc., a name used by 19th-century potters for strong earthenware. The original patent ironstone china, patented by C. J. Mason 1813, was at first hard, white, thinly potted, slightly translucent. But with a change of formula it soon became the widely familiar tough heavy ware for inexpensive table services, conservatory vases, seats, etc., boldly and brightly decorated with 'Oriental' flowers. Continued from the late 1840s by F. Morley & Co. and from 1862 by G. L. Ashworth & Brothers. They might include the mark *Mason's Patent Ironstone China* and the name has been continued in Mason's Ironstone China Ltd.

Italian Comedy figures *See* Harlequin.

Italian quilting On bedcovers, etc., patterns in relief achieved with double rows of stitching through both fabric and lining to form narrow tunnels filled from the underside with soft cord or candlewick. Popular in the early 18th century.

Ivory (Fig. 107) Mainly from elephant tusks (African: glossy, close-textured; Indian: whiter, easier to work). Identified by minute, inconspicuous lozenge-shaped spaces between tiny curving lines within its texture, in contrast to the splintering lines of bone. Substitutes taken from hippopotamus, wild boar, walrus and sea-unicorn or narwhal. *Vegetable ivory* was used for small carved ornaments in the mid 19th century, being the seed of a dwarf South American palm tree, but the material soon lost its whiteness. More enduring Victorian imitations included ceramics (*see* below) and glass (Queen's ware).

Ivory porcelain In mellow ivory tones introduced by Worcester in 1856, evolved from parian ware for figures, etc.; also their glazed parian called stained ivory used for late Victorian japonaiseries and further developed for iridescent and 'shaded pink' effects and for Sabrina ware. Ivory-toned glazed parian porcelain was used also by several other potters, notably W. H. Goss.

Iznik pottery Turkish pottery made at Iznik, south-west of

Istanbul, in the 15th–17th centuries and widely imported into Europe, influencing, e.g., Italian maiolica. Distinguished by coloured ornament, especially flowers, underglaze, on an opaque white ground, at first including much in blue-and-white, later especially turquoise and cool green tones and still later also black and vivid scarlet.

Jacaranda *See* Rosewood.

Jacinth A clear wine-red gem form of zircon, becoming an unreliable blue when heated.

Jackfield wares *See* Jet ware.

Jacobean period Reign of James I (1603–25); sometimes also (as 'late Jacobean') the 1660s–80s including the reign of James II (1685–88).

Jacobite glass (Fig. 105) Engraved drinking-glasses supporting the cause of the Old and Young Pretenders, especially the 1745 rebellion. With more or less cryptic motifs including rose, jay-bird, crude portraits, inscriptions such as *Fiat* or *Revirescit*. *See* Amen glass. Much modern engraving on old glasses.

Jacquard weave Elaborate loom-woven patterns resulting from an invention of J. M. Jacquard (1752–1834) hand-operated until *c*.1835. *See* Paisley shawls; Picture ribbons.

Jade Semi-precious stones – nephrite from Central Asia, New Zealand, Canada, U.S.A., etc., and jadeite, mostly from Burma. Nephrite, dark 'spinach' green to greenish white, and grey, often with striations and brownish patches, some rusty red, is harder than steel and cannot be cut with a knife; it was worked by the ancient Chinese mainly from pebblestones, using friction and abrasives (undercutting only from the 13th century onward). They especially like subtle whitish tones and silky polished surfaces (never faceted) – colour and texture often likened to mutton fat. Modern Chinese work is usually in jadeite, bright or deep green, brown and other colours, mined since the 18th century, glossier than nephrite and more nearly translucent, including sharply cut and brightly polished intricate carvings from the later 19th century. Thin vessels should 'ring' when struck. Not to be confused with other minerals such as chrysoprase, soapstone and serpentine. Beginner-collectors may be confused by modern jade carvings from Canada and the U.S.A. where it is widely sought; they should realize that it is very difficult to value jade or tell the genuine from substitutes.

Japanning Glossy, richly coloured and black surfaces decorated in gold and colours in the style of Oriental resinous gum lacquers, greatly admired in England from the 17th century. 1. On wood. Applied to English furniture from the 1660s and on early Georgian longcase clocks, using for the best work some 10 or 12 coats of heat hardened spirit shellac varnish (shellac and spirits of wine – later sometimes cheaper oil varnishes). Notable work in the later 18th century and through to the 1860s on Clayware and papier mâché. 2. On metal. Sometimes called tôle peinte. Became important for trays, etc., when heat-hardened varnishes were applied to tinned plate (tinned sheet iron) from early in the 18th century. Some particularly fine work is associated with Pontypool and Usk. But Birmingham and Wolverhampton became the world centre of the trade from late in the 18th century, using improved 'tin iron'; drop-hammer shaping was introduced *c*. 1820 for coal scuttles, etc.

Japans Chinoiseries as applied to ceramic ornament – inconsequential handling of Oriental themes in brilliant colours, by the Japanese for export to Europe and in imitations by many English potteries such as Worcester from the 1760s into the 19th century, copying styles that ranged from delicate Kakiemon to gold-glinting red-ground Kutani and brocaded Imari. Also by Chelsea, Derby, Spode, etc.

Japonaiserie (Figs. 114, 297) Through the second half of the 19th century, following the widespread invasion of Japanese arts and crafts into the western world. These influenced the art and design of, e.g., William Burges, Edward Godwin, J. M. Whistler, Christopher Dresser, etc., and were expressed in silver, ceramics and home furnishings from bamboo and lacquer to cork pictures and paper fans, and including many imitations of ivory.

Jardinière 19th-century stand of wood, metal or ceramics for a pot plant or flowers; could be as elaborate as the 'support for a small room garden' described by P. & M. A. Nicholson in 1836.

Jargoon *See* Zircon.

Jasper Form of quartz popular in Victorian 'Scotch pebble' jewellery, mainly opaque red or brown or ribbon-banded; some yellow or green. Harder than Welsh crimson jasper marble.

Jasper ware, Jasper dip Dense, fine-grained, fine-stoneware introduced by Josiah Wedgwood in 1774, needing no glaze. Used for medallions and plaques (low relief portraits and Neo-classical figure scenes in white on coloured grounds), jewellery cameos, table-wares, etc. In solid jasper the white ware was tinted a single colour throughout the body – soft blue, green, lilac, etc.

In less costly *jasper dip* from 1785 the colour was merely surface-applied by dipping in jasper-ware slip. Comparable work came from William Adams, John Turner and others. Popular with Victorians (solid and dip) and ever since.

Jelly glass (Fig. 79) The earliest, 17th century, was a small round bowl; a rim foot from *c*.1700; followed by a range of styles with trumpet and bell-shaped bowls on domed and knopped feet, and with increasingly elaborate cut ornament from the 1750s. The foot was small for close placing on the dessert pyramid.

Jelly mould From the later 18th century designs included a two-part pattern in earthenware – a fluted casing and a central cone or pyramid. Hot jelly was poured into the casing and into it was inserted the flower-painted cone point downwards, so that it would support and decorate the clear jelly at table when the casing was lifted off. In the 19th century, moulds of copper (tinned inside) were supplemented by more intricate, elaborate shapes in Britannia metal, some being made to lift off the set jelly in parts, allowing for undercut patterns. Alternatives then included cheap heavy stoneware and earthenware.

Jennens & Bettridge *See* Clay ware; Papier mâché.

Jeroboam 1. Large bowl or goblet, 2. Now also a large wine bottle.

Jet Hard black form of lignite (itself a form of coal) still found on English beaches. Greatly favoured by Victorians for carved and polished mourning jewellery etc., copied in cold black glass, moulded wood powder and ebonite or vulcanite.

Jet ware Brownish-red earthenware covered in deep blue glaze and fired in a smoky kiln until lustrous black. Associated with Jackfield, Shropshire, but widely made in the 1750s–70s and revived in later 19th-century Staffordshire (using much harder red earthenware).

Jewelled embroidery Craze of the 1880s for pincushions, tea cosies, costume ornament, etc., using imitation jewels and pearls with fragments of coral, mother-of-pearl, sequins, beads, beetles' wing-cases, etc., with silver-gilt and metal threads, purls etc.

Jewelled porcelain Foil-backed glass imitation jewels and pearls set into porcelain by Sèvres; an improved process for fixing them was patented in 1872 by W. H. Goss. Raised dots of white and coloured enamels were more simply applied as 'jewelling' on plate rims, etc., by Victorian–Edwardian Copeland, Mintons, Worcester and others.

Jewellery Personal ornament of precious metals and/or precious or semi-precious stones, pearls, enamels, etc. 1. *Art jewellery*: late Victorian–Edwardian, tending to avoid the glitter of faceted stones and polished metal, using dulled silver or pewter, baroque pearls, etc. 2. *Costume jewellery*: modern term for less valuable daytime ornament in materials ranging from coral to Tunbridge ware and 'Ruskin stone'.

Joey Small wineglass or dramming glass for spirits, usually with a short thick stem and a wide heavy foot. Some of fine quality but mainly thick-bowled, of cheap glass, associated with early 18th- and 19th-century crazes for duty-free gin, frequently with pontil marks until Victorian times.

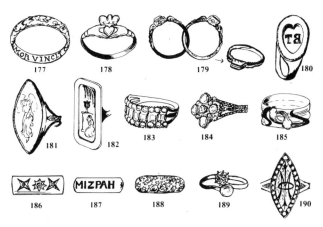

Jewellery illustrated by finger rings. TOP ROW: **177** Tudor posy ring engraved inside. **178** Fede (faith) ring (hands clasping crowned heart). **179** Gemel ring (two interlinked, shown open and closed). **180** Seal or signet. CENTRE ROW: **181** Late 18th-century marquise shape (with Wedgwood medallion). **182** Mourning, *c.* 1800. **183** Regency, popular shape. **184, 185** Early Victorian, flowers in half pearls and intertwined snakes. BOTTOM ROW (All mid to late Victorian): **186** Gipsy setting. **187** Mizpah (Biblical reference to Laban and Jacob). **188** Ivy-engraved keeper. **189** Cross-over diamond and pearl. **190** Mourning (black enamel and pearls), 1890s.

Joggled ornament Outline patterns on soft pewter; engraved by making a series of small curved cuts using a rocking motion.

Joined furniture. Joinery With parts fitted strongly together using mortise-and-tenon joints; more refined than carpentry.

Kakiemon style (Fig. 176) 17th-century Japanese potter's adaptations of the Chinese *famille verte* colour scheme to white porcelain, most popularly in simple asymmetrical sketches of

141

flowering branches springing from rocky crevices with occasional exotic birds and animals. Widely copied by Chelsea, Worcester, etc. *See* Famille rose.

Kaendler, J. J. *See* Meissen.

Kaolin *See* China clay.

Kauffmann, Angelica (1741–1807) Swiss-born painter, in London 1766–82. Portraits, etc., also murals and ceiling designs in the Neo-classical manner for Robert Adam. Her paintings were widely engraved and the prints copied by furniture decorators, etc. She married the decorative painter Antonio Zucchi.

Kelmscott Press *See* Morris, William.

Kent, William (1686–1748) Architect, a pioneer in reviving the Palladian style; designer of heavily scrolled and pedimented furniture, interiors, gardens, silver in the grand manner, out of step with his period's advancing Rococo trends.

Kent, William Maker of Victorian-style flat-back earthenware figures and dogs in Burslem; continuing use of old master-moulds until the 1960s.

Kerr & Binns *See* Worcester porcelain.

Key pattern *See* Fret.

Kick In a glass bottle or decanter, a hollow rounded dome in the base to aid annealing, mainly pre-1760.

Kidderminster carpets Early work was smooth-faced, without pile. A double-cloth, reversible two-ply or three-ply was usual from the 1730s and a Brussels or moquette type was also made from 1753. *See* Axminster; Wilton.

King's blue Strong purplish-blue glass of the 1820s–30s, coloured with refined cobalt, named for George IV. *See* Zaffre.

King's Lynn *See* Norwich glass.

Kingwood. Violet wood Hard, close-grained Brazilian wood, deep brown to purple. Known by these names from the 19th century (previously might be prince's wood) and sometimes confused with an allied species, rosewood. Used in veneer with satinwood for banding, etc.

Kit-Cat drinking glass With heavy funnel bowl and baluster stem on folded foot as depicted by Kneller in portraits of members of a Whig club (founded 1703) at a London tavern run by Christopher (Kit) Catling.

Klismos Ancient Greek chair fashionable during Neo-classical revivals in the late 18th and early 19th centuries. The line of the concave sabre-curve legs balanced by low back verticals crossed by a concave back-rest.

Knife case (Fig. 202) Small serpentine-fronted chest with forward-sloping lid and partitions to hold table knives, forks and spoons vertically, making loss or theft conspicuous. In some demand by the 17th century. Exquisite specialist workmanship from mid Georgian days (in silver-mounted wood marquetry, shagreen, etc.), when a pair would stand on sideboard pedestals. Sometimes shaped as a Neo-classical urn with a rising lid on a central stem.

Knop (Figs. 222, 250, 252, 258) 1. In wood, a lathe-turned rounded knob. 2. In stemmed table glassware, a swelling more pronounced than a baluster curve, named as an acorn knop, mushroom, cushion, etc., some containing air-bubbles 'tears'. 3. in silver, an ornamental finial – such as a lion sejant, maidenhead, seal, etc. – soldered to the straight handle of a pre-1660s spoon.

Knotting Fashionable hobby from the late 17th century and through the 18th when knotted trimmings replaced loose silken fringes on upholstery. Simple finger work at first; elaborated in the later 18th century using a shuttle (often of attractively decorated ivory, tortoiseshell, etc.) to make fringes and ornament for couching upon coverlets, etc. – 'candlelight work' and occupation for coach journeys and other situations that precluded embroidery. *See* Tatting.

Knurling *See* Gadrooning.

Kovsh Russian vessel with high looped handle, basically for measuring drink, but often enriched as an ornament from the late 18th century.

Krater Ancient two-handled wide-mouthed bowl, a Grecian vessel for mixing wine and water, popular in Neo-classical designs.

Kronheim & Co Colour printers associated with attractive Victorian Christmas cards, etc., in clear colours with line-and-stipple engraving. From 1849 were licensed to use George Baxter's technique.

Labelled decanter (Fig. 85) Wheel-engraved or enamel-painted with flourishes framing a wine name and suggesting a chain round the vessel's shoulder, as found in silver wine labels. Mainly 1750s–80s.

Labels On furniture, silhouettes, Tunbridge ware, etc. Always worth looking for and preserving intact, however shabby or poorly printed, as indication of maker and date. *See* Bin labels; Wine labels.

Labradorite A soft grey feldspar showing a rich play of colours – blues, greens, yellows – with almost the sheen of closely related moonstone and similarly used for minor jewellery, cameos, etc.

Laburnum wood Hard, heavy, greenish-yellow with pinkish-brown shading. Slices from branches showing marked concentric growth rings were widely used from the 17th century onward in oyster parquetry. Used for handles in Edwardian Arts and Crafts furniture.

Lace Developed in England, from the Continent, from the 16th century, the term covering four textile products. 1. patterned mesh created in a single thread with needle stitches. *See* Needlepoint lace; Venetian lace. 2. Mesh created with a multiplicity of threads wound on bobbins. *See* Bobbin lace; Bone lace; Honiton lace; Pillow lace. 3. Costume trimming of gold or silver-gilt braid. 4. Ancient costume tying cord of variously plaited threads.

Lace box Name now given to shallow, flat-lidded, rectangular boxes suitable for gloves, etc. Handsome in the late 17th and early 18th centuries, covered in marquetry, embroidery etc.

Lace, ceramic Rouen technique used by Mintons, e.g., for decorative mid 19th-century parian figures. Machine-made lace was dipped in wet slip; when dried and kiln-fired it left a finely perforated pattern in the ware. *See* Chiné ware.

Lace glass *See* Latticinio.

Lacis Darned netting, forerunner of lace, recollected in Victorian guipure d'art.

Lacquer Ancient Chinese craft from the Chou dynasty (1027–221 BC) onwards, using the sap of the tree *rhus vernicifera*, brilliantly developed by the Japanese and the inspiration for European 'japanning', including so-called Coromandel lacquer from the 17th century.

Ladder-back chair. Slat-back Modern term for a chair with a tall back composed of horizontal rails. Included: 1. An 18th-century rush-seated country chair; 2. More sophisticated work with pierced shaped and carved cross-rails.

Ladle *See* Punch-ladle; Tea-caddy ladle.

Lalique glass and jewellery Associated with French artist René Lalique, 1860–1945, who trained as a jeweller (with two years' study in England) and worked as a brilliantly original jewellery designer and manufacturer, 1881–1905, before becoming absorbed with glassware including Art Nouveau and Art Deco styles. His factory and styles since continued by his son Marc.

Lambeth delft Usual name for London-made delftwares.

Lambeth 'faience' Doulton plaques, tiles, pilgrim bottles, etc., attempting a Victorian interpretation of the early Italian maiolica technique, *c.*1872–1914. In fine earthenware with painted ornament under a warm-toned lead glaze – colder leadless glaze from 1900.

Lambrequin *See* Pelmet.

Lamerie, Paul de (Figs. 159, 160) Influential Huguenot silversmith, b.1688. Apprenticed in London 1703, and continued working there until he died in 1751. Continued using Britannia standard silver until 1732. Associated with elegant design ranging from early simplicity to highly decorative Rococo chasings and castings.

Lamps Until the 19th century development of gas lighting (a novelty in the 1820s) the term implied open flame lamps with fibrous wicks burning oil such as train oil from whale blubber or sluggish colza oil from rape seed. While candlemakers monopolised wax and tallow, the cottage and workshop relied on such primitive lamps as the *slut* and *crusie* (or *chill*), the

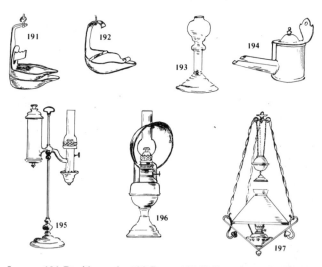

Lamps. **191** Double crusie. **192** Betty. **193** Hollow glass. **194** Double spouted. **195** Argand style (intended to have shade over its glass draught shield) that continued into 20th century. **196** Paraffin reading lamp, Victorian–Edwardian. **197** Edwardian hanging lamp (height adjustable and duplex burner).

smelly oil burning in an open bowl pinched into one or more beak-spouts to support floating wicks. The *double crusie* had a duplicate vessel under it to catch drips. A ratchet arrangement tilted it to feed the wick. The *Betty lamp* was 'better' because fitted with a hinged lid. The *spout-lamp* from *c*.1720s had a spout for the wick, often with a drip-gutter and an iron pick-wick chained to the lid. The later 18th century saw considerable design improvements in the wick, as in the *Argand*, *Liverpool* and *duplex* lamps. Oil flow was aided with clockwork in the early 19th century *Carcel* or French lamp and from the 1830s by a spring mechanism in the *moderator* lamp. Dangerous camphine was in use from the 1830s (a distillation of oil of turpentine) followed by paraffin *c*.1850. *See* Night-lights.

Lancashire chair (Fig. 308) Name often given to a heavy style of hoop-back Windsor, often wholly of yew wood with decoratively turned arm supports, legs and stretchers.

Lancashire snuffbox 19th century, in brass or copper with crudely engraved watch-dial figures around its circular lid and traditionally associated with out-of-work Prescot makers of watch units. Typically with a keyless lid-locking mechanism worked by manipulating a domed sun and crescent moon, to thwart pilferers.

Lantern Iron or brass framework often with sheets of horn to shield a candle from draughts, made from the Middle Ages to the present century. Ornate designs (Chippendale, etc.) glazed and gilded, to hang in halls, etc., from the 18th century.

Lantern clock. Birdcage clock (Fig. 66) Worked by hanging weights, so hung on the wall, forerunner of the longcase clock. Metal frame (iron, later brass) with a bell dome and corner pillars.– the earliest English domestic clock.

Lap dovetail *See* Dovetail.

Lapis lazuli Semi-precious stone, bright azure to deep blue with occasional golden iron pyrites sparkles. Ancient source of ultramarine blue powder. Opaque, used for seals, beads, buttons, ornaments, often as a veneer and for jewellery including Victorian–Edwardian art jewellery.

Lath-back chair *See* Windsor chair.

Larchwood Yellowish to reddish brown, durable but liable to warp. Used like pine as a carcase wood and in rustic furniture.

Late Georgian *See* Georgian period.

Latten Vague Medieval term eventually specifying brass in tough close-textured sheets produced by laborious hammering. Some English-made by late 16th century.

Lattice Net-like tracery with straight members crossing diagonally, e.g., in brass in Regency cupboard doors.

Latticinio Lace glass. Fine threads of white or coloured glass in filigree mesh effects enclosed in clear glass. Ancient technique perfected by Venetians and found, e.g., in some millefiori paperweights and Nailsea glass.

Laurencekirk woodwares Kincardineshire souvenir craft popularised by Charles Stiven, snuff-box-maker from 1783, whose firm continued to 1868 (name-stamped Stiven boxes from 1819). Stiven improved the traditional 'invisible' wooden hinge cut as an integral part of both box and lid – the so-called Scottish hinge usually in sycamore wood, associated with James Sandy but widely found in Northern Europe. *See* Mauchline ware.

Lava ware Very hard-glazed, heavy ceramic ware strengthened with blast-furnace slag and coloured with oxides of iron, cobalt and manganese. Early to mid Victorian, seldom marked.

Laymetal. Leymetal *See* Pewter.

Lazy tongs In metal or wood, thumb-and-finger loops pressed together would extend trellis-work arms and grasp a small object two to three feet away.

Lead Heavy, grey, soft metal, its weather-resistance prompting some use for cast garden ornaments. William Storer's hardened lead, patented 1770, was used for some Adam gilded mirror frames. *See* Flint-glass; Glaze, lead; Pewter.

Lead crystal. Lead glass *See* Flint-glass.

Lead glaze *See* Glaze.

Leather Tanned or boiled hides and skins, among the most ancient chest and furniture coverings; also embossed and gilded for wall hangings. *See* Blackjack; Coffer; Morocco leather; Roan; Shagreen.

Le Blond prints Issued by Abraham Le Blond, b. 1819, using plates and blocks sold in 1868 after the death of George Baxter to make less well finished full-colour prints (called Le Blond Baxters); remembered also for his own, named, colour print 'ovals', etc.

Leeds Pottery (1760–1878) Notable for smoothly glazed cream-coloured earthenwares including elaborate table-centres, etc., often with hand-punched pierced decoration and twisted handles, from 1760. Light in weight for successful export to the Continent. Made also pearlware, including figures, black stoneware, etc. Continued to 1878 but no association with original company after 1820. *See* Castleford; Senior.

Leek Embroidery Society Founded 1879 as one of many efforts to improve embroidery standards, the work being done on printed tussore silks in embroidery silks from the same source – a Leek fabric-printer and dyer, Thomas Wardle, husband of the founder.

Leer. Lehr Glassmaker's oven for slowly toughening ware; improved designs led to more ambitious glass ornament from the 1740s and from the 1780s.

Leopard's-head mark on sterling silver (Figs 138, 139) Used from 1300 and became the recognised mark of London silver. Many consecutive styles of a more or less lion-like head, crowned from *c*. 1450 to 1821.

Liberty & Co (Fig. 298) Fabrics, metal wares, etc. sold by Arthur Lazenby Liberty, (1843–1917) at his Regent Street shop from 1875, encouraging then current interest in Oriental wares. *See* Cymric silver; Tudric pewter.

Lignum vitae Immensely strong wood in contrasting deep brown and greenish black. An early import from the West Indies and long retained its medicinal reputation. Used for machinery, fine turnery such as loving cups from the 17th century and some veneers.

Limed oak In contrast to fumed oak. Wood treated with lime, leaving it speckled white, usually unpolished, as part of the Edwardian cottage mood.

Limerick 'lace' 1. From *c.*1830, designs in tambour embroidery on machine-made net in flax thread, cotton, shiny silk. 2. Patterns on net in close-running needle stitches. Both may have needlepoint fillings comparable with muslin embroidery.

Limewood Creamy tones, soft, close-grained, excellent for undercut carving; favoured by Grinling Gibbons and his school.

Limited, Ltd in ceramic marks Not included with the manufacturer's name until after the Limited Liability Act had been passed, 1860; hence an aid in dating.

Limoges enamels Associated with the French town from the 12th century, soon becoming commercialised, but long retaining a unique reputation, first for champlevé enamels and, from the 15th century, for painted religious scenes, etc., in and on enamels on a copper base. From the 16th century both secular and religious subjects were mainly in grisaille, some on dark blue or brown grounds, but with ornaments restricted to filmy layers of white, brush-painted to reproduce cameo effects in slightly rounded modelling, sometimes tooled for delicate detail. *See* Worcester.

Line engraving *See* Engraving.

Linenfold carving 19th-century name for a formal pattern derived from hanging folds of cloth, used for carved furniture panels, etc., from the late 15th century.

Linthorpe Pottery Near Middlesbrough-on-Tees. Pioneer art pottery, 1879–90, under Henry Tooth who, together with the pottery's 'art advisor' Christopher Dresser, applied crackle effects and secret experimental glazes to many original slip-cast shapes, though Dresser soon lost interest and Tooth went to Bretby in 1883.

Linwood, Mary Tireless Leicester needlewoman remembered for *c.* 60 full-size embroidered copies of famous paintings worked in irregular stitches in specially dyed crewels. These were exhibited in London for nearly 50 years and sold after her death in 1845.

Lion marks on silver *See* Britannia standard; Leopard's-head; Scottish silver; Sterling.

Liquid gold *See* Gilding.

Lithograph Print taken from lithographic stone (or metal) often suggesting a pencil drawing. Basic principle was that the artist could draw freely with a suitable greasy or oily substance on the prepared stone which, when wetted, could be inked all over. The drawing retained the ink, while the wet stone repelled it. Simpler than engraving or etching; developed in the 1790s by Aloys Senefelder (1771–1834) of Munich.

Lithophane 'Picture' formed in intaglio-moulded glassy porcelain, for window panel, hand screen, etc. Against the light the thicker areas of porcelain appeared shadowy while the deepest hollows, where it was thin, provided highlights. Widespread in Europe; patented in 1828 in England when they were made by the Grainger firm, Worcester, followed by other firms from 1842, such as the Kennedy Porcelain Co., Burslem.

Lithotint Surface tone or wash effect in lithography achieved by preparing the stone with a ground of powdered resin as used for aquatints. *See* Chromolithograph.

Littler's blue Distinctive ultramarine blue invented by potter William Littler (1725–84) for use on salt-glazed stoneware. He became proprietor of Longton Hall from 1751, but porcelain so coloured may be associated with his subsequent Scottish (West Pans) factory.

Liverpool lamp *See* Argand lamp.

Liverpool ceramics Earthenware from late in the 17th century; delftware from the 1700s; cream-coloured earthenware from late in the 18th century. *See* Herculaneum. Soft-paste porcelains from the mid 1750s by eight or more potters including William Reid,

William Ball, Richard Chaffers, Philip Christian and Seth Pennington (one of three brothers, at work 1770s–90s).

Livery cupboard Ill-defined furnishing where, through the 16th and early 17th centuries, a household would find food and candles for the night. Probably in the style of a court cupboard, but with a small closed cupboard in the upper section.

Locke & Co., Worcester Minor china factory, 1895–1905, established by Edward Locke, formerly of the Grainger factory. Never a part of the Worcester Royal Porcelain Co., but for a time used a confusingly similar mark.

Locket Small ornamental case, usually gold or silver, for a miniature portrait, lock of hair or similar keepsake usually worn on a necklace chain or as a brooch or pendant. Very small in the late 18th and early 19th centuries; larger, cheaper, when in fashion again in the 1860s, often containing a tiny photograph.

Loggerhead Circular inkpot on a wide flat base, with holes in the rim for pens.

Longcase clock. Grandfather clock (Fig. 64) Long-pendulum, weight-driven household clock wholly enclosed in a free-standing wooden frame, often over seven feet tall. Made from the 1660s, tending to become larger, more ornate, through the early 18th century. Dated by style of case, dial (e.g. often arched from *c.*1720; often white instead of brass, in the later 18th century). Maker's name appeared on the dial from the 1690s – many being listed in books by, e.g. W. Britten, G. H. Baillie. Grandmother clock, less common, was smaller.

Longchain *See* Sautoir.

Longton Hall Obscure factory making Staffordshire's first soft-paste porcelain, established *c.*1749 and continuing to 1760, mainly directed by William Littler. Made table-wares including covered dishes in fruit-and-vegetable shapes, and mugs and jugs with ill-designed, recognisable handles. The factory's figures included some white, thickly glazed primitives – 'snowman figures' to the collector. *See* Littler's blue.

Looking-glass (Fig. 205) In the 17th and early 18th centuries in costly massive framing (silver, tortoiseshell etc.) to make the most of a small shallow-bevelled glass. Through the 18th century in better (cast) glass, but still requiring separate craftsmen to grind and polish it, to 'silver' it with foil and tin-and-mercury amalgam, and to make its carved and gilded frame in fashions ahead of other furniture, (including over 250 designs by Robert Adam). *See* Plate glass.

Loo table From the early 19th century, a circular table on a central pillar and a spreading pedestal or feet, seating up to eight people for the 18th- to 19th-century card-game lanterloo or loo.

Lopers. Runners Rails drawn out to support the open flap of a desk.

Louis XIV (1643–1715); Louis XV (1715–74); Louis XVI (1774–89), (d. January 1793) French kings associated with Baroque, Rococo and Neo-classical styles in furniture, silver, etc. English use of their names (Louis quatorze, Louis quinze, Louis seize) often refers to Victorians' immensely popular imitations.

Love seat Modern name for late 17th- and early 18th-century chair (French *marquise*) wide enough for extravagant costumes, but developed as a small twin-back settee – 'half settee' in the 1740s.

Lovespoon Welsh. Through the 18th century a betrothal gift, hand-carved from a single piece of wood by the giver. On sale through the 19th century, some machine-carved from the 1840s (some with early dates.) Double spoons from *c.* 1850. Recognisable 19th-century motifs include Menai Bridge (opened 1826) and the turnbuckle-and-chain.

Loving cup Victorian name for a vessel known in early silver as a grace cup (passed round at feasts after grace had been paid) and subsequently as a toasting cup. A two-handled, footed vessel found in silver, pewter, glass, ceramics. In Leeds and other earthenwares of the 1770s–1870s it was often painted overglaze with the owner's name and date, but fakes exist.

Lowestoft, Suffolk 1757–*c*. 1800. Small factory making soft-paste bone-ash porcelain, mainly useful wares with blue and embossed ornament, including transfer-printing from the 1770s. Made many minor items such as caddy ladles and miniature wares as well as individually inscribed birth plaques, mugs, etc. and souvenir 'Trifles'. No association with 'Oriental Lowestoft', a term for Chinese armorial porcelain decorated to British commission.

Lozenges Diamond or rhomboid shapes, often incised on 17th-century furniture panels.

Lunettes Half-moon or semicircular shapes often found as repetitive borders on 17th-century furniture.

Lustres Glass pendant drops or Victorian ornamental vases hung with these.

Lustre-wares Ceramics, collectors differentiating between elaborate early work (Iznik, Hispano-Moresque, maiolica) that inspired, e.g., William de Morgan, and the simpler English lustres made from the 1800s and popular throughout the early 19th century. These were oily solutions of metallic salts brushed on to earthenware or bone china and skilfully kiln-fired.

Gold provided tones from bright gold to purplish pinks (using gold-and-tin purple of Cassius) and 'copper' (low carat gold darkened by being applied over deep red earthenware).

Platinum oxide produced untarnishing 'silver' including highly prized resist lustre with a pattern in white or colour against the 'silver' ground. From the 1820s tea-pots, etc., might be mould-shaped and all-over lustred to suggest sterling silver plate; with white-glazed interiors from the 1840s. (Also a short-lived cheaper electro-silvering process in the 1850s.)

Spattered lustre (with the oily solution sprayed through muslin) is associated with Sunderland, but was made also in Staffordshire and elsewhere.

Wedgwood introduced his mottled '*moonlight*' lustre in 1810.

Lyre Ancient stringed musical instrument, its horseshoe shape

198 C. R. Mackintosh design for chair, 1897. **199** C. F. A. Voysey design for writing-cabinet. (Both V. & A. Museum.)

used in Neo-classical furniture such as Adam-style chairs, Regency sofa-table supports, Victorian canterburies.

Macaroni 1. Foppish young man of about the 1760s and hence his extravagent dress. 2. A hookless chatelaine hung over a tight belt, its chain of gold, jewelled or enamelled, with ends, of equal length, weighted with a watch and either a tassel or a sham watch (*fausse montre*).

Mackintosh, C. R. (1868–1928) Architect, house decorator. Around 1900 he worked with H. MacNair and two craft-students Margaret and Frances Macdonald (whom they married) to create the 'Glasgow style' as an impressive interpretation of the period's Arts and Crafts and Art Nouveau trends. Remembered for his early sensuous ethereal ornament and for tall austere furniture, every piece designed for a specific setting, such as Glasgow's Cranston tearooms.

Macramé Victorian hobby developed from knotting, for fringes, etc., with cords and metal threads, finger-twisted and plaited, using pins and a lace-maker's pillow.

Madeley, Shropshire (1825–40) Soft-paste porcelain made by Thomas Randall, former London porcelain decorator. This resembled then-fashionable early Sèvres, but he refused to add Sèvres marks. Bone china from the late 1830s.

Mahogany Warm brown wood from the West Indies and Central and South America, hard, heavy and of huge girth, from several fairly similar trees. Became important in England from the 1730s although walnut long remained fashionable.

Included early *Spanish or San Domingo*, dark, very heavy, with little grain pattern, but very strong in intricate carving.

Cuban was welcomed around the 1750s for its fine ripple or curl grain, much used in veneers.

Honduras or baywood, easily fading, lighter in weight, with an open grain, was used through the later 18th century and onwards for cheaper work and under veneers.

Maiolica, Italian Basically the same as Dutch and English delftware and early French faience – all stemming from the Hispano-Moresque tin-glazed ware (first imported via Majorca). All had the same purpose of giving crude earthenware a clean opaque white surface, using costly tin, for ornament in colours and lustres. So named from the 16th century and continuing in widespread production through the 17th and 18th centuries until successfully challenged by English cream-coloured earthenware. Especially noted for early 16th-century lustres and distinctive pictorial ornament. *See* Engobe; Majolica, English.

Majolica, English Popular colourful relief-moulded ware, often in naturalistic shapes covered in various types of opaque white ground to secure glowing effects with brush-painted colour glazes, clear or opaque. Products ranged from umbrella stands to dishes of fruit or nuts. Evolved at the Minton factory in 1851 under art director Leon Arnoux, who might use parian ware for majolica figures etc. Widely produced, with little similarity to the Italian Renaissance ornament although some designed for Mintons by the artist Alfred Stevens was inspired by such motifs.

Malachite Stone in many tones of bright copper green attractively

156

veined and banded, rather fragile with a texture resembling agate. Used as furniture inlay or veneer, and in jewellery.

Maltese lace Term now implies a type introduced to Malta in the 1830s – black-and-white silk guipures in simple abstract patterns, made also elsewhere including England.

Mandarin fan Hundred-faces fan. 19th-century Canton export, the embossed and richly painted leaf including over 100 tiny figures with glued-on painted ivory faces and glued-on brocaded robes. Some ornate copies assembled in France.

Mandarin porcelain From late in the 18th century, Chinese export ware decorated with 'mandarin' figures, some in full relief, their colours including pinks, reds and gold in harsh juxtaposition.

Mantel clock From the 18th century onwards, a spring clock to stand on a shelf or mantel, usually implying an ornate case of gilded metal, porcelain, marble.

Mantilla Spanish head-and-shoulders shawl of black or white silk lace or blonde, or of black silk.

Manwaring, Robert Remembered for his book of designs *The Cabinet and Chair Makers' Real Friend and Companion,* 1765.

Manx table Tripod table with carved legs resembling those in the arms of the Isle of Man.

Maple Pale, fine-grained wood often flecked and taking a good polish, attractive for veneers. Knotty burr growths were excellent for small turnery. *See* Mazer. American sugar maples include the Victorians' favourite bird's-eye maple, lustrous golden colour with small dark spots. *See* Sycamore.

Maps Age and quality judged by their paper (including watermarks), style of decoration, colouring (often modern – wrong in tones and texture). Printed dates suggest only the year that the original copper plate was prepared. A few were printed on white satin from the later 17th century onwards for embroiderers, and others may be found copied in print-like stitchery as map-samplers.

Marble Usually taken to include all such limestone rocks as are white or attractively coloured or veined and take a high polish. Popular in Georgian and Victorian furnishing. Substitutes included scagliola and Victorian painted slate. *See* Alabaster; Marble mosaics; Serpentine.

Marble mosaics Commonly 'scrapwork', forming a veneer of marble fragments for souvenirs in holiday regions, followed by conventional patterns and bird-and-flower motifs. Derbyshire produced more intricate inlays set into hollows shaped in the marble base, for early Victorian snuffboxes, etc., and even table-tops.

Marbling, ceramic Streaky mixing of colours on the surface of the earthenware as distinct from solid agate ware. In slipware, from the 16th to the end of the 18th centuries; in coloured glazes especially from the later 18th century including Wedgwood's 'granite' and 'porphyry.' *See* Tortoiseshell ware.

Marbling, paper Colours intermingled on the surface of a trough of size, taken up by a sheet of unsized paper laid over them. Such paper, polished, was used for wall coverings, book end-papers, etc. The method was adapted to book fore-edges (*see* Fore-edge painting) from about the 1670s.

Marcasite Name commonly given to crystalline cubic sulphur ore or iron pyrites (fool's gold) when used for jewellery, 18th to 19th centuries. Pale yellow with brilliant lustre, cut, polished and mounted as individual stones. Rarer, true marcasite is the same chemically, but paler yellow with radiating crystal structure. Not to be confused with cut-steel.

Marcella cloth Cotton woven with a quilted honeycomb effect popular, 19th to early 20th centuries, for bed covers.

Marks (Figs 71–76, 138–161, 232) Inconspicuous symbols, figures, initials, etc., offering clues to makers, dates, tax payment, protection of design against copying. Easily forged and sometimes deliberately misleading but always interesting to collectors. Rare on English furniture, glass (*see* Irish glass; Pressed glass); useful on silver (*see* Hallmarks). In ceramics, incised marks have proved most difficult to fake; painted marks are occasionally altered (e.g. 'England' mark erased) or misleading (*see* Coalport). *See also* 'Limited' mark; Potteries; Registration marks and references to individual firms.

Marlboro' leg (Fig. 124) On late 18th-century furniture. Tapering square-section leg (thermed) with a square-cut projection either as the foot or as a collar slightly above a plain foot.

Marqueterie ware Earthenware made by Doulton, late 19th century, surface-patterned with a mosaic of coloured clays comparable with Tunbridge ware marquetry mosaic.

Marquetry (Fig. 288) Furniture ornament, more elaborate than inlay. Patterns of flowers, birds, scrolls, 'seaweed' (or endive) etc. composed in veneer with fragments of different woods glued over smooth furniture surfaces. Notable in the late 17th and early 18th centuries; in the later 18th century Neo-classical style, and in Victorian imitations, with paint as an obvious substitute. *See* Tunbridge ware.

Marquise (Fig. 181) Ring with a stone cluster in the popular late 18th-century shape of a pointed oval or ellipse (shuttle shape); hence marquise cut (navette cut) for jewels.

Marquise chair *See* Loveseat.

Marriage commemoratives Include, e.g., 17th-century pewter and furniture marked with a triangle of initials – surname at the apex, husband's and wife's first names below. Also 18th- to 19th-century ceramics inscribed by the china-seller, such as loving cups and suitably painted fans, etc. All popular with fakers.

Marrow scoop In silver, etc., from late in the 17th century onwards, for extracting savoury marrow from beef bones. Usually with a long narrow bowl and a still narrower flute as its handle.

Martin lacquer *See* Vernis Martin.

Martin brothers (Fig. 12) Four brothers running their own studio pottery from 1873; marked wares are from their Southall pottery, 1877–1915. Pioneer studio potters applying new techniques to salt-glazed stoneware; remembered for grotesque 'Wally birds', etc., but also for restrained gourd vases, etc.; influenced by Japanese pottery that they observed at the 1900 exhibition.

Mary Gregory glass Mainly Bohemian from *c*. 1870s onwards. Cheap glass painted with child figures in white enamels (sometimes with tinted faces) named after an American glass decorator.

Mask 1. In furniture-carving, silver-casting, ceramic jug spout, etc., a face shaped in relief – human, animal, mythological, grotesque. 2. In ceramics, included character jugs and mugs. *See* Bellarmine; Rodney mementoes.

Mason china *See* Ironstone china.

Match boxes, Vesta boxes (Fig. 225) Tiny boxes for the waistcoat pocket or to hang on the watch-chain, made first in base metal for the various wax-match manufacturers' 'fusees', and 'vestas'. Became collectable items in gold, silver, etc., in many imaginative shapes especially from the 1870s into the 1920s. Early specimens might be compartmented for both matches and tinder. Easily identified by inclusion of a roughened striking surface, provided that this has not been added to an outmoded tinder or snuffbox. Mainly serrated slot strikers from the 1890s. Some dual-purpose (as cigar-cutters, etc.) and some with trick safety fasteners.

Matting Delicately roughened surface created by close, evenly spaced hammered punching. Skilled work producing a dull non-reflective background, e.g., behind polished silver ornament, furniture-carving or the hands on a brass clock dial. *See* Chasing.

Mauchline ware General term for small Scottish souvenir woodwork developed in Ayrshire (Mauchline and Cumnock) and Kincardineshire (Laurencekirk). Became widely popular in the 1820s–30s, including small boxes in finely grained sycamore with 'invisible' Scottish hinges. Some were hand-painted or pen-drawn with meander lines, prompting ruled patterns in tartan colours for which the firm of W. & A. Smith devised multiple pens and varnish colours, patented 1853 and 1856, often surrounding local views. Soon the tartans were painted on paper pasted to the boxes and the views, local and foreign, were transfer-printed; some boxes were decorated with varnished photographs. Eventually the skill formerly used for making snuffboxes was applied to a wide range of souvenirs – glove-stretchers, wool-winders, ring stands, egg cups, notebooks, napkin rings. Some pieces were labelled by W. & A. Smith or by Davidson Wilson & Amphlet. *See* Laurencekirk; Scoto-Russian ware.

Mazarine 1. Flat perforated plate fitting inside a serving-dish, mainly for fish from *c.*1770, in silver, earthenware, etc. 2. Rich smalt blue applied in wet washes to soft-paste porcelain biscuit by Chelsea, Derby and Worcester, imitating Vincennes, and later used on bone china.

Mazer From Middle Ages, turned wooden bowl named from the speckled markings of the most suitable unshrinking wood, found in burry excrescences of the maple tree. The resultant vessel, unavoidably shallow, was often deepened with a rim of silver or pewter.

Measure *See* Weights and measures; Wine measures.

Mechlin lace Early name for nearly all Flemish lace. From the 1700s and in the Regency it was popular in England for trimmings, as a simple, light-textured lace distinguished by flat threads outlining the pattern – this and the hexagonal ground being made together on the pillow.

Medallion Typical feature in Neo-classical ornament as an oval or circular panel in painted furniture, jasper-ware plaques and fan decoration (usually three, painted on fine silk).

Medullary rays In timber, lines of dense tissue radiating from the centre of a log crossing the annual ring marks. Early carpenters split newly felled oak along these rays, such riven timber showing desirable 'silver grain'.

Meerschaum 'Sea foam', a lightweight porous white hydrous magnesium silicate lending itself to elaborate carving for tobacco-pipe bowls, from the 18th century onwards.

Meigh, Charles *See* Old Hall.

Meissen Porcelain factory near Dresden. Made Europe's first hard-paste porcelain, *c.*1710. Great period 1730s–50s, but disrupted by the Seven Years War. Production has continued ever since, including the reissue of popular early models, but gradually the lead passed to Sèvres. Meissen's J. J. Kaendler, chief modeller 1731–75, originated the style of figure modelling copied throughout Europe, including Chelsea, etc.

Melodeon. Melodium American organ with double keyboard. Same principle as the accordion but with bellows worked by foot pedals. From the mid 19th century.

Melon shaping Rounded vertical lobes or corrugations on late 16th- to early 17th-century furniture bulbs. Found in silver and other metal vessels of the early 18th and early 19th centuries, as it strengthened soft or thin metal against denting.

Memento mori (Fig. 182) 'Remember you must die' – tiny skulls, coffin pendants, etc., as macabre ornament, especially popular among personal mourning jewellery in the 16th to 17th centuries. The late 18th century favoured tomb scenes; in the 19th-century snake motifs and jet cameos (especially of veiled faces) were approved among a general fashion for memorials in jewellery.

Mendlesham chair. Dan Day chair (Fig. 318) Suffolk variant of the saddle-seated Windsor, its low back having a double crest-rail and double cross-rail, each often framing a row of small balls and with the rails linked by flat pierced splats.

Mercury gilding *See* Gilding.

Mercury twist *See* Air twist.

Merese (Fig. 252) In a drinking-glass, a collar or disc linking bowl and stem, occasionally stem and foot.

Méridienne Regency name for classical couch with one scrolled end higher than the other and usually paw feet on castors.

Mezzotint Print suggesting the painter's tone gradations instead of lines. Taken from a copper plate prepared by being roughened all over until it would print velvety black. The artist's skill lay in scraping away some of this burr to achieve the required range of tones and burnished highlights.

Mica. Talc Silicates found in granite, etc., important for their perfect cleavage, splitting into thin, elastic, greasy-feeling plates, translucent and showing a pearly lustre. Common transparent mica is generally known as talc – used for lanterns, early sets of 'transformation' pictures, etc.

Miers, John (1756–1821) Important silhouettist working mainly in Leeds and London, painting in exquisite diaphonous detail in black on card or white-plaster medallions, neatly framed, or mounted in tiny silhouette jewellery. Printed labels gave his address and price. His most important assistant was John Field, later a partner with his son, William Miers, until 1830, using 'Miers & Field' labels. Some of Field's work was pencilled with bronze; he died in 1841.

Mignonette lace Named as endearingly light, fine pillow lace, its ground resembling tulle, widely exported from France and Flanders.

Milk glass *See* Enamel glass; Sunset-glow glass.

Millefiori glass 'Thousand flower' ornament using an ancient Roman process taken up in 16th-century Venice. Popular in England from the late 1840s (Bacchus, Powell and other firms) copying the work of notable French factories (Baccarat, St Louis, Clichy), using canes of many-coloured glass. Patterns such as concentric circles made with thin slices from these canes were enveloped in clear flint-glass by fusion and could be used for domed paper weights, bottle-stoppers, etc. Collectors must realise that, while Clichy went out of business in the 1880s, Baccarat and St Louis revived the craft in the 1960s and modern paperweights, based on similar traditional patterns, may also come from English, Scottish and American glassworks.

Millegrain setting In jewellery, the gemstone girdle gripped by a circle of minute metal beads.

Ming dynasty (1368–1644) First period in Chinese history to include exports to Europe. Ceramics especially important, with underglaze blue and copper-red ornament and magnificent translucent overglaze enamels (including dragons, phoenix, etc.). Notable floral textiles in colour and gold thread, in embroidery, weaving and silk tapestry, such as flowers of the four seasons (peony, prunus, lotus, chrysanthemum); also carved and painted lacquers, cloisonné enamels, etc.

Miniatures, painted Most usually a small portrait painted on vellum, paper, ivory, card or enamel. Elegantly boxed as costume ornament from the 16th century. Some fine work, occasionally signed, but much by copyists for sitters to give away. Increasing use of ivory in the 18th century, stipple painted from *c.*1730.

Minster jug *See* Old Hall pottery.

Minton (Fig. 7) (Mintons from 1872 to 1951.) Potters, of Stoke-on-Trent from 1793 to the present day, marking wares with impressed year symbols from 1842. Thomas Minton, d. 1836, was joined by his son Herbert in 1817, making blue-printed and richly coloured earthenwares and bone china. Under Herbert's control, 1836–58, manufacture improved to include cabinet porcelains, parian statuary, English majolica. Later Victorian successes included acid gilding, pâte-sur-pâte ornament, Palissy and Henri-deux wares. Minton flower-encrusted wares are often mistaken for Coalport. *See* Tiles.

Miser purse (Fig. 269) Modern name for stocking purse.

Mitre Diagonal line at the right-angle meeting of two mouldings or bands of veneer — a detail expected of the English cabinet-maker. Also a V-shape incision in deeply cut glass.

Mocha stone. Moss agate Decorative form of chalcedony showing moss-like markings of iron oxide.

Mocha ware Cheap table-wares with bands of markings suggesting mocha stone, no two identical, achieved by allowing acid-based colour to diffuse through wet clay slip before glazing and firing. From the late 18th century onwards. Made also on the Continent.

Moco ware Substitute for mocha ware – cheap earthenware merely spattered with coloured clay slips before glazing.

Modeller, ceramics The maker of the original figure model for shaping a master mould, source of the working moulds that would shape a figure's different parts. These parts were finally assembled into the figure by a 'repairer'.

Moderator lamp *See* Lamps.

Mohs's scale Arbitrary order of hardness for stones devised by Friedrich Mohs, late 19th century – from 10 for hardest (diamond) to 1 for softest (talc).

Moiré Fabric with a wavy sheen associated especially with watered silk; hence *moiré metal.* patented 1816 by Edward Thomason, Birmingham manufacturer, who applied hard varnish to preserve the wavy figure in tinned iron plate, for tea canisters, etc. In the 1830s, colour-stained and painted by china-decorators, it was known as *crystallised ware.*

Monarch's-head duty mark (Figs. 156, 157). In profile, among silver hallmarks, 1784–1890, indicating payment of silver duty by the manufacturer. Provincial assay offices were sometimes slow to change their punches when a monarch died. *See* Drawback silver.

Money box With a slit for coins, traditionally and into the 19th century consisting mainly of primitive designs in pottery, smashed to recover their contents. Crude representations of hen-and-chicks, beehive, chest of drawers, etc.; cottages in the 19th century. Copper coin required larger boxes from the end of the 18th century. Mechanical contrivances found mainly from the later 19th century and in modern copies.

Monkey orchestra Hard porcelain monkeys dressed as musicians, made at Meissen from 1747 onwards. In soft porcelain by Chelsea, 1756, Derby, 1760s; in bone china by Copeland & Garrett, 1830s–40s.

Monopodium (Fig. 239) 'One foot' implying an animal's head and leg (usually a lion's) forming a single unit, as a table leg, etc.

Roman ornament popular through the Regency and late Georgian years.

Monteith Large silver bowl with notched or undulating rim (often detachable) for iced water to cool wine glasses suspended into it by their feet. From the late 17th century onwards, copied in pewter, delftware and earthenware such as Leeds creamware, also 18th century 'glass trays'. Some oval, in pairs, from *c.* 1760, but soon outmoded by individual wineglass coolers.

Moon *See* Cresset.

Moons. 'Grease spots' Small discs of greater translucency seen in some early soft-paste porcelain, when viewed against the light, indicating imperfect blending of materials.

Moonstone Softly translucent gemstone (a variety of feldspar) with an opalescent-to-pearly lustre. Cut *en cabochon* for minor jewellery, much favoured by late Victorian-Edwardian art jewellers.

Moorfields carpets, London Hand-knotted in the Turkish manner, made by Thomas Moore from *c.* 1760, including Robert Adam designs.

Moresque Decoration in Moorish style – applied to much Spanish and Portuguese work reflecting Moorish occupation of the Peninsula. *See* Hispano-Moresque wares; Turkish style.

Morgan & Sanders From 1801 large-scale London manufacturers of much then-popular multi-purpose and similar 'patent' furniture including sofa-beds and globe writing-tables. Some illustrated in *Ackermann's Repository*. *See* Trafalgar fashion.

Morocco Fine-grained goatskin leather, originally Moorish. Used, dyed red, by bookbinders from the 16th century; red, green or blue for desk tops, etc., from the 18th century.

Morris chairs (Fig. 317) Two styles associated with the Morris firm although not designed by William Morris: 1. Adaptation of the Sussex spindle-back with slender, duplicated cross-rails and stretchers and with arm supports extending several inches below the seat. 2. Adjustable upholstered chair, with backward extensions of the arms, these being notched for a movable crossbar to support the hinged back at any required slope. Balance maintained by extending the seat-rails to form the back legs, as in a steamer chair.

Morris, William (1834–96) A leading figure in the 19th-century art world, important at the time as a poet and social reformer as well as for his enthusiasm in encouraging the period's handicrafts revival. *See* Arts and Crafts movement. Was a craftsman as well as designer, e.g., in embroidery, weaving and printing of textiles and high-warp tapestry; he controlled the Merton Abbey factory from 1881 and his love of fine book production found expression in his private Kelmscott Press (including his own type-design) from 1889. The firm of Morris, Marshall, Faulkner & Co., 'fine art workmen in Painting, Carving and the Metals', launched in 1861, continued with him as successful sole proprietor from 1875.

Mortar 1. Timeless heavy bowl – stone, bronze, etc. – for substances pounded with a round-headed pestle. 2. Primitive floatwick lamp. 3. 19th-century night-light candle, thick, slow-burning.

Mortise-and-tenon joint In wood, to join end-grain into side-grain. A square-section tenon or tongue driven into a matching hollow cut in the side of a piece of wood and secured by pinning through both pieces with a headless wooden dowel-pin. Draw-boring, with the dowel-pin holes slightly out of line, fixed the joint extra tightly. In English furniture by the 16th century.

Mortlake, Surrey, tapestry factory Established 1619, employing expert Flemish weavers, producing some of the period's finest tapestries, using fine English wools in the slow high-warp process. Sold to Charles I, 1637, encouraged under the Commonwealth and active into the 1680s; its mark, St. George's cross, continued by other factories. Included copies of designs by Rubens and Vandyck, Raphael cartoons and royal portraits; also many elegant garden and landscape scenes with tiny mythological figures, and sets of the Months (haymaking, shearing, etc.) *See* Soho.

Mortlock, J. London china-sellers and decorators from 1746; as Mortlocks Ltd, 1893–1934. Marked much ware from Coalport, Derby, etc. so that the style of their mark aids dating.

Mosaic work (Fig. 289) Pattern or picture formed of small cubes (tesserae) or pieces of marble, glass, stone, etc., set into mastic or stucco, including minute work for mosaic jewellery (earrings, etc.) Used by Egyptians, Romans; also, later for floors, walls, table tops. Not much in England but *see* Marble mosaics; Tunbridge-ware mosaics.

Mote skimmer (Fig. 267) From the late 17th century and frequently found in the 18th-century tea equipage. A long teaspoon with a decoratively pierced bowl for skimming tea-leaf debris from poured tea and a barbed finial to clear leaves from the spout-strainer inside the teapot. Associated by some collectors with the service of punch.

Mother-of-pearl. Nacre Certain conch and bivalve shells with their outer coverings scraped away to reveal iridescent shimmering linings. Widely found in decorative use from the 16th century including nautilus shells mounted as stemmed cups. Also small pieces of shell (scales) exactly cut to shape and riveted all over the surface of silver vessels or applied as furniture inlays. In the 18th century the shell was carved and pierced in English and Oriental games-counters, knife-handles and foil-enriched fan sticks, again with Victorian copies. The great Victorian demand was met by increasing supplies including thicker, less lustrous Australian shell for card cases and tea caddies and for encrustations on papier mâché and other furniture: these were shaped by grinding and acid from about 1840, instead of the traditional clumsy filing. *see* Card cases; Fans; Jewelled embroidery.

Mother-of-pearl ware Ceramics with iridescent glaze. *See* Belleek porcelain; Glaze.

Moulded glass *See* Blown-moulded glass; Pressed glass.

Mouldings Lengths of wood cut in decorative section for cabinet-making, along cornices, in panel-framing, etc., their outlines usually based on classical architectural design.

Mounts Usually of metal applied to wood, ceramics, coconut cups, etc., such as handles, locks and protective corners to furniture. *See* Fans; Ormolu. In *Sheffield plate* they were necessary to hide the copper core in cut edges: from *c.*1775 they were of silver wire, followed by some solid silver castings in the 1780s and stamped silver (with lead-alloy fillings) from the 1790s, becoming more elaborate from 1815.

Mourning jewellery (Figs. 182, 190) Painted miniatures, locks of hair, initials, dates of birth and death, later Victorian photographs and similar personal details incorporated in pendants, lockets, rings, generally dominated by black (enamel, onyx, jet, etc.) Only lost their importance near the end of the 19th century. *See* Memento mori.

Moustache cup Victorian teacup from the mid 1850s onwards with a guard projecting inside the rim to keep the drinker's moustache dry.

Muffineer Small castor on a stemmed foot for sprinkling cinnamon on toasted muffins, from the 1760s through Victorian days (when the term was also used for a lidded muffin-dish.) With a lower perforated dome from the 1780s; kitchen castor shape from the 1790s, sometimes with a pierced body to show a blue glass lining.

Muffle kiln Small box kiln for firing enamel colours on ceramics, etc., without direct exposure to the flames, at temperatures from *c.*750° to 950° C.

Mug Handled drinking-vessel. With a base rim, so no saucer required. In a wide range of materials through the 17th to 20th centuries, dated by shape, ornament, etc. *See* Frog mug.

Mulberry wood Yellowish brown with dark streaks, heavy, tough, occasionally used for veneers.

Mule chest Modern term for a chest with one or two drawers in the base, mainly 17th century, forerunner of the chest of drawers, and Victorian.

Muntins *See* Stiles.

Mural Wall painting other than a fresco.

Murano glass From the Venetian island where glassmakers attempted to keep the secrets of their skills, renowned from the Middle Ages.

Musical box With clockwork mechanism, producing tunes from vibrating metal strips struck by pins set in a revolving cylinder. Weak-toned in the 1800s, but showing frequent improvements through the 19th century such as a loud-soft movement, 1838, and flute, drum and bell notes from *c*.1850.

Muslin Now a general term for delicate plainly woven cotton cloth. Important to embroidery collectors as the basis of much superb white embroidery.

Mutchkin *See* Tappit hen.

Nacre *See* Mother-of-pearl.

Nail-head work *See* Close nailing; Piqué.

Nailsea glass (Fig. 113) Name for jugs, gemel flasks, bells, rolling pins, and imitative nonsense such as tobacco pipes and walking

200 Nailsea glass ornaments: bell, walking stick and giant tobacco pipe.
201 Papier mâché letter rack, hand-painted in Wolverhampton style.

sticks, some in low-taxed dark-toned bottle glass, but many more brightly decorated with flecks and lacy stripes in white or colours; flint-glass might be used after tax abolition in 1845. Nailsea glass factory near Bristol was noted, 1788–1873, for crown glass and bottles (not flint-glass), but this fancy work was widely made at Sunderland, Newcastle, Stourbridge, Wrockwardine (Shropshire), Alloa, etc. *See* Latticinio.

Nantgarw and Swansea porcelain, Wales Soft-paste porcelains, highly translucent, finely glazed, but costly in wasters; made by William Billingsley at Nantgarw, 1813–14 and 1816–19 and at Swansea, 1814–16, including renowned 'duck-egg' porcelain with a greenish translucency. Some London-decorated with hard, brilliant colours and gold; and remaining stocks by Thomas Pardoe at Bristol after Nantgarw's closure.

Nappy plates To place under a glass for catching froth from foaming 'nappy ales.' Listed in records of Bow, Leeds, etc.

Nautilus cup *See* Mother-of-pearl.

Nautilus ware Dessert services shaped as nautilus shells, catalogued by Wedgwood, 1774, in queen's ware. Made in bone china by other potters from *c.* 1820.

Nécessaire Etui in box shape for the dressing-table.

Needlecase 1. Carried by women from the Middle Ages. Through the 18th to 19th centuries they were usually variants of a damp-proof screw-cap tube in a range of attractive materials including ivory, shagreen, Tunbridge ware, etc. in such shapes as a parasol, peapod, etc. 2. In the 19th century a small rectangular needlebox, which might be decorated with a Baxter colour print, known as a *needle print*.

Needlepoint lace Developed from drawn-thread embroidery in the 16th century and distinguished from lighter pillow laces by being worked with a needle and a single thread, using a loop or buttonhole stitch.

Nef Gold or silver ship model for the dining-table, important in early ceremonial dining, holding spices, knives, etc., from the 14th

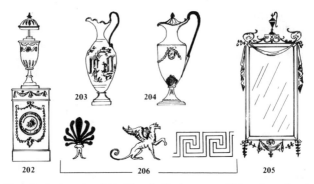

Neo-classical style. 202 Urn knife box on sideboard pedestal. **203** Porcelain vase painted with scenes of classical ruins. **204** Sheffield plate hot water jug. **205** Looking-glass with gilded composition ornament. **206** Three ornamental details: anthemion, griffin, Greek fret.

century. Some English-made from the 16th century. Some on wheels for serving wine in the later 17th century. English and Dutch models were used as table centres for sweets from the later 18th century, but remaining specimens more often date to the 19th century.

Neo-classical style. Adam style (Figs 29, 48, 86, 124, 125, 162–164, 181, 182, 209–213) From the 1760s, appearing as a reaction against Rococo excesses in furniture, silver, ceramics. Led by Robert Adam in Britain, inspired by excavations (Herculaneum, etc.) and his own studies of classical antiquity, but more superficial, less factually archaeological, than Neo-classical design in the 1800s. Associated with simple flowing curves, vase and urn outlines, straight tapering reeded legs, ornament flat or in low relief such as anthemion, patera, husk, swag, etc.

Neo-Gothic *See* Gothic taste.

Nephrite *See* Jade.

Nest of tables *See* Quartetto tables.

Netsuke A small Japanese carving originally corded and intended as a toggle for a man to attach an inro to his belt. *See* Inro.

New art *See* Art Nouveau.

New Canton Name given to new soft-paste porcelain factory at Bow, Essex *c*. 1750, following experimental work under Thomas Frye. Indicated current fashion for Chinese (hard-paste) porcelain. *See* Bow.

Newcastle-on-Tyne glass Important glassmaking centre including flint-glass table-wares. Light style of drinking-glass associated with the period 1730–80 in a soft flint-glass popular with Dutch glass-engravers. Increased production from the end of the 18th century. *See* Beilby; Pressed glass.

New Chelsea Porcelain Co (Fig. 76) Present century bone china manufactory reproducing early porcelain shapes and decorations of Chelsea, Sèvres, Meissen, etc., including an anchor and 'Chelsea' in some printed marks.

New Hall, Shelton (Fig. 279) Made porcelain from *c*. 1781 using a hard-paste formula, but fired at a lower temperature, with a wet-looking glaze. From *c*. 1810 to 1835 bone china, some marked New Hall in a circle. Remembered for unusual silver-shaped teapots.

New stone china *See* Stone china.

Nickel Hard, whitish malleable metal available from the 1750s, taking a brilliant polish. Used mainly in alloys.

Nickel silver Most usual name for nickel alloys (mainly copper, zinc and nickel: no silver). Much used under silver in electro-plated wares. A cheap substitute for table silver, often called German silver or argentan plate (advertised from 1835). *See* British plate; EPNS mark.

Niello Black compound of heated lead-silver-copper-sulphur used from the Middle Ages onwards as a decorative filling for engraved metal. Sometimes called Tula work from the Russian town where it originated.

207 Night-light (Clarke's fairy light). **208** Pastille burner, flower-encrusted cottage.

Night-lights 1. Especially from the 1830s, using slow-burning non-guttering candles in decorative holders such as china cottages and churches, with cut-out windows; also with lithophanes. 2. Simple wax lights patented by George Clarke, 1844 and developed by Samuel Clarke as *fairy lights*, 1886; these had the wax contained in coloured glass bowls for hanging in the conservatory, etc. *See* Queen's Burmese glass.

Nonsuch chests Made by 16th- to 17th-century Flemish or German craftsmen, perhaps working in England, with fronts inlaid as building façades. Named for supposed resemblance either to Henry VIII's Nonsuch Palace or to Nonsuch House on London Bridge.

Northwood, John *See* Cameo glass.

Norwich glasses. Lynn glasses Name artbitrarily given to tumblers and wine glasses horizontally ribbed or grooved.

Nottingham lace Machine-woven, imitating pillow lace, mainly from early in the 19th century and more elaborately by the Jacquard machine patented 1837, but flimsy, with weak edges.

Nottingham stoneware Salt-glazed like common brown stoneware, but given a smooth surface with clay slip containing iron oxide, resulting in an intensely rich brown with a slight metallic lustre. Process evolved, 1690s, by James Morley, who used incised decoration and made some double-walled vessels, the

174

outer wall with perforated patterns. Imitations by Derbyshire potters to the 1800s, but inferior.

Nutcracker Early tool with two levers pivoted at the end, crushing the nut between them; from the late 17th century also a screw-action type, the alternatives then being a lever or pincer style, often with the nut crushed between the jaws of a carved human head. All lent themselves to imaginative ornament in Europe's woodcarving regions; some had a lead-weighted handle to hammer the extra tough nut.

Nutmeg grater Silver, etc., in pocket size (smaller than a snuff rasp) for the toddy drinker, the design usually including a compartment for the nutmeg. The grater was hand-pierced in silver or sheet steel until *c*.1770s, then in blued steel. Shapes included cylinder, oval, heart, egg, urn, mace.

Oakwood Pale, darkening in use to glowing brown. Much European oak imported as wainscot and clapboard, easier to work into furniture than English oak. Hard, enduring wood, found in much remaining Tudor-Stuart furniture ('age of oak') and 19th- to 20th-century imitations. *See* Bogwood; Medullary rays.

Obsidian Glassy volcanic rock, black (iron) with glossy sheen, sometimes carved for ornaments or jewellery.

Objets d'art Ornamental items in general, frequently implying articles that are small and valuable.

Octavo *See* Folio.

Oeil de perdrix On porcelain, 'partridge eye' painted as a regularly spaced minor ornament, each a circle of colour ringed by smaller dots. A Sèvres fashion copied by Madeley, Minton, etc.

Oenochoe Ancient Grecian shape exaggerated by Victorians for claret jugs, coffee-pots, etc., with arching handle, flaring lip, narrow neck and wide-shouldered egg-shaped body tapering to a small foot.

Ogee. Cyma recta (Fig. 101) The flowing S-shaped double-curve, concave above, convex below, of classical moulding, found in furniture mouldings and bracket feet, drinking-glass bowls (and double-ogee), etc.

Oil gilding *See* Gilding.

Oil lamp *See* Lamps.

Old Crown Derby China Works (Fig. 72) Established by former workmen as Locker & Co. when the Derby factory closed in 1848, using old models and patterns and continuing until absorbed by the Royal Crown Derby Porcelain Co. in 1935. *See* Hancock, Sampson.

Old English (Fig. 262) 1. Spoon pattern from *c.* 1760. *See* Spoons. 2. Surface ornament on silver around the 1880s–90s, perhaps intended to recall 17th-century work, with heavily embossed flower and fruit motifs crowded closely over tea caddies, sugar castors, scent bottles, etc.

Old Hall (Fig. 75) Long-lived Hanley pottery, using 'Old Hall' marks, some with their 'founding date', 1790. Run by the Meigh family 1790–1861; most notably by Charles Meigh (1835–49), remembered for Neo-Gothic jug designs in white stone china, known as the 'York Minster jug', etc. Firm was the Old Hall Earthenware Co., 1861–86; Old Hall Porcelain Works, 1886–1902.

Old Hall, Wolverhampton *See* Wolverhampton style.

Oleograph Chromolithograph varnished and pressed to suggest the texture of oil painting on canvas. Late 19th-century German notion for Christmas cards, postcards, etc., used in England by, e.g., William Dickes.

Olive wood Hard, yellow to greenish brown with dark markings. Used for parquetry veneer, turnery, 18th to early 19th centuries.

Ombre table Three-sided for a Spanish card-game popular in England through the later 17th and 18th centuries.

Omnium *See* Whatnot.

On-glaze. Overglaze Ceramic ornament applied after glazing, usually in enamel colours unsuited to the glazing kiln heat and fixed by additional firings at lower temperatures.

176

Onslow spoon *See* Spoons.

Onyx Variety of chalcedony with structure of grey and white in parallel bands or planes suitable for cameos; often darkened (known as nicoló) and used for mourning jewellery.

Opal Gemstone, a soft glassy form of hydrated silica, with a wonderful play of colour due to dispersion of light by innumerable microscopic prisms, from white and pale iridescent pinks through reddish-orange tints (fire opal) to deep glinting blue-greens (black opal). Popular with late Victorian art jewellers. *See* Doublet.

Opal glass. Opaline glass Found among the early Victorian's range of semi-opaque ornamental glass, with a fiery glow when held against the light. Could not be cut, but was painted, gilded, mounted with colourful clear glass motifs in relief (reptiles, etc.)

Opaque twist *See* Air twist glass.

Opaque white glass *See* Enamel glass; Sunset-glow glass.

Open-flame lamps *See* Lamps.

Opus anglicanum Pre-Reformation church embroidery, England making the finest in Europe through the 13th and early 14th centuries, much still preserved among church vestments. Characteristic Gothic figure-ornament in rhythmic designs exquisitely stitched, especially in exacting split-stitch and against backgrounds shimmering with underside-couched gold thread.

Orange glass 1. Large top-glass for a dessert pyramid, holding an orange or orange-chip sweetmeats. 2. Sometimes a Williamite glass.

Orders of architecture Classical system controlling proportions in architectural design, the orders being the Doric, Ionic and Corinthian (Greek), Composite (combining features of the Ionic and Corinthian) and Tuscan (Roman). Revived interest from the Renaissance; more scholarly from the 17th century. Debased versions found, e.g., in furniture pillars and pilasters, silver candlesticks, etc. The entablature (cornice, frieze and architrave) sometimes surmounted by a pediment, rested on its appropriate capital (including abacus), pillar and base.

Orders of architecture. 209 Tuscan. **210** Doric. **211** Ionic.
212 Corinthian. **213** Composite, showing (a) cornice, (b) frieze,
(c) architrave, (d) entablature, (e) abacus, (f) capital, (g) shaft, (h) base
(i) column, (j) pedestal.

Original engraving *See* Inscriptions.

Ormolu Named from the powdered gold leaf used in fire-gilding;
hence bronze or refined golden brass gilded to protect it from
tarnish. Cast into ornate mounts for clocks, furniture, vases,
candelabra, etc., in the 18th to 19th centuries, notably by
Matthew Boulton. Later imitations might be cheaply lacquered
with gold-toned varnish. Or copied in bronze-finished cast iron.

Orrery Clockwork device showing movements of the planets, first
made by George Graham for Charles Boyle, Earl of Orrery,
*c.*1700.

Ottoman Late Georgian-Victorian. Basically a fully upholstered
back which serves seats on two or four sides. Sometimes circular
('chaperone's seat'); or in units assembled around a central ornament; or as a backless box. Wooden framework sometimes visible
from the 1840s.

Outside decorators In ceramics, specialist independent
enamellers who received porcelain 'in the white' to ornament it in
their own workshops.

Overglaze *See* On-glaze.

Overlay glass *See* Cased glass.

Ovolo In furniture, mirror frames, etc., convex moulding in quarter-circle section.

Oyster veneer Form of parquetry, each section showing a wood-grain pattern suggesting an oyster shell, typically the irregular concentric markings found in slanting cross-grain cuts from branches or saplings of such trees as laburnum.

Pad foot *See* Club foot.

Padouk wood Hard, heavy, purplish-red to brown, sometimes found in furniture made for Europeans in the East Indies.

Painted enamels *See* Enamels.

Pair-case watch With a second, protective outer case (sometimes protected by a third case). Frequent in the later 17th and 18th centuries.

Paisley pattern. 'Indian pine' Repetitive use of comma-shaped motifs filled with flower sprig detail introduced on costly late 18th century shawls imported from Kashmir, variously described as palm or mango leaf. Paisley shawls were hand-loom woven from the 1800s, at first plain with narrow border patterns; by the 1830s technical advances permitted price-cutting copies of increasingly elaborate Kashmir patterns, the characteristic motifs eventually lost in debased, elongated over-elaboration. Some printed from *c.*1850. Pattern was woven for wearing the shawl folded diagonally: reversible patterns from *c.*1860. Best had a weft of fine 'cashmere' wool with wool-and-silk warp; others were all-wool, silk-and-cotton or cheaper all-cotton. *See* Shawls.

Paktong. Chinese silver Silver-toned alloy of copper, zinc and nickel used from the 1770s for hearth furniture, etc.

Palimpsest Parchment re-used after attempted erasure of original writing, or brass as in brass memorial tablets re-engraved on the back.

Palissy ware Made by French Huguenot Bernard Palissy, *c.*1510–89 and his descendants – dishes, etc., with applied ornament of figures, masks, grotesques, arabesques, lizards, ferns, etc., modelled in relief and using a range of high temperature colours. The name was revived by Mintons and widely applied to Victorian wares, including figures with richly colour-glazed relief ornament, much like the period's English majolica. Considerable modern reproduction.

Palladian style Roman architecture as interpreted by 16th-century Italian Andrea Palladio influencing early Georgian architecture and furniture, as reaction against the Baroque. Monumental interiors, ponderous furniture, expressed especially by William Kent.

Panels In furniture usually rectangular, of flat wood within framing of thicker vertical and horizontal stiles, muntins and rails, as in a panelled chest. Especially suited to construction in oak.

Pap boat Small spouted feeding-bowl for child or invalid.

Paper filigree *See* Filigree paper work.

Paper knife Decorative desk detail, blunt-bladed, in metals, ivory, tortoiseshell, etc., for delicately opening folded and sealed letters and for slitting uncut pages of books, journals, etc. and for Victorian envelopes.

Paper lace Embossed borders on, e.g., Regency valentines, prompted development of perforated patterns by such London firms as Dobbs & Co. Paper pressed between dies and hand-filed to remove unwanted background.

Paper mosaic Ornament built up into realistic low relief by knife-cutting and pasting fragments from sheets of coloured paper: an 18th century hobby prompted by professionals who cut armorials, etc., in vellum.

Paper ware *See* Clay's paper ware; Papier mâché.

Paperweights Wide 19th-century range in local marble souvenirs, weighted metal celebrity figures, etc. Glass weights included costly crystal cameos and millefiori; also cheap pressed work and dumps.

Papier mâché (Figs. 201, 292) Used first for architectural ornament and from the later 18th century also for trays, coach panels (*see* Carton pierre; Clay's paper ware). More widely remembered for early 19th-century firescreens and other minor furniture, trays, boxes, etc., suggesting Oriental lacquer, mainly japanned glossy black and brilliantly decorated with gilding, paint, bronze powders, mother-of-pearl, etc. Chairs and tables might be reinforced with iron or made partly of japanned wood. Clay's sturdy ware was rivalled by cheaper pulp mixed with glue and resin, equally light in weight, free of warping, with attractively glossy surfaces of stove-hardened japan varnish (fadeless black from the 1830s). Shaping between metal dies patented 1832; bronze powder ornament patented 1812; mother-of-pearl encrustations patented 1825, with more delicate acid-shaping from 1840. Occasional marks of notable makers include Birmingham's Jennens & Bettridge (who made early papier mâché furniture and frequently marked their wares) and Wolverhampton's Alderman & Illidge. *See also* Spiers; Wolverhampton style.

Parcel gilt Silver ware or furniture partially gilded.

Parchment Ancient material for writing and painting, prepared from animal skin, mainly of sheep and goats. Inferior to vellum made from skins of lambs, kids, etc.

Parian ware. 1. Statuary parian, a highly vitrified porcelain suggesting lustrous whitish Grecian marble from Paros, made from 1842 by Copeland & Garrett and the Minton firm and eventually by *c.* 50 firms, especially for small white figures and busts (shaped in moulds, from designs by well-known sculptors and sometimes mistaken for individual sculptures). *See* Carrara ware. 2. Cheaper variant, domestic parian, was in production by 1850. lacking a silky texture and with its surface protected by smear glazing. It was used for relief-moulded jugs, vases, etc., many including flat areas of colour – blue, green, brown – with 'orange skin' surface.

Parquetry Furniture wood veneers cut into balanced symmetrical patterns popular in the late 17th century, the Regency, etc. On boxes in Tunbridge ware, small diamond shapes in contrasting colours and grains were used to suggest three-dimensional cubes.

Partridge wood. Brown ebony Hard, heavy, straight-grained, with brown and dark red parallel streaks suggesting bird plumage. Sometimes used for late 17th-century parquetry.

Parure Suite of matching jewellery, becoming fashionable during the Renaissance, typically a necklace, two bracelets, earrings and a brooch or pendant.

A *demi-parure* included fewer items, such as a pendant and matching earrings.

Passementerie Like early lace, a word first used also for braids and cords, eventually accepted for lace of gold and silver and more generally for gimps and beaded trimmings.

Paste. Strass 1. In ceramics, *see* Body. 2. In jewellery, artificial gem stones. Pastes of special lead-glass (a development from English flint-glass) were lapidary-cut to fit together closely in any required pattern (more amenable than diamonds). To make the most of their refractive fire they were backed with metal foil, necessitating protection from corrosion by air-tight close-setting. *See* Culet. Leading maker was jeweller G. F. Stras (1701–73) of Strasbourg; hence the alternative name, stras or strass. Fine 18th-century English work, but Victorians treated them merely as substitutes for precious stones, sometimes even giving them open settings. Paste feels less cold than diamond, topaz, rock crystal.

Pastel Coloured chalk crayon, used mainly for sketches. *See* Crayon etching.

Pastille burner (Fig. 208) Form of cassolet, now generally implying early 19th century's popular bone china cottage, castle, summerhouse or other model, often flower-encrusted. This was usually lifted from its base to insert a smouldering pastille, its fragrance emitted through chimneys, etc. Many reproductions exist.

Patch box Small shallow container for variously shaped silk 'beauty spots' worn by fashionable 18th-century ladies. Distinguished from generally more substantial snuffboxes by a 'steel' mirror inside the lid. (*See* Speculum.)

Patchwork From Medieval days to the present, with some confusion in dating, due to the use of outmoded fabrics. Small pieces of different textiles edge-joined to form a pattern, with no background material visible in contrast to applied (appliqué) ornament. Usually composed of matching geometric shapes (hexagons especially from the 1850s). Centrepieces for bedcovers, etc., were specially printed, *c.* 1800–17, some with commemorative dates. Some Victorian pictorial work and autograph or album cushions. *See* Crazy quilts.

Pâte de verre Late 19th-century French technique: 'glass paste' of crushed glass, coloured and mould-shaped into figures, etc., and individually hand-finished with a spatula after slow firing.

Patent glass *See* Queen's Burmese glass; Queen's ware glass.

Patera Popular Neo-classical motif, e.g., on furniture (painted, cast brass, etc.) with concentric ornament often suggesting a rosette, flat or in low relief.

Pâte-sur-pâte Ceramic ornament: 'paste-on-paste'. Layers of white semi-transparent watery slip painted and hand-tooled upon a coloured ground to build up a cameo effect fixed by firing and glaze. Ancient technique introduced from France to the Minton firm, *c.* 1870, by M. L. Solon (1835–1913) who continued until 1913, his pupils including Alboine Birks (1861–1941).

Patina Dark greenish encrustation on antique bronze and copper, difficult to fake. More generally, the attractive effect of time on, e.g. long-polished furniture.

Pattern numbers On ceramics, metalwares, not to be confused with dates, but different styles of numbering may aid in identifying a maker and the date of a pattern's introduction.

Pavé setting In jewellery, close-setting of gems, concealing underlying metalwork.

Pavilion In jewellery, the lower section of a cut gemstone, below the girdle, frequently held by the mount.

Pear-drop arcaded moulding On cabinet furniture, often below the cornice, a series of arches separated by small swellings.

Pear-drop handle Small pear-shaped hanging handle, usually brass, popular on furniture in the late 17th century, but much reproduced.

Pearls (Figs. 183, 184, 189, 190) Smooth, lustrous organic gems usually round, white, formed in shells of molluscs, often deliberately cultured. Widely used in jewellery, including half-pearls; irregularly shaped Baroque pearls were favoured by art jewellers; local fresh-water mussel pearls were popular in Scottish jewellery. Imitations are common. *See* Seed pearls.

Pearlware Hard white earthenware evolved 1779 by Josiah Wedgwood. Tended to replace cream-ware because excellent for blue transfer-printing.

Pearwood Pinkish tones with fine smooth grain, harder than lime. Used for carved furniture (frames, etc.) and stained and polished as an ebony substitute in inlays.

Pedestal (Figs. 164, 202) Architectural term applied to furniture indicating a solid support in contrast to legs; hence pedestal desk; pedestal sideboard on two solid supports containing cupboards or drawers, and pedestal bookstand, early 19th century, with shelves on all four sides.

Pediment Architectural feature; in cabinet furniture generally describes any decorative frontal structure above the cornice. *See* Break; Swan-neck.

Pedlar doll Man or woman on fixed base displaying a hawker's licence and carrying a tray of miniature jewellery, household items, printed broadsheets, etc. From late in the 18th century; many modern or with modern wares.

Peg tankard Communal drinking-vessel containing a vertical line of marker studs.

Pellatt, Apsley *See* Crystal cameo.

Pelmet. Lambrequin Horizontal drapery to conceal a curtain rail over a window or below the cornice of a curtained bed.

184

Pembroke table (Figs. 23, 276) Light table from *c.*1750s, often elegantly decorated during the Neo-classical vogue. With a drawer in the underframing and small falling flaps supported on fly brackets, the open top often shaped as a round-cornered squarish rectangle, occasionally a rounded oval.

Pendant Hanging ornament; hence a jewelled motif hanging on a necklace or brooch, pendant earrings, etc.

Pendeloque (Fig. 38) In gemstones, a pear shape, facet-cut.

Penrose *See* Irish glass; Waterford glass.

Penwork Arabesques, flowers, chinoiseries, etc., in white on black japan or vice versa. Hand-painting, the final details added with a quill pen and Indian ink. Late 18th century and early 19th centuries, on cabinets, tables, etc.

Perfume burner *See* Cassolet; Pastille burner.

Peridot For jewellery, transparent soft green gem-form of the mineral olivine, easily scratched, less valuable than the demantoid garnet, but popular with late 19th-century art jewellers.

Perpendicular style English, late Gothic, *c.*1380–1520, characterised by long slender vertical lines.

Petit-point embroidery *See* Tent stitch.

Petuntse China stone. *See* China clay.

Pew group Modern name for primitive hand-shaped figures often with musical instruments, supported by a high-backed settle (no church association.) Usually white salt-glazed, with dark clay eyes, buttons or other trimmings; a few lead-glazed with touches of colour. Many reproductions.

Pewter (Figs. 10, 284) Alloy composed mainly of tin. Brightly polished, it was a cheaper table-ware alternative to silver, but was largely ousted by increasingly serviceable 18th-century earthenwares. The Pewterers' Company was established in London in 1348 (*see* Touch) with strict rules regarding the quality of its wares which included: *sadware* (plates and similar flatware) consisting of tin strengthened with a little bismuth and copper – later antimony – mould-cast, lathe-trimmed and toughened by

Pewter. 214 Scottish tappit hen measure. **215** Baluster wine measure. **216** Irish early 19th-century haystack or harvester measure. **217** Two Victorian ice or dessert moulds. **218** Liberty Tudric pewter clock. **219, 220** Clasp and hatpin in art pewter for amateur tooling, 1900s.

prolonged hammering; *trifle* of medium hardness for casting drinking-vessels and 'trifles' such as buckles; and *ley metal* for measures, candle-moulds, etc., often heavily leaded – up to 40% until reduced to a 10% maximum in 1907. Leadless pewter became important again in the later 18th century, but was differently handled. *See* Britannia metal; Vickers metal. A late Victorian demand for cast-pewter tankards, etc., and the vogue for antique pewter from the 1890s onwards resulted in ornamental and domestic wares including amateur work, but also reproductions and fakes, such as many spoons.

Phelps, W. Late 18th-century silhouettist with a wide range of techniques, painting and cutting his likenesses and sometimes introducing touches of colour such as pink, blue or green to costume details.

Photographs 1. On ceramics, *see* Decalcomania. 2. On woodwork, *see* Mauchline ware.

Picot Small loop of thread decorating the edge of lace.

Picture ribbons Pictorial work woven on jacquard looms in glossy silks, achieving three dimensional effects with vivid patches of foreground colour and minute background detail such as crowds at sporting events. Made famous by silk-weaver Thomas Stevens, Coventry, established 1854, who produced bookmarkers, valentines, Christmas cards, etc.

His most elaborate *Stevengraphs*, from the late 1870s, were mounted on titled, gilt-edged cards, including series of historical scenes, coach and railway scenes, celebrity portraits, etc. Some restricted to black, white and grey tones. Several other makers.

Picture trays In japanned tin-plate, hand-raised, from Pontypool and from John Baskerville of Birmingham by the 1750s, later rivalled by lighter 'paper trays'. Several distinctive rim shapes are aids to dating. *See* Clay's paper ware; papier mâché; Spiers; Wolverhampton style.

Piecrust table Pillar-and-claw with its rim shaped in a series of cyma curves.

Piecrust ware Lidded ceramic vessels shaped and decorated to suggest standing pies, contributing to the expected dinner-table spread of alternative dishes during the flour shortage of the Napoleonic war. Made in cane-ware by Wedgwood, J. & W. Turner, E. Mayer, C. Meigh, etc. Less clear-cut detail is to be noted in moulded work by J. & W. Ridgway from the 1830s. Heat-resistant pie dishes for oven use were made in Derbyshire from *c.*1850.

Pier glass. Pier table Often placed together against a pier – a wall space between windows in formal Queen Anne and Georgian rooms. A tall mirror in an elaborate gilded frame hung above a D-shaped table, often finely veneered or painted. Both frequently made in pairs. ·

Piggin Staved, cooper-made wooden dairy vessel for milk or cream.

Pilasters Architectural ornaments attached to the front corners of case furniture, often with the characteristic details of a Neo-classical column.

Pilgrim bottle *See* Costrel.

Pilkington's Tile & Pottery Works Clifton Junction, near Manchester. Founded 1892. Under William and Joseph Burton developed from tile works to art pottery (1897–1938 and 1948–57), exploiting a notable range of glazes including brilliant lustres. Gordon Forsyth became chief designer in 1906.

Pillar-and-claw furniture 18th-century name for small tables, kettle stands, firescreens and dumb waiters in a tripod design with a central pillar ornamentally turned and often carved resting on three out-jutting legs (in a succession of shapes that aid dating.) Some tables with removable tops. *See* Birdcage.

Pillar moulding. Roman pillar moulding Glass ornament of vertical convex ribs or reeding adding weight, e.g., around the body of a Regency decanter, associated with Irish glass before it became subject to tax-by-weight from 1825.

Pillow lace Bobbin-wound threads fashioned into ornamental motifs and background mesh by intermingling them among pins stuck into a small padded pillow. Machine-made imitations mainly from the early 19th century. *See* Bobbin lace; Bone lace; Needlepoint; Nottingham lace.

Pill slab For apothecaries' work – of marble or delftware, blue-painted, sometimes with the Company's arms. ·

Pinchbeck An improvement on ordinary copper-zinc brasses, claimed to be almost indistinguishable from gold. Invented by

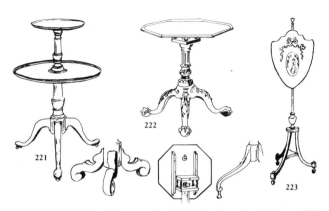

Pillar-and-claw furniture. 221 Dumb waiter with dished trays. **222** Mid 18th-century table with, *below*, two details of earlier and later claw arrangements flanking 'birdcage'. **223** Pole screen, 1790s–1800s.

watchmaker Christopher Pinchbeck, whose son advertised a wide range of 'toys', 1733–47. But the name was soon applied to much gold-coloured copper-zinc brass by the Birmingham toy trade.

Pinched plate Ribbon of flattened silver wire, popular in the 16th to 17th centuries among purls, etc., on wear-resistant professional embroidery for book covers, glove gauntlets, etc.

Pincushions From Medieval days lidded cylindrical pin-poppets. From the 17th century, gifts of pins often spelt out greetings on tiny pin-fringed cushions ('Bless the babe', etc.). In the 1800s small flat shapes rimmed with pins for the reticule, followed by massive Victorian cushions of lace, patchwork, etc.

Pine wood. Scots pine In pale tones, was known as yellow deal; in warmer tones, as red deal or pine. *See* Deal.

Pinxit *See* Inscriptions.

Pinxton, Derbyshire First small pottery launched by impecunious

William Billingsley in 1796. Made highly translucent, finely potted soft-paste porcelain, but proved unprofitable and he soon left. Factory petered out *c*.1812.

Pipe stopper For pressing tobacco into the pipe bowl, a small tool, frequently cast in brass, pewter or lead, in most use from the 17th to the mid 19th centuries, the essential flat end or press becoming larger to suit changes in pipe bowl design and often cross-hatched for secondary use as a letter wafer-seal. Some on loop handles for the watch-chain, some imaginatively shaped, as celebrity caricatures, etc.

Pipkin Metal or earthenware cooking-vessel.

Piqué 16th-century Neapolitan invention: tiny gold or silver studs inserted into tortoiseshell or ivory to form a smooth glinting pattern, for snuffboxes, fan sticks, jewellery, etc. Heavier version known as *clouté* (nailhead) *piqué*; scenes, etc., inlaid in strip gold known as *posé d'or*.

Pitcher Large jug, usually earthenware.

Plane wood Whitish, close-grained. Sometimes used instead of beech for painted furniture. Sycamore is sometimes called Scottish plane.

Planishing Using heavy hammer with slightly rounded face to give a smooth and polished surface to metal such as hand-raised silver or brass.

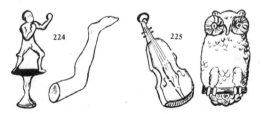

224 Two pipe stoppers. **225** Two match boxes.

Plaque Round, oval or rectangle of metal, ceramic ware, etc., mounted or inlaid as decoration on furniture, etc.

Plasma Dark green variety of chalcedony often with light or darker spots and stains. Used for cameo carving.

Plaster of Paris Calcined gypsum. *See* Alabaster. Shaped by moulding while damp, for copying sculpture, etc. and for moulds in pottery factories from *c.*1745. Dried harder, smoother than common lime-and-sand plaster.

Plate. Plating *See* Electroplate; Sheffield plate; Silver plate.

Plateau In silver or ceramics, a flat-surfaced tray, circular or oval, on plinth or small feet. Often made in sections to suit the size of the dining-table where it supported an épergne or other centrepiece. *See* Sand picture.

Plate glass Sheet-glass ground flat and polished on both sides. Could be made by casting from the 1690s; large scale development in England from the 1770s, including looking-glass.

Plate mark In a print, indicates engraving, etching or other intaglio process, being the pressure mark left on the area of dampened paper covered by the copper plate, distinctively lower than surrounding margins. If incomplete, the print is 'clipped'.

Plate pail Wooden bucket for carrying a stack of dinner plates, its straight sides including a vertical slit for easy plate removal. Handsome in 18th- to 19th-century brass-bound mahogany.

Platinum Precious metal, costlier than gold, clean, white, hardened with iridium for cobweb-fine jewel settings. Increasingly popular in the early 20th century, but lacked hallmarks through the collectors' period. *See* Lustre-wares.

Playing cards From the Middle Ages. Patterned backs from the 1830s, with rounded corners from the 1860s. Marked with figures from the 1860s, letters from the 1880s. Double-headed court cards from 1867. Dating is also aided by tax marks on the ace of spades. *See* Duty ace.

Plinth Base of a classical column; hence a footless square or rectangular base to case furniture.

Plique-à-jour Skilled enamel work that returned to favour in Art Nouveau jewellery, e.g., by R. J. Lalique, the enamel delicately framed in gold wire with no backing to mar its translucent colours.

Plumtree wood Hard, heavy, yellowish tones around reddish-brown heartwood. Found in early country furniture and some inlay.

Plush Fabric with a deep pile, especially popular with Victorians.

Plymouth porcelain Patent for first English hard-paste porcelain obtained by William Cookworthy, 1768, after he had located suitable ingredients in Cornwall. Production included table-wares, ornaments and many figures. In 1770 he moved to Bristol.

Plywood Two or more wood veneers glued together with their grains running in different directions to avoid warping. Mainly 20th century.

Point d'Angleterre *See* Brussels lace.

Point lace *See* Needlepoint lace.

Pokerwork. Pyrography Ornament burned into wood with heated metal tools, the hollows neatened with sandpaper. Late 18th- and 19th-century hobby given impetus by Arts and Crafts Movement with suitable small furniture, etc., supplied by department stores. As a commercial wood finish it was ousted by the use of acid. Not to be confused with the more difficult hobby xylopyrography.

Pole screen (Fig. 223) Moveable firescreen (frequently framed embroidery) on a vertical pole with a pillar-and-claw or pedestal base reflecting fashions of 18th to 19th centuries. Early Victorians included oil paintings on copper and papier mâché and elaborate carving in the Warwick style.

Polychrome Many-coloured.

Polygonal Many-sided.

Pomander Spherical openwork box of gold, silver, enamelled, etc., containing ambergris or spiced wax, carried in the 15th to 16th centuries to counteract disease and ill-odours. From the later 16th century, compartmented for perfume powders. Fancy shapes – skull, book, etc. – in the 17th century, reproduced by Victorians. *See* Pouncet box; Vinaigrette.

Pompadour fan With the guards and some of the sticks *battoir* shaped – with one or two swellings for medallion ornaments.

Pompeiian style Mainly 19th-century term for Neo-classical ornament based on excavated work at Pompeii, an Italian town engulfed by Mount Vesuvius, AD 79.

Pontil mark. Punty mark Scar on base left when a glass vessel was broken from the iron pontil rod used to hold it during construction. Smoothed on good quality glasses after *c.* 1750, but frequent on cheap ware for another century and on fakes.

Pontypool and Usk japanning Snuffboxes, chestnut servers, charcoal braziers, etc., in brilliant colours under heat-hardened varnish unaffected even by a charcoal fire. Finest quality work evolved from the 1730s by the Allgood family using local tin-plate (sheet iron soaked in molten tin) and their own lustrous varnish. Expanded *c.* 1770s–1800s, with rivals (same family) at Usk. Some fine decoration is associated with Benjamin Barker. Less costly ware made in Birmingham and Wolverhampton might be sold as 'Pontipool'.

Poplar wood Whitish with yellow or grey tinge, close-grained, but soft, used for some early inlay.

Porcelain *See* Bone china; Bone porcelain; China clay; Hard-paste porcelain; Soft-paste porcelain.

Porphyry Volcanic rock, most usually red or purplish, scattered with paler feldspar crystals; some dark olive-green. Takes a high polish, for pillars, table-tops, etc.; hence imitative marbled glaze by Wedgwood and others from *c.* 1770.

Porringer. Pottinger Sometimes now called a bleeding bowl. Term usually restricted to a shallow, single-handle bowl, in 17th-century silver, etc., for individual servings of spoon-foods, as distinct from the deeper posset pot and caudle cup intended for thinner spicy gruels.

Portable barometer Patented by Daniel Quare, 1695. Brief minor fashion: a stick barometer mounted on folding tripod feet with a moveable cover for the open end of the mercury tube. *See* Barometers.

Portland vase. Barberini vase Cameo glass in the British Museum probably from Alexandria, *c*. 50 BC, copied in Wedgwood jasper ware (many issues) and in 19th-century cameo glass.

Posset pot Name now given to 17th- to 18th-century handled, lidded and often spouted pot for the serving or shared drinking of hot spicy drinks. Handsome examples in slipware, delftware, stoneware. *See* Caudle cup.

Postcards With picture and conventional greeting from the 1880s; for sale unstamped from 1894, followed by P.O. acceptance of messages alongside the address, offering full scope for pictorial work by such popular artists as Phil May, (1864–1903), Donald McGill (1875–1962) and cat-fascinated Louis Wain (1860–1939). An attempt at an art form was made in Raphael Tuck's Connoisseur series, 1903; Edwardians also enjoying photographs, tricks and novelties, political cards, valentines, etc.

Posy holder Mainly in 19th-century use from the 1820s to carry a small bunch of fresh flowers, their stalks pinned into a tube, cornucopia or stick-handled cup. In silver, gilt metal, etc., including filigree, with a handle of mother-of-pearl, amber, porcelain, etc.,

226 Posy holder. **227** Prattware: crude Wellington commemorative jug.

sometimes with folding legs to stand upright when put aside during a dance.

Potichomania Minor Victorian craze from France for imitating fashionable Oriental ornaments by lining glass vases (and some rolling-pins) with decoratively printed paper cut-outs or transfers varnished and backed with white.

Pot-lids Shallow covers (slightly domed from 1848) of earthenware pots (for hair pomade, fish paste, etc.) collected for their full-colour transfer-printed pictures. These were made by a process evolved by Jesse Austin for the Fenton firm of potters F. & R. Pratt, followed by more than a dozen other potters. The same process was applied to plates, vases, etc. Many 20th century re-issues.

Pot-pourri vase Decorative jar or bowl for sweet-scented dried flowers, etc., recognised by its pierced cover, sometimes with a close cover also to retain the fragrance.

Potteries Staffordshire region especially associated with ceramics, described as the 'Five Towns' by author Arnold Bennett. Confusingly a ceramic mark may include an inconspicuous town initial following those of an individual firm (intended to indicate an address for direct re-ordering of replacement table-wares; hence unwelcome to the china retailer). The six towns especially associated with this practice were Burslem, Cobridge, Fenton, Hanley, Longton and Tunstall. All, together with Stoke-upon-Trent, are now included in the area Stoke-on-Trent.

Pottery 1. Usually accepted as a general term for earthenwares and stonewares as distinct from translucent porcelains. 2. A factory where any of these are made.

Pottle Two-quart drinking-vessel.

Pouch table (Fig. 240) Work-table with a pleated fabric bag hanging from a drawer in the frieze for needlework, often in addition to fitted compartments under a hinged table-top. Late 18th to 19th centuries.

Pounce pot Accompanying inkpot on inkstand, with perforated (pounced) top. Held gum sandarac powder ('sand') used to check ink-flow on parchment and unsized paper, especially after erasures; subsequently held white sand, to blot slow-drying ink on sized, shiny writing paper.

Powder blue Underglaze granular effect on porcelain, such as some early Worcester, achieved by blowing powdered smalt blue through a muslin-covered tube on to the ware's oiled surface.

Prattware (Fig. 227) Now associated with the potter Felix Pratt (1780–1859), but introduced c.1790s and made by many potters into the 1830s. Popular jugs, etc., which could have bold relief-moulded ornament (often commemorative) because the ware's characteristic 'high temperature' colouring was protected by strong glaze.

Pre-Raphaelites Attempt at a Medieval artists' brotherhood, founded 1848 by D. G. Rossetti, W. Holman Hunt, John Millais and others with support of John Ruskin, aiming to paint exactly what they saw in defiance of academic convention.

Pressed glass Cheap substitute for free-blown cut glass, thicker and heavier, made in England from the 1830s (e.g. by W. H. Richardson), but mainly from the 1860s. Hot glass was forced by a plunger into a patterned mould making the outer surface sharply indented while the inside remained smooth, unlike blown-moulded glass. Finish was improved by fire-polishing. Pressed table-wares in clear glass patterned to suggest elaborate cutting were made in vast quantities including much for export, especially by Sowerby's Ellison Glassworks Ltd. Midlands makers included Bacchus & Sons, Rice Harris & Sons, Thomas Hawkes.

Makers who marked their glass included J. G. Sowerby (peacock's head mark, registered 1876); Henry Greener & Co. (lion with halberd); George Davidson & Co. (demi-lion rampant over turret) all in North-East England (*see* Sunderland), J. Derbyshire of Manchester (J. D. and anchor) and the Kilner firm, near Wakefield. Other firms in Manchester and the North-

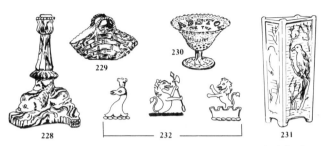

Pressed glass 288 Marbled slag candlestick. 229 Typical basket.
230 'Gladstone for the Million' (by Henry Greener). 231 Sowerby spill
vase (design registered 1877). 232 Marks used by (*left to right*) Sowerby,
H. Greener, George Davidson.

East can sometimes be identified by Patent Office registration
marks.

Pricked pictures Young ladies' hobby from late in the 18th
century until the 1860s. Portrait prints, often hand-coloured, were
given added realism by slight relief effects achieved by pricking
with wooden-handled needles, outlines being emphasised from the
front and filled in from the back. Developed commercially as
roulette pricking with a many-pointed wheel, preceding
embossing and paper lace.

Prie-dieu chair (Fig. 293) Tall-backed, low-seated, single chair,
early to mid Victorian, with a broad top and splayed back legs.

Princes plate High quality electroplating.

Princess Charlotte souvenirs The only child of George IV and
Queen Caroline, born 1796, married Prince Leopold of Saxe-
Coburg in 1816. Her wedding followed by her death in childbirth
in 1817 prompted portraits, etc., on ceramic plaques, in ivory and
crystal cameo glass, even as printed centrepieces for patchwork.

Printed fabrics English imitations prompted by restrictions on
imports of Indian chintz. Linen and cotton cloth block-printed
with fast dyes from the late 17th century. Notable 18th-century

197

monochrome printing from copper plates, 20 years earlier than the renowned French *toile de Jouy*. Roller printing from the 1780s. Colours: frequently purple-brown; substantial black only from the 19th century; greens until *c.*1810 in pencilled yellow over printed blue; stippled shadows from *c.*1815. Some printed snuff handkerchiefs – humorous, political, topical. *See* Patchwork.

Printie (Fig. 78) Small circular hollow, shallowly wheel-ground in early Georgian glass and more heavily among the deep-cutting of the 1800s. Known as a bull's eye in Victorian pressed glass.

Prismatic cutting In glass, among the deep-cutting of the 1800s, parallel grooves cut in V-section, elaborated, e.g., into blazes.

Prisoner-of-war work By Frenchmen (including Dieppe ivory carvers) held in England during the Napoleonic wars, permitted to sell what they made in, e.g., bone (ships, automata, games), straw-work, paper filigree.

Profile *See* Silhouette.

Proofs. States Trial prints from an engraved plate, differentiated as: 1. *Artist's proof*, with no printed lettering, but signed by the artist and probably numbered; this is different from a *signed proof* which may be any finished print that the artist has signed. 2. *Proof before letters*, the print including the names of artist, engraver and publisher, but no title. 3. *Open letter proof*, which includes the title in outline lettering, before the printer issues the final version with a professionally engraved title.

Provenance Proof of an antique's source and history, hence its authenticity.

Prunts (Fig. 77) Small glass bosses attached to some early drinking-glasses, sometimes tooled as 'strawberry prunts'. Also found among glass trailings on 'Nailsea' fairings. *See* Roemer.

Prussian decanter (Fig. 88) A favourite shape of the 1780s–1820s, with a broad-shouldered, inward-sloping body, its lower half usually comb-fluted. With a flat mushroom stopper finial followed in the 19th century by target, pinnacle and globe.

Pulled-thread embroidery Usually worked in white on fine white muslin, stitched into lacy perforated patterns, background diapers, etc., without pulling out any fabric threads. These were merely drawn aside and whipped into groups with a needle and very fine cotton.

Pulvenated Rounded outward like a cushion, an architectural term sometimes applied to a convex frieze on case furniture from late in the 17th century.

Punchbowl For serving wine-based or spirit-based drinks from the 17th century. An opportunity for a handsome ornamental vessel in silver, delftware, glass, etc.

Punch-ladle. Toddy-ladle Serving-spoon accompanying the punch bowl from late in the 17th century, its bowl in successive cylindrical, goose-egg, oval, double-lipped, circular and shell shapes (by the 1750s). A coin inserted in the bowl may suggest a misleading date. Later, many lightweight, factory-made, fluted or pattern-embossed. Handles of silver, ivory or hardwood. Hot toddy, popular from the 1770s, affected wood so whalebone was used, with a twist-turned grip. *See* Toddy lifter.

Punch pot. Punch kettle Stoneware and other ceramics for serving hot punch or toddy, suggesting a large teapot but lacking a strainer inside at the base of the spout. Late 18th and early 19th centuries.

Punchwork Silver, especially late 18th century. Thin rims strengthened with rows of punched hollow beads instead of soldered-on mouldings.

Punty *See* Pontil mark.

Purdonium (Fig. 233) Wooden coalbox with a hinged lid at the front, a removable metal lining and a slot at the back for a shovel, from the mid 19th century.

Puritan spoon *See* Spoons.

Purled glass Ribbing added around the base of a drinking-glass bowl.

Purls 1. In lace, picots or 2. work in metal thread. 3. In

233 Purdonium. 234 Puzzle jug in delftware.

embroidery from the 16th century, tiny flexible tubes made of closely-coiled wire for applying among spangles, etc., to take the rub of wear. Silver-gilt or cheaper silk-covered copper.

Puzzle fan Brisé fan which shows two different painted scenes on each face, depending on which way it is opened. Has additional blades so that opening reveals only half of each at a time.

Puzzle jug Stoneware, slipware, delftware, bone china. Made from the 17th century but many are of the 19th to 20th centuries. With a pierced neck so that the liquor had to be obtained from one of several spouts around the rim, these being linked with the hollow handle. For success the drinker had to block the other spouts and sometimes an additional inconspicuous hole.

Pyrography *See* Pokerwork.

Pyrope Gemstone garnet of deep crimson colour.

Pyramid Arrangement of glass salvers for the informal 18th-century dessert. Two or three on top of each other in decreasing size held an array of individual sweetmeats – jellies, custards, syllabubs, dry sweetmeats in appropriate dessert glasses.

Quaich Early Scottish drinking-bowl of staved wood with lug handles. Style continued from the 17th century in silver and pewter, with pierced handles.

Quaint style Art Nouveau as crudely interpreted by commercial furniture makers in the late 1890s to 1900s, with writhing forms,

200

heart-shaped apertures, frequently in fumed oak or stained birch.

Quartetto tables Four, or three, small tables in graduated sizes to fit into each other for drawing-room use from the 18th century.

Quartz Most common mineral. Used in jewellery, etc., as colourless rock crystal; less commonly pinkish 'rose quartz'; and as amethyst, cairngorm, citrine, etc. *See* Aventurine.

Quartrefoil Shaped as four lobes, as in Gothic tracery where they are separated by cusps.

Queen Anne style Strictly 1702–14, but extended to cover the 1700s–20s' change to well-proportioned arching curves and smooth surfaces, observable in case furniture, bended-back chairs with cabriole legs, silver teaware. Confusingly much table silver and other domestic furnishings of the later 19th century were described at the time as 'Queen Anne' – the name now given to the original 'picture-book' architectural style of *c.*1860–1900.

Queen's Burmese glass Made from the late 19th century by T. Webb & Sons under US patent – heat-shaded pale yellow to deep pink, coloured with gold and uranium. Used for table-wares and for shades for the new electric lighting. Was opaque in contrast to alexandrite glass. *See* Night-lights.

Queen's plate A high standard of electroplating.

Queen's ware Named by Wedgwood, 1765, for Queen Charlotte, wife of George III. Great improvement on earlier earthenwares with strong, uncrazing cream-coloured glaze, but further improved by Wedgwood in 1780 and by his successors from 1846. Widely made as cream-coloured earthenware by other potters such as Leeds.

Queen's-ware glass. 'Patent Queen's ware' Patented in 1878 by Sowerby & Co. of Gateshead, notable makers of art glass and pressed glass. This was one of the period's attempts to imitate carved Japanese ivory in an opaque, yellowish-tinted material.

Quill cleaner On inkstand, small vessel with holes in its lid for inserting quill pens. Its filling of lead shot steadied the pot and helped to clean the nibs of clogged ink.

Quilling Row of cylindrical pleats or gathers in ribbons, ruffles or lace; hence a series of small blobs in trailed glass ornamenting 'Nailsea' vessels. *See* Filigree paperwork.

Quilting (Fig. 304) For costume (from Medieval armour to Georgian dress), bedcovers, etc. Two layers of fabric, often with interlining, strongly held together by lines of plain stitching through all layers, forming patterns in low relief. See Italian quilting.

Quintal vase For flowers, late 18th century. Fan shape composed of five conjoined tubes on a heavy base. In Leeds creamware, etc.

Quizzing fan Late 18th century, with peepholes around the border of the leaf; sometimes also with a spyglass set in the base of the guard. The cockade fan opening to a circle had the spyglass in its substantial rivet.

Rails In furniture-framing, horizontal members as in, e.g., chair-cresting, table frieze.

Raising Process of shaping metal such as silver from flat sheet to hollow-ware by long hammering with frequent annealing and final planishing.

Ram As a horned head, a frequent Neo-classical ornament. Actual horn used for snuff mulls. *See* Horn.

Rasp *See* Nutmeg grater; Snuff rasp.

Ratafia glass Distinctive small-capacity flute now associated with this almond-flavoured cordial, but more probably originated as a surfeit water glass.

Rat-tail *See* Spoons.

Ravenscroft, George Associated with the important Savoy Glasshouse, London, from 1673. *See* Flint-glass.

Reading chair *See* Cockfighting chair.

Red stoneware Made by Wedgwood, called rosso antico. *See* Elers red ware.

Reeding Parallel mouldings in convex profile, opposite of fluting; frequent as Neo-Gothic ornament.

Reed top *See* Tambour.

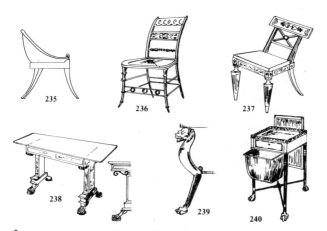

Regency furniture. 235 Thomas Hope chair design. **236** Bedroom chair from Ackermann's *Repository of Arts*, 1814. **237** Grecian style from *Modern Costume* by Henry Moses, 1823. **238** Sofa table (including end view) by George Smith from his *Designs for Household Furniture*, 1808. **239** Lion monopodium. **240** Pouch work – table with adjustable firescreen.

Refectory table Modern term for Tudor-style long dining-table with massive legs and low stretchers.

Refractive brilliance Important feature of gemstone: a measure of the extent to which light is reflected back from the surface of the stone or bent (refracted) when entering the stone. An important consideration when working on a colourless stone's back facets. Hence the superiority of the diamond's brilliant cut (Fig. 37) over the flat-based rose cut (Fig 35). Here a measure of comparable importance is the stone's *dispersion* of white light into its constituent rainbow colours.

Regency period (Figs. 31, 78, 107, 126–128, 135, 183, 243–246, 288, 290) Strictly 1811–20, but a style covering *c.* 1795–1825.

Archaeological attempt to imitate classical form as well as ornament. Much fine furniture in low, plainish outlines, rich veneers,
brass mounts; heavy silver; ornate gilded porcelain; deeply cut
glass. Included Egyptian ornament and some escapist Oriental
bamboo and Neo-Gothic ornament.

Registration marks. Registration numbers *Rd* in diamond shape
indicates registration of a design at the Patent Office against
copying between 1842 and 1883. The exact date this was done
can be worked out from the letters and figures in the points of the
diamond, but articles so marked may be considerably later. The
Roman figure at the top indicates the class of goods: I for metals,
II for wood, etc. From 1884 the mark was merely 'Reg. No.'
Beginning that year at 1, this had reached 351, 201 by the end of
1899.

Relief print Opposite of intaglio: parts left projecting from a wood
block were inked to make an impression on the paper. Less pressure was required than for an intaglio print, so such prints show no
plate marks and were cheaper, using a type press. *See* Woodcut;
Wood engraving.

Rembrandt prints High quality prints issued in monochrome at
the end of the 19th century and in colour early this century by a
Lancaster company.

Renaissance 'Rebirth' of classical spirit (banishing Gothic trends)
and revival of art and letters – in Italy from about the mid 15th
century, in England by the 16th century, with periodic renewed
impetus. *See* Neo-classical style.

Rent table Later name for round or octagonal table with drawers
all round the frieze, made from the second half of the 18th century.

Repairer Confusing name for the assembler of ceramic figures
who puts together the parts shaped separately in moulds. *See*
Modeller.

Repoussé work *See* Embossing.

Reproduction Exact copy of an antique, but without deliberate
deception. *See* Fake.

REGISTRY OF DESIGNS

Index to the letters for each month & year from 1842 to 1867

1842	X	January	C
1843	H	February	G
1844	C	March	W
1845	A	April	H
1846	I	May	E
1847	F	June	M
1848	U	July	I
1849	S	August	R
1850	V	September	D
1851	P	October	B
1852	D	November	K
1853	Y	December	A
1854	J		
1855	E		
1856	L		
1857	K		
1858	B		
1859	M		
1860	Z		
1861	R		
1862	O		
1863	G		
1864	N		
1865	W		
1866	Q		
1867	T		

a - Class
b - Year
c - Month
d - Day
e - Bundle

For Sep 1857
2y Letter R used
From 1st To 19th Septr.

For Decr 1860 a very
Letter K used.

July 1st 1842

J. Wong
Registrar

Registration marks, china. 241 Keys to the letters and figures found on diamond-shaped marks used for registering designs, 1842–67.

242 Keys to letters and figures, 1868–83.

Resist Wax or other material applied to ceramics, cloth, paper, metal or glass to repel a colour, dye or acid, etc., from certain parts of a design, as in resist lustre (*see* Lustre-wares).

Restoration period The 1660s, following restoration of the monarchy under Charles II. Associated with many furnishing innovations from the Continent. *See* Cabinet-makers.

Reticule Very small handbag for use with skimpy dress around the 1800s when pockets were taboo. Many delightful designs.

Rhodium Brilliant untarnishable metal, harder, whiter than related platinum, sometimes used to plate silver jewellery.

Rhodonite Manganese spar; when rose-red it may be cut and polished for jewellery.

Ribband-back chair Clever mahogany carving to suggest twisted ribbons illustrated, 1754, but not invented by Thomas Chippendale and continuing through the 1770s–80s.

Rice-grain porcelain With grain-like perforations filled with clear glaze.

Richelieu embroidery White openwork: the pattern outlined in buttonhole stitch and linked by bars (often with picots, like needlepoint lace) with the fabric background cut away.

Ridgway family Far-ranging Shelton–Hanley potters important through the 19th to 20th centuries, making china, fine stonewares, earthenwares, etc.

Riesener furniture By important French cabinet-maker, J. H.

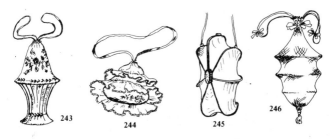

Reticules, Regency. 243 With basket base. **244** White embroidery.
245 On folding wire frame. **246** Network.

207

Riesener (1734–1806) including elaborate marquetry showing musical instruments, etc. and fine chiselled bronze mounts.

Rivière Necklace consisting of a row of graduated single stones.

Roan Soft flexible sheepskin for upholstery, cheaper than Morocco.

Rocaille 'Rockwork' as in garden fantasies with shells as a motif; origin of 'Rococo', *q.v.*

Rock crystal Pure quartz, water-clear, most usually found in hexagonal prisms. Highly valued and worked into luxury vessels richly engraved from the Middle Ages onwards. Cut for jewellery, but lacks sparkling brilliance; softer than diamond or white topaz. *See* Bristol diamonds.

Rock crystal glass Introduced 1878 by Thomas Webb & Sons and associated with the West Midlands. Characterised by deep wheel engraving in flint-glass, but whereas wheels and abrasives usually left the pattern matt, here every detail was polished to limpid clarity. Thinner, cheaper glass by 1900 although the work continued to *c.*1910 as 'bright polished engraving.'

Rockingham Swinton Pottery, Yorkshire, established 1745; associated with the Brameld family from 1778 – most notably from *c.*1813 under three brothers led by the eldest, Thomas. Remembered for bone-china ornaments, table-wares, etc., much magnificently coloured and gilded, made from *c.*1825 and marked with a griffin from 1826. Closed 1842, but one brother, J. W. Brameld continued as a decorator in London to 1854. Much unmarked china attributed to Rockingham, probably wrongly.

Rockingham glaze *See* Glaze.

Rococo (Figs. 27, 28, 59, 104, 273, 285, 295) Term introduced *c.*1830. Eventually the accepted name for a style deliberately invented in the early 18th century in Paris, to defy accepted symmetrical ornament. Popular as the 'modern style' in mid 18th-century England as an escape from heavy Baroque. Expressed in asymmetrical cartouches, opposing C-scrolls, fantasies suggesting waterfalls, rocks, shells and chinoiserie (decoration at the

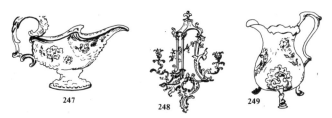

Rococo style, mid 18th century. 247 Bow sauceboat. **248** Chippendale candle bracket or girandole. **249** Silver cream jug.

expense of form). There was an attempted late Georgian and early Victorian revival.

Rodney mementoes 1. In glass, *see* Ships' glass. 2. In ceramics, included Derby's mask jug from 1782, with a mask of Admiral Lord Rodney forming the spout, commemorating his popular victories over the Spanish and French. Many copies.

Roemer. Romer (Fig. 77) From the 1670s, the English version of the German pale green glass for hock. Nearly spherical bowl on a wide stem at first studded with raised blobs or prunts, a style repeated in the Regency. *See* Rummer.

Rolled gold Base metal covered on both sides with a thin layer of

250 Roemer, *c.* 1690s. **251** Toddy lifter and, *below*, sugar crusher also used by rum drinker. **252** Rummer, *c.* 1790s.

gold – less valuable even than 9 carat gold, but preferable to electro-gilded gilt metal.

Rolled paper work *See* Filigree paper work.

Rolling-pin Pastry roller, becoming a collector's item when treated as a love-token or souvenir and made, e.g., of 'Nailsea' glass (from Sunderland, Newcastle, Alloa, etc.). In dark glass with coloured flecks; in blue, green or amber with painted ornament; in opaque white painted or transfer-printed. Around 1800, early rollers were filled with heavily taxed salt; later filled with sweets or made without an opening. Many reproductions.

Roll-top desk Office desk with quarter-circle tambour top of narrow strips of wood on a flexible backing.

Rope turning *See* Trafalgar fashion.

Rose cutting (Fig. 35) Gemstone cutting especially for diamonds evolved around 1640 as an improvement on early cabochon cutting, with a wide flat base and faceted sides rising to a point with a tiny flat facet on top, the facets triangular, usually 16 or 24. Developed from the diamond's natural eight-sided crystal shape, at first merely cut in half. Early in the 18th century the more wasteful but effective brilliant cut came into increasing use; the rose cut continued even in the 19th century for smaller diamonds, often mounted in clusters, pavé set. *See* Brilliant cut; Cabochon cut; Diamond; Refractive brilliance.

Rosenberg, Charles (1747–1844) Silhouettist (including jewellery work), in Bath from 1787. Painted in intensely black pigment usually on the inside of flat or convex glass, backed by orange or fading pink card.

Rose engine-turning *See* Engine-turning.

Rose quartz *See* Quartz.

Rosewood Heavy, dense, dark purplish-brown with pronounced nearly black figure. For furniture in solid and veneer, especially from the early 19th century and much favoured by early Victorians. May be confused with kingwood. Sometimes called jacaranda.

Rosewood marble English marble suggesting rosewood. Dark brown, richly veined, taking a high polish.

Rosso antico *See* Red stoneware.

Rout chair Hired out for routs – fashionable evening assemblies as described by Sheraton, 1803: small, painted, with rush seats. Continued in Victorian days as rout or soirée chairs, often with cane seats and back panels.

Royal Crown Derby Porcelain Co Name adopted in 1890 by Derby Crown Porcelain Co. (founded 1876) makers of fine bone-china table-wares, plaques, figures and also (to 1914) 'Derby Crown Earthenware'. *See* Crown Derby.

Royal Doulton *See* Doulton wares.

Royal Worcester *See* Worcester.

Royle's self-pouring teapot (Fig. 281) Patented 1886. Worked on hydraulic principle to avoid lifting a large family-pot; a somewhat similar notion may be found in silver. Lid was raised, then a small hole in the knob was closed with the finger so that lowering the lid caused tea to flow from the spout. Made by Doulton whose mark included the name of the patentee, J. J. Royle of Manchester.

Ruby. Oriental ruby Rare gemstone variety of corundum, crystallised alumina, the second hardest mineral, as is sapphire, its magnificent clear red colouring due to traces of chromium. May be confused with spinel and, when a paler rose red, with balas ruby.

Ruby glass Clear deep red glass for ornaments coloured with expensive gold chloride from the late 17th century. In Victorian cased glass the layer of ruby glass might be as thick as $\frac{1}{8}$ inch. *See* Cranberry glass.

Ruching Stitching along a ribbon or band drawn tight to produce frilled or box pleated edges for trimming valances, etc. In flounces or ruffles the stitched gathering is along only one edge.

Rudd table Late 18th century. Fitted dressing-table illustrated by Hepplewhite, its drawers containing two swinging mirrors at different angles for complete self-viewing.

Rule hinge For the table-flap that closed over the fixed table-top as in typical 18th-century card tables. Hinges were attached each side to the edges of top and flap, to leave both flat surfaces unspoilt.

Rule joint In a drop-leaf table or folding screen, the edges of adjoining parts shaped in corresponding profile so that folding would leave no gap.

Rumblers *See* Horse bells.

Rummer (Fig. 252) Distinct from the roemer. A goblet for long drinks such as rum-and-water grog with a large, deep bowl on a short stem and small foot, often handsomely engraved from the later 18th century. *See* Toddy glasses.

Run moulding In furniture, a moulding consisting of continuous groovings made with a moulding plane along the solid wood of, e.g., the stiles or muntins of a panelled chest.

Running sideboard. Dinner wagon Three tiers of open shelves with end supports, most often on castors. In dining-room use throughout the 19th century.

Rushlight holder Metal grip with scissor action counter-weighted to ensure a safe hold near the burning tip of a slender rush (partially peeled and dipped in kitchen grease). Through the 17th to 19th centuries, appropriately mounted for table, floor and hanging use as a weak substitute for the highly taxed tallow candle.

Rushbottom chair Cheap and popular through the 18th- to 19th centuries, the seat often painted. Also fashionable with art-conscious Edwardians.

Ruskin, John (1819–1900) Critic, author of *The Stones of Venice*, etc., greatly influencing Victorian ideas on design.

Ruskin Pottery, Smethwick Established 1898 by W. Howson Taylor (1876–1935), who won international recognition for his attempts to copy the delicate brilliance of Sung and Ming glazes. His tall vases in notably thin ware were shaped wholly on the wheel and on principle, too, his broken, splashed and flambé glazes were lead-free, in a range of fine ruby, brown, purple and light blue tones. He also produced lustres and single-colour and mottled soufflé wares. The rich colours showed to good effect even in such minor products as furniture bosses, jewellery mounts ('Ruskin stones') and cards of buttons.

Russia leather Calf skins impregnated with oils distilled from birch-bark.

Rustic furniture From the mid 18th century, made with gnarled branches for arbours, etc. In the mid 19th century also copied in iron and ceramics.

Sabicu Hard, heavy wood somewhat resembling rosewood, but easier to work; used for cabinet work.

Sabre leg. Scimitar leg. Waterloo leg (from 1815) (Fig. 128) Chair legs in forward and backward concave curves copying ancient klismos.

Sabrina art ware With elusive ornament shimmering in the depths of a parian porcelain paste. Made by Worcester, *c.* 1897–1930s.

Saddle seat Typical Windsor chair seat of solid wood such as non-splitting elm (for taper-tenon legs) and shaped with depressions to the sides of a slight ridge. Even when polished it allowed the sitter to lean back without sliding forward.

Sadler & Green, Liverpool Early transfer-printers in monochrome on ceramics, for potters such as Wedgwood. On tiles from *c.* 1756.

Sadware *See* Pewter.

Salamander Iron disc on a long handle fire-heated and held over food to brown it. Sometimes with small legs to support it in the heart of an early down-hearth fire.

Sales catalogue conventions Seller of painting, print, ceramic ware, etc., considers an attribution to be exact when the item is described as *painted by* the artist (name in full – not just a surname) or *signed*, or *dated*. Phrases such as *bears signature* or *bears date* imply only probability. *After* (artist's surname) implies probable copy. The suffixes *-pattern* and *-ware* imply that the item is probably not from the factory named, but is in the style of its wares. *A.f.* (as found) implies obvious need for scrutiny before purchase.

Salopian China Manufactory. *See* Caughley.

Salt, Ralph *See* Walton, John.

Salver *See* Trays.

Sampler From the 16th century a record of stitches, elaborated in the 17th century as a narrow band sampler sometimes 36 inches long, covering the full range of a girl's needlework skill, including marking alphabets, drawn-and-cut work, etc. In the 18th century it became a child's showpiece with borders, verses, etc., frequently worked on moth-attacked worsted tammy cloth. Some attractive darned work. Early 19th-century work often poor, in cross stitch. Many fakes.

Sampson Mordan & Co. A name found on innumerable minor silver and silver-mounted items coming from the City Road, London, workshops established in 1815 by 25-year-old Sampson Mordan, the firm continuing until 1941. His original patented 'ever-pointed' pencil, with several variants, remained an important item, but the firm's range covered dressing-cases (with the firm's own locks), vinaigrettes, card cases, vesta boxes and many novelties, such as their familiar inkpot shaped as a tortoise.

Samson porcelain Made by E. Samson & Cie, Paris, from 1845. May confuse a collector by imitations of Chelsea, Worcester, Sèvres, etc., but in hard-paste porcelain.

Sand *See* Pounce pot.

Sandalwood Aromatic, mellowing to a warm light brown. For boxes, etc.

Sand burning Wood dipped in hot sand to shade and mark its surface, as in marquetry detail. Described by John Evelyn, tree authority, in 1664.

Sand-glass *See* Hour-glass.

Sand picture. Marmortinto Began *c.*1780s as a basis for dinner-table decoration by 'table deckers' who made patterns in dyed powdered marbles and mica. Soon these were made permanent, stuck to shallow trays and supplied by china sellers. Early Victorians used sands from the Isle of Wight, etc., for 'paintings' after Morland, etc.

Sang de boeuf 'Oxblood'. *See* Glaze.

Sapphire Precious blue gemstone variety of corundum coloured with titanium. See Ruby. Can be made artificially.

Sardonyx A reddish (iron-tinged) and white banded chalcedony.

Satin glass. Victorian fancy glass in many colours given a satiny surface with hydrofluoric acid.

Satinwood Golden tone with a satin sheen, fashionable through the later 18th century and *c.*1860–85, the West Indian variety having the richer grain, the East Indian paler with dark streaks.

Satsuma ware. Japanese pottery (as distinct from porcelain). Made by Koreans who settled on the island of Kyushu from the end of the 16th century making a creamy, crackle-glazed earthenware which became more ornately decorated in coloured enamels and gold. Was so popular with English Victorians that it was imitated in Kyoto, etc. Late decoration included dragons and story-telling figure scenes in colours mellowed by great use of pencilled gold.

Saucer Small dish for sauce or pickles (stoneware, delftware, etc.); adapted during the 18th century to hold a tea or coffee cup.

Sautoir. Longchain Lightweight chain with variously decorated links and clasp, often worn to carry a watch, scent bottle or pencil tucked into the girdle. Early Victorian and Edwardian.

Save-all *See* Candlestick.

Scagliola Roman substitute for marble and mosaics, used for pedestals, table-tops, etc. Italian imports from the 17th century; made in England from late in the 18th century with a special coloured plaster, isinglass and marble chips, highly polished.

Scale pattern. Salmon scale In ceramics, a diaper of formal repetitive curves suggesting fish scales, used as a background, mainly underglaze, e.g., on Worcester porcelain from *c.*1760.

Scallop *See* Escallop shell; Shells.

Scent bottle *See* Smelling bottle.

Scimitar leg *See* Sabre leg.

Sconce Mainly from the 17th century onwards. Candle sockets or branches supported by a bracket or wall plate often of looking-glass, silver, gilded gesso, brass or other reflective surface; occasionally embroidery. *See* Girandole.

Scoto-Russian ware By the Smith firm of Mauchline from the 1840s. Souvenir boxes imitating Russian niello and silver inlay. Boxes were covered with paint over metal foil so that engraved lines showed a pattern in glinting foil preserved by varnish (gold medal in 1851). Variants included their Scoto-Damascene ware.

Scottish hinge *See* Laurencekirk wares.

Scottish silver (Figs. 150 – 153, 280) Edinburgh silver marked with a three-towered castle from 1485. Standard thistle mark from 1759 for sterling silver. Glasgow used a town mark of a bird, tree, bell and fish from 1681, adding a lion rampant standard mark from 1819; the thistle added 1914. Aberdeen, Banff, Dundee, Inverness, etc., also assayed Scottish silver.

Scrapbooks Through the 19th and early 20th centuries, young ladies' albums for mounting personal arts and crafts, increasingly supplemented with professionally prepared and advertised items (scenes, flower groups, etc.), e.g. scissor-cuts by profilists, 1820s–30s; steel engravings from the 1840s; vividly coloured lithographs, varnished and embossed increasingly from the 1870s onwards.

Scratch blue. On ceramics. *See* Sgraffito.

Scratch carving On furniture, simple lines incised into the wood surface. Mainly country-made and pre-Georgian.

Screen *See* Banner firescreen; Candle screen; Cheval glass; Polescreen.

Screen writing-table Term could imply a writing-table with a vertical sliding screen at the back. Or it might be a tall cheval firescreen a few inches thick, the upper part fitted with small drawers (or a mirror) revealed when the front was let down on metal braces to serve as a writing-board and with shallow cupboards below, as in Shearer and Sheraton designs.

Screws In furniture from the late 17th century, brass, hand-filed with slotted heads. Lathe-turned from *c*.1760; machine-made, sharply pointed, from *c*.1840.

Scrimshaw Sailors' work (love-token stay-busks, etc.) using jack-knife and sail-needle on whale bones and teeth and walrus tusks, for carving and incised work picked out with lamp black.

Scriptoire. Scrutoire *See* Secretary.

Scroll Spiral ornament of classical origin; hence, in furniture, recurring fashions for scroll arms, legs, feet.

Sealed bottles From the 17th century until *c*.1830 many a wealthy customer supplied his vintner with bottles embossed with his personal crest or cypher, having provided the bottle-maker with a brass die for such seals.

Seals (Figs. 2, 180) Used from ancient times as marks of authority and sharing in neo-classical revivals. Found in rings (some with revolving bezels) and as fob pendants. Some with impersonal patterns for Victorian watch-chains (but even then sometimes serving more interestingly as tiny hinged cases for miniatures or silhouettes). Also handsomely mounted as desk seals. Personal motifs were more finely cut when sealing wax was improved from the late 17th century. Materials include silver (hallmarked from 1791), gem stones, marble and, through the 18th to 19th centuries, glass, hardened steel, fine stonewares.

Secessionists Breakaway movement of young Viennese artists and craftsmen from 1897, modelled on the work of C. R. Ashbee and the British Arts and Crafts Movement. Led to the founding of the 'Vienna workshops', 1903, by influential J. Hoffmann and K. Moser, developing a severely angular, geometric style.

Secessionist ware (Fig. 7) Introduced in 1902 as a cheap Minton earthenware by Leon Solon: fluid Art-Nouveau shapes, moulded and slip-trailed in colourful flowing glazes.

217

Secretary. Secretaire. Scriptoire Desk fittings covered by a hinged vertical front opening downwards on metal braces to form a flat writing-board. Was made as tall cabinet furniture from *c.*1670, mounted on a stand or chest of drawers. More commonly found in the later 18th-century version as a fitted 'secretary drawer' with a drop-front, as the deep top drawer of a chest of drawers. Defined by Hepplewhite as differing from a desk 'in not being sloped in front'. Known also as a scrutoire, escritoire and other spellings – the name revived by George Smith in 1808 as scrotore. *See* Croft; Screen writing-table.

Sedan chair Introduced from Italy, 1634. Seat enclosed in coach-like framework carried on horizontal poles by two chairmen. Occupant could enter and leave inside his own home.

Seddon, George (1727–1801) Notable London cabinet-maker and upholsterer in Aldersgate street from 1750, producing great quantities of pleasantly simple furniture, some labelled. His grandson, Thomas, was a furniture-designer in the Gothic style.

Seed pearl Round pearl of less that $\frac{1}{4}$ grain weight. Used in Tudor-Stuart embroidery. Through the early 19th century they were made into elaborate jewellery parures, stitched with white horsehair or silk on to pierced and fret-cut mother-of-pearl in patterns of vine, honeysuckle, etc.

Self-pouring teapot *See* Royle.

Semi-porcelain *See* Stone china.

Senior, James At work in the 1900s, making finely pierced earthenware, using shapes and marks associated with the renowned Leeds Pottery. W. W. Slee, antique dealer, is often credited with this clever work, which he merely handled.

Sequin Small spangle or disc often in fancy outline, of light shiny metal used by embroiderers for decorating dress, gloves, fan.

Serpentine (Fig. 23) Shape much favoured in 18th-century furniture for the fronts of sideboards, etc., with a convex curve flanked by two concave curves.

Serpentine rock Hydrous magnesium silicate in green (suggesting jade) and in colour mixtures of red, green, black, brown, yellow, often veined with white. Soft and much used for ornaments, as e.g., in Cornwall's Lizard area and in West Ireland (green 'Connemara marble'.)

Settee From the late 17th century. Shape suggests a row of three chairs fused together, upholstered or bar-back; early Georgians expected two settees to match a suite of chairs. For sitting rather than reclining (compare sofa).

Settle Forerunner of settee. From Norman days shaped as a bench with panelled back, high or low, arms and sometimes also a cupboard overhead. Frequently the seat covers a chest; otherwise it may be criss-crossed with cord passing through the seat-rails to support a mattress. Less fashionable country work from the 18th century, revived among late Victorian-Edwardian 'cottage' furniture.

Sévigné Brooch or bodice ornament shaped as a ribbon bow (and often suspended by ribbons.) From the 17th century onwards and later named after Madame de Sévigné, French letter-writer (d. 1696) who popularised sets of three in graduated sizes.

Sèvres Renowned French porcelain, brilliantly white with rich colours and gilding, also bisque figures, etc. Soft-paste (pâte tendre) porcelain made at Vincennes from 1745 using a mark of two crossed Ls from 1753. Factory moved to Sèvres in 1756. Some hard-paste porcelain from 1769 and this became the main product from 1772, showing a high level of artistic and technical achievement, state subsidies ensuring that it dominated Europe as Meissen had in the 1730s–40s. But some soft-paste continued until 1800 and was reintroduced c.1847.

Sgraffiato. Sgraffito 'Scratched' or incised ceramic ornament especially on slip-covered ware. Some collectors restrict the term *sgraffiato* to ornament where the slip covering the background areas is scraped away, leaving lines of slip pattern against the red earthenware body.

Sgraffito then consists of ornament where only the lines of the pattern are cut through the slip to show the underlying red earthenware body.

In *scratch blue* the ware might be colour-dipped to show blue pattern where the slip was scraped away; or incisions might be filled with powdered colour before firing.

Shagreen Tough, waterproof skin, frequently dyed green, glued on to instrument- and jewel-cases, tea-chests, etc. The wild asses' skins used in the 17th to 18th centuries were more cheaply imitated in other animal skins artificially 'grained' with pressed-in seeds. But from the 18th century these became increasingly superseded by spiny sharkskin (dog fish, ray fish, etc.), the spine bases filed smooth, but leaving a distinctive mottled surface.

Sham Of deceptive appearance; e.g., furniture drawer-fronts introduced for symmetry where none could possibly fit, as on the left side of a davenport (which has full-depth drawers on the right side).

Sham-dram Deceptive spirit glass for a tavern keeper. Short, sturdy, often with the early style of folded foot on a 19th-century glass.

Sham watch *See* Macaroni.

Shank (Figs. 177-190) 1. In jewellery, the loop of a ring. 2. On a button, the back loop for attaching it. 3. In glass, refers to a stem, as in the straw-shank (Fig. 100) drinking-glass where the stem is drawn out from the bowl, and the stuck-shank (Fig. 94) where bowl, stem and foot are separate units fused under heat.

Shawls Costly Kashmir work welcomed by fashion from the 1780s, prompting Norwich shawl-weaving from 1784. Became essential wraps over increasingly voluminous dress, *c.*1820s–70s, in wool, silk, cotton. Associated especially with Paisley. Typically two yards square; the plaid shawl four yards by two yards; three-quarter plaid, three yards by four feet. Also made in lace at Honiton, etc., imitated in tambour-worked net and in machine-made Nottingham lace.

Shearer, Thomas (Figs. 22, 165) Furniture-designer associated

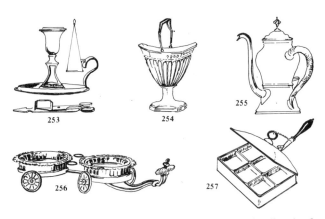

Sheffield plate. 253 Chamber candlestick with, *below,* the snuffers that fit the slot under the candle. **254** Wirework glass-lined sugar basket. **255** Argyle. Late 18th century. **254** Double wine-coaster (the small rings to hold the decanter stoppers). **257** Cheese toaster. Both early 19th century.

with engraved plates in *The Cabinet Makers' London Book of Prices*, 1788, re-issued under his name as *Designs for Household Furniture*.

Sheffield plate Invented 1742 by Thomas Bolsover of Sheffield and used for table-wares, candlesticks, etc., resembling solid silver, but much cheaper. Ingots of sterling silver and copper were first heat-fused together, then rolled into sheets to be hand-raised, die-pressed, spun, drawn into wire, even pierced, like silver. Silver was usually applied to both sides of the copper ingot from the 1760s, but some articles were merely tinned on the underside or interior. The line of copper showing on every cut edge was masked with increasing skill that aids dating. (*See* Mounts.) For cheapness the silver was much thinner than its copper core, but might be thickened on areas that had to be engraved (inscriptions,

221

etc.) This is usually detectable. In every way Sheffield plate is entirely different from electroplate where pure silver is applied last, obscuring all signs of construction processes. Marks mainly after 1836. *See* British plate.

Sheldon tapestry Rare, from the earliest tapestry works in England, established by William Sheldon at Barcheston, Warwickshire, in 1561 with a Flemish-trained manager. From 1570 the work was continued by his son through the early 17th century. Included remarkably detailed maps within magnificent borders of pillars, trellised arches, grotesque figures and masks.

Shells Motifs for furniture ornament through the 18th to 19th centuries. Actual shells were professionally carved as cameo jewellery; and mounted on caskets, arranged in grottoes, etc., as an amateur hobby, especially in the later 18th century. But examples now found are mainly Victorian or later, including: patterns in tiny iridescent shells as 'rice work'; posies under glass domes; shell-dressed dolls; and 'albums' consisting of shallow boxes with shell arrangements inside lid and box, sometimes called sailors' valentines. *See* Escallop shell; Mother-of-pearl.

Sheraton, Thomas (Figs. 166, 167) (1751–1806) Designer of light Neo-classical furniture with emphasis on vertical straight lines, dainty detail, ingenious contrivances such as a harlequin table, as described and illustrated in his four-part *Cabinet Maker's and Upholsterer's Drawing Book*, 1791–4, *Cabinet Dictionary*, 1803 and the more bizarre *Encyclopaedia*, first volume 1805. No record of his making furniture after coming to London, *c.* 1790, from Stockton-on-Tees.

Sherratt, Obadiah (1776–1840s) Burslem maker of ambitious earthenware story-telling figure groups on footed bases. Followed by his widow and son.

Sheveret. Cheveret Narrow tables with writing space backed by a set of drawers or pigeon holes. At its most distinctive this drawer unit lifted off, to leave a larger writing area, being placed on a shelf provided for it between the table-legs.

Ships' glass For officers' use at sea. 1. *Decanter* (Fig. 87) with a wide heavy base, the sides slanting sharply to the base of the neck, now known as Rodney decanter after his victories of 1780 and 1782. 2. Stumpy *drinking-glass* with an extremely wide, substantial foot.

Shoe-piece In a chair, a shaped projection housing the base of the splat. In the late 17th century this was attached to the chair's lower cross-rail; through much of the 18th century, attached to the back seat-rail. Only in reproductions is it found made in one with cross-rail or seat-rail.

Sideboard Medieval Tudor Stuart side-table or shelving to set out plate, glass, etc. Acquired its modern implication of fitted drawers and cupboards only in the 1770s when the table might be made as a single unit with flanking cupboarded pedestals, as illustrated by Shearer, 1788.

For smaller rooms from the 1790s and onwards *cellaret sideboards* were made with cupboards between their four front legs, leaving space for a central wine cistern. From the 1820s increasing height and elaboration characterised the back board, followed by Victorian carving such as that of the Warwick school. Some with ever-taller mirrors from the 1840s on.

Side chair. Single chair One without arms.

Signet ring (Fig. 180) Finger ring intaglio-cut for use as a personal seal.

Signpost barometer See Yard-arm barometer.

Silenus Frequent figure in jug ornament, etc., as a fat, bald drunkard, usually riding an ass, accompanying his youthful pupil Bacchus, god of wine, among satyrs, maenads, etc. *See* Bacchantes.

Silesian stem (Figs. 46, 94) On candlesticks, drinking-glasses of the early 18th century and some until the 1780s. Modern name for a pedestal stem tapering inwards from a pronounced shoulder, sometimes inverted; four or six sided – some eight sided from *c.*1740.

Silhouettes. Shades, Profiles Named after Etienne de Silhouette (1709–67) for the extreme austerity of his financial programme for France; hence portraits reduced to minimal profile outlines, usually in solid black, mainly head-and-shoulders, but some full-length and some extra tiny for jewellery. Knife-cut in England from late in the 17th century, but mainly popular from the 1770s onwards. Methods then included: painting on plaster of Paris, ivory or white card, often in late work touched with bronzing; painting on glass backed with coloured composition, or inside convex glass to throw the shadow on white plaster; scissor-cutting in black paper or silk mounted on card and sometimes with the outlines softened with brushwork; cutting the profile out of white paper and backing the hole with black paper or cloth. Many profilists used simple 'machines' to reduce their shadow outlines and/or make additional copies.

In a late Georgian revival showier work was produced, often full-length, the blackness mitigated by touches of metallic bronzing on hair and costume – sometimes using real gold. Many flourished in Brighton and other resorts or 'toured' with considerable publicity and there was often a showground atmosphere to their work, which might include painting or cutting tiny scenes for scrapbooks. Books of printed silhouettes were issued and a cutting from one of these may confuse the beginner. *See* under individual entries – Beetham, Buncombe, etc.

Silicon china Opaque earthenware by Booths Ltd., Tunstall, early 20th century, imitating 18th-century porcelains.

Silicon ware Vitrified brown stoneware, hard, smooth, variously carved, perforated, coloured, decorated with pâte-sur-pâte slip, etc., as a Doulton art ware from 1880.

Silver. Silver plate Precious white metal, harder than gold, but most frequently further strengthened with alloy. *See* Britannia standard; Sterling. Pure silver was used in electroplate. Term 'silver plate' implies ware constructed of silver, in contrast to Sheffield plate and plated silver (electroplate).

Silver-gilt Article made in silver and finally gilded.

Silver grain *See* Medullary rays.

Silveria glass Ancient technique developed *c.*1890s by the glass firm Stevens & Williams. A gather of clear glass, lightly tinted, was rolled over a layer of silver foil, sealed in with more hot glass. For greatest brilliance this was then blown to shape, shattering the foil into glittering fragments, as an alternative to rolling the hot glass in metallic spangles.

Silver-lustred ceramics *See* Lustrewares.

Singing-bird musical box Costly, exquisite form of musical automaton from about the 1770s. Early birds enamelled; later feathered. Cheaper from the 1860s.

Skewer Wood or metal spike for meat. Often in lignum vitae wood from the 1680s. Some in silver through the 18th to 19th centuries, becoming flat and tapering with a die-struck ornamental loop finial from *c.*1770.

Skillet Early saucepan for the down-hearth – hence with feet and a long handle. Some in silver for charcoal braziers.

Skirt guard Decorative little metal clamp fixed to the Victorian-Edwardian lady's skirt hem and linked by a chain to the waist. A pull on the chain would raise her skirt above puddles.

Slag glass *See* End-of-day glass.

Slat-back *See* Ladder-back chair.

Slate Greenish or purplish non-absorbent rock, popular on early Victorian furniture in place of heavier marble. Japanned to resemble marble inlay or papier mâché.

Slice *See* Fish server.

Slide. Slider 1. *See* Candle slide. 2. *See* Wine coaster.

Slip Potter's clay watered down to a creamy consistency, different clays showing different colours when fired.

Slip casting From the 1730s, hollow-ware and figures shaped by pouring slip into a revolving porous plaster mould. This absorbed moisture from the outermost thin layer of slip which formed a crust on the inside wall of the mould, whereupon the remaining wet slip was poured away leaving the shaped hollow article to be dried and removed from the mould for firing.

Slipware Coarse earthenware covered or ornamented with slip. Methods included: trickling or dotting from a spouted pot; applying to hollows in press-shaped wares; combing in marbled effects; incising. 17th-century work was much copied in the 19th century. *See* Barum ware; Fishley; Sgraffiato; Toft ware.

Smalt A refined deep blue glass prepared from zaffre, used in colouring ceramics, etc. (and for whitening linen). *See* King's blue; Mazarine; Powder blue; Zaffre.

Smear glaze *See* Glaze.

Smelling bottle (Fig. 104) Early name for scent bottle. Implies small decorative bottle for the chatelaine, sautoir, reticule, etc., through the 18th to 19th centuries in silver, glass, porcelain, painted enamels, etc., most usually in a flattened pear-shape, sometimes a flattened sphere. To some Victorians it was a substitute for the late Georgians' vinaigrette, to contain reviving scent based on liquid ammonia perfumed with lavender, clove, etc. *See* Double scent bottle.

Smith, George (Figs. 135, 238) London furniture-maker at work by 1804, remembered for influential books of designs including Gothic, Egyptian and Grecian ornament, published 1805–36.

Smith, W. & A. *See* Mauchline ware.

Smock. Smock-frock Strong outer garment of linen or cotton drill for shepherds, drovers and other outdoor workers. Stitched gathering – 'smocking' – ensured easy movement without clumsiness; additional embroidery might have regional or craft associations. Conspicuous in the early 19th century; popular with Arts and Crafts ladies of the 1880s onwards.

Smoker's bow chair Low-backed variant of 19th-century farmhouse and kitchen Windsor, on splayed, turned legs, but with back and arms forming a continuous horizontal hoop above the back and sides of the saddle seat, supported by turned spindles. Padded version known as Eaton Hall chair.

Snakewood Hard, difficult to work, red with darker veins and spots. Sometimes used for veneers around 1800.

Snuffboxes (Fig. 104) Small, flattish for the pocket, larger to stand on the table, usually hinged, but generally too well made to require a fastener. In all convenient materials from the late 17th century onwards. *See* Enamels; Lancashire snuff box; Laurencekirk and Mauchline wares.

Snuffers *See* Candle-snuffers.

Snuff handkerchief Usually cotton, some silk, some printed from the 1750s; *see* Printed fabrics. Many that remain date from *c.*1820–70. Spotted bandana introduced by James Bayley, 1790s.

Snuff mull For rasping and storing snuff powder from a plug of tobacco. Ram's horn cut inside with ridges and fitted with a hinged cap of silver, horn or bone. Pocket and table sizes. From the late 16th century, but many are 19th century or modern.

Snuff rasp Largely outmoded in the 18th century by commercially ground snuff. Iron or steel grater with a frame and hinged or pivoting cover in silver, boxwood, etc. and with a spouted cavity below to pour the powder into a snuffbox.

Soapbox Of silver, brass, turned wood, etc., its body and hinged lid forming a nearly spherical shape on a wide foot, frequently with perforations in the lid or base. Held a scented soapball, or wig powder.

Soapstone Steatite, a natural mixture of china clay and magnesium silicate, slightly soapy to the touch, soft and much carved by the Chinese, Eskimos and others.

Soapstone porcelain Soft-paste porcelain for useful wares containing 35–45% steatite – denser, heavier than other soft-porcelains, seldom crazing and less vulnerable to boiling water. Made at Bristol, Worcester, Caughley, Liverpool.

Sociable (Fig. 58) Victorian upholstered seat on S-plan for two people to sit half facing each other.

Social table *See* Horseshoe tables.

Soda-lime glass In world-wide use for windows, bottles, etc. (silica and carbonate of lime fluxed with sodium carbonate). Was the quick-cooling glass of early Venetian fame, its fragility prompting English development of flint-glass.

Sofa Symmetrical, like a settee, but tending to be longer, wider, for reclining, made mainly from the 1760s onwards, including heavy overstuffed Victorian versions only gradually showing more of their wooden framework. *See* Couch; Méridienne.

Sofa table (Fig. 238) Elongated version of the Pembroke, with small flaps to the end of the main table top and trestle supports with out-jutting castor-mounted feet. Often with frieze drawers and a section of the top reversible for games which two could play seated side by side. Popular from the late 1790s to the 1820s.

Soft-ground etching Somewhat resembling a crayon etching. Paper was applied over the acid-resist wax on the etcher's copper plate. Pencil pressure on this paper removed the acid-resist in soft-edged lines, ready for the normal etching processes.

Soft-paste porcelain. Frit porcelain White, translucent, but fragile and costly, imitations of Chinese hard-paste porcelain. It lacked correct ingredients, introducing instead a glassy frit. The paste was kiln-fired before and after covering with a lead glaze at lower temperatures than those of hard-paste, so that the paste can be scratched with a file. Made from the 1740s until eclipsed by bone china. *See* Bow; Caughley; Chelsea; Derby; Liverpool; Longton Hall; Lowestoft; Madeley; Nantgarw; Pinxton; Worcester.

Softwoods All timber from coniferous trees. *See* Deal; Spruce.

Soho, Birmingham *See* Boulton, Matthew.

Soho tapestry Absorbed Mortlake weavers from *c.*1685, and continued to use Mortlake mark. Under John Vanderbank (1689–1727) this establishment became world famous at a prolific period for tapestry (including chinoiseries). Followed by Paul Saunders to 1758 (romantic landscapes, etc.). Elusive Joshua Morris (notably fine flowers, birds, grotesques) at work in London in the 1720s, also used the Mortlake mark. *See* Tapestry.

Sovereign boxes, purses Range of small containers, especially Victorian–Edwardian, to attract today's collector, from chain-link purses to spring-loaded boxes.

Spade foot *See* Thermed foot.

Spandrel (Figs. 64, 67) Triangular space between the curves of a circle or arch and the right angle of its surrounding frame, as, e.g., the decorated corners of a longcase clock dial outside the chapter ring (late 17th-century brass cherubs followed by scrolling; painted ornament on later 18th-century white dials, such as the four continents.)

Spangle *See* Sequin.

Spanish foot *See* Gadrooning.

Sparvers Bed hangings. *See* Tent bed.

Spatter glass Small ornaments, etc., mottled with bright specks of red, green, brown, yellow enamel glass, against an opaque glass lining.

Spavin leg (Fig. 127) Graeco-Roman line popular in Regency furniture, its outline adapted from the back leg of a lion, frequently modified into a meaningless jerky curve.

Speculum Shiny silver-coloured copper-tin alloy long used for 'steel' mirrors (in patch boxes, etc.)

Spelter Crude zinc, much softer than bronze, but found in cast figurines, etc., plated to resemble antique bronze or silver.

Sphinx Mythological monster variously adapted by Assyrians, Greeks and Romans from an Egyptian creature with wigged human head and recumbent lion's body (as in some Regency furniture). Neo-classical ornament frequently included Graeco-Roman version with a woman's head and bust on the recumbent body of a winged lion.

Spider-leg table (Fig. 275) Delicate gate-leg table often with eight legs, all slender turnings, left square for all joints – two at each end of the fixed framing and two for each gate. Fashionable in the third quarter of the 18th century.

Spiers & Son, Oxford Notable Victorian decorators of papier mâché blanks (trays, tables, etc.) especially with Oxford views.

Spigot Barrel vent-peg; hence the tap near the base of an urn or water filter.

Spill jar (Fig. 231) Lidless wide-mouthed ornamental vessel for pipe-lighters.

Spindle In furniture, a turned rod, straight or with a slight central swelling, as in the turner-made spindle-back chair. Split lengthwise for glued-on ornament, especially on 17th-century chest furniture.

Spinel. Balas ruby Gemstone, its clear red variety confusingly similar to the more valuable Oriental ruby. Balas ruby is a paler rose colour.

Spinet Musical instrument, wing-shaped like a small harpsichord – a 17th century development from the virginal, with a small keyboard and plucked strings.

Spinning wheel Horizontal spindle turned by a treadle-worked wheel, twisting the thread as the spinner drew it from a prepared mass of flax, wool or cotton. Improved from the 17th century with the addition of a faster-turning bobbin to wind the thread at a controlled tension.

Spit. Spit-jack Iron bar with sliding fork prongs or a basket for roasting meat over a fire. Mechanical *spit-jack* replaced the dog to keep it turning – weight-driven from the late 16th century, or using hot air from the fire to turn a rotor in the chimney (18th-century *smoke jack*). Weighted rotating *dangle-spit* to hang in front of the fire was improved when turned by clockwork, acquiring cylindrical casing as a *bottle-jack*. Useful in a Dutch oven.

Spitalfields silk London silk weaving from the 1580s, associated with Flemish and French refugees; their guild was founded 1629 and the business continued until the early 19th century.

Splat (Figs. 306–309) Central vertical member of a chair-back, in baluster, etc. outline, widely used through the 18th century.

Splayed leg Chair or table leg curving outwards.

Spode, Josiah (Fig. 282) (1735–97) Had his own Stoke-upon-

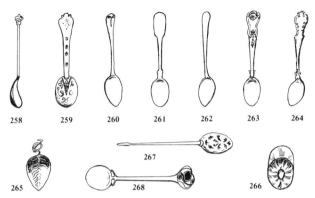

Spoons, chronological series. 258 15th-century writhen knop. **259** Trifid, back view. **260** Hanoverian. **261** Fiddle. **262** Old English. **263** King's pattern. **264** Victoria pattern. **265, 266** Caddy spoons (leaf and jockey cap) flanking **267** Mote skimmer and **268** Liberty Art Nouveau spoon (silver and enamel).

Trent earthenware factory from 1770 and was followed by his son and grandson (d. 1829), same name. Continued by W. T. Copeland and his successors. *See* Copeland china. Spode was important for his development of transfer-printing underglaze; bone china from 1794; feldspar porcelain from *c.* 1800. *See* Stone china.

Spoons Collected in silver, pewter, brass, wood, horn, etc. Early fig-shaped bowls on straight, *knopped stems*, followed by mid 17th-century plain ends (*puritan* and *slipped-in-the-stalk*). By the late 17th century oval bowls had flat-faced stems in a slight S-curve from a forward-curving stem-end in *trifid* or dognose shape. The bowl had a characteristic rat-tail tapering from the stem-bowl junction to a point on the back of the bowl.

By the 1720s–30s, in the *Hanoverian pattern*, an egg-shaped bowl was backed instead by a rounded drop and on the front of the spoon a narrow tapering ridge extended from the up-curved stem-end.

A major change, *c.* 1750, gave the spoon-end its first hint of a backward curve – presumably because cleaner home conditions meant that the table could be laid with spoon bowls upward (accounting also for subsequent concentration of ornament on the front of the spoon.) Forks retained the earlier shaping.

One 1750s spoon finial was the *Onslow scroll* (compare Rococo 'paper scrolls' on chair crest-rails).

More plainly, from *c.* 1760, the simple backward-curving spoon stem became the most enduring favourite as the *Old English shape*, giving the stem a slightly arching outline.

Minor stem ornament included thread, feather and bead edgings and, from *c.* 1780, bright-cutting, q.v. Hall-marks, previously low on the stem and usually distorted in finishing the spoon, were moved nearer the stem-end.

The square-shouldered *fiddle shape* of *c.* 1800 has persisted but soon might be elaborated – in the *shell pattern*, for example that developed into the *king's* and *queen's* patterns and from 1840 the scroll-edged *Albert*, and many variants.

Spornberg, Jacob Swedish silhouettist working in Bath in the 18th century. Likenesses painted on glass, often outlined in Etruscan red pigment against a black background.

Spout lamp *See* Lamps.

Sprigged ornament In ceramics, relief ornament shaped separately in small moulds and applied to the ware before firing, for clear undercut effects, as on jasper ware, impossible by ordinary mould-shaping.

Sprimont, Nicholas (1716–71) Came to England from Liège, 1742, working first as a silversmith, then as Chelsea porcelain factory's influential manager from the late 1740s (where the ware might reflect silver shapes).

Springs Of spiral coiled wire for mattresses, chair seats, first patented, 1828, by Samuel Pratt and soon in wide use by upholsterers.

Spruce. Fir Soft white wood for joinery. Term in early documents probably meant chests, etc.; shipped from Prussia.

Spun glass. Lampwork Popular cheap ornaments, long made with bunsen lamp and coloured glass rods by street-corner showmen. Victorians welcomed more elaborate models, such as scenes of ship and lighthouse or birds around a fountain, now all sold as friggers.

Spun metals For speedy shaping of thin hollow-wares in silver, Sheffield plate, base metals, long despised by silver craftsmen. A steel or hardwood tool held a disc of flat metal against a wooden block or chuck revolving in a lathe until it acquired the shape required. Mainly 19th century.

Squab seat Chair seat with a low rim to hold a cushion (squab) from the 17th century. *See* Yorkshire chair.

Square (Fig. 92) Square-sided glass decanter made from the 1720s in a range of sizes for medicines, spirits (pint and quart) and wines (half gallon), mainly in sets of three or four for a silver or mahogany gardevin or a Victorian tantalus.

Staffordshire blue White earthenware or bone china painted or transfer-printed in blue underglaze. Associated with North Staffordshire as the centre of the British pottery industry. *See* Blue and white.

Staffordshire figures Generally the term implies cheap little earthenware figures including people, dogs, lambs, often with a nostalgic flavour, hawked through the streets in the early 19th century. Forerunners of flatback ornaments. *See* Sherratt; Walton.

Stained glass 1. Solution of metal oxide deposited on the surface of a glass vessel, fixed by firing; yellow (oxide of silver) especially popular. 2. Mosaic of coloured glass for windows, furniture insets, firescreens, popular with late Victorians and Edwardians.

Stamped metal (Figs. 29, 285) Important from the late 18th century onwards for shaping, embossing and piercing wares of thinly, evenly rolled metal (made possible by the improvement in hardening steel for tools.) Articles in, e.g., Britannia metal could be machine-stamped with hammer and die in sections and assembled, some being weighted with tin-lead fillings.

Standish Early name for inkstand – a tray or box for writing equipment elaborated to include bell, sealing taper stick with its extinguisher, wafer box (used by Victorians for postage stamps). *See* Pounce pot; Quill cleaner; Wafers.

Statuary porcelain Early Copeland name for parian ware.

Staunton chess set Most familiar conventionalised shapes designed by the Hon. Howard Staunton, son of the Earl of Carlisle, registered 1849. London-made by J. Jacques & Sons in natural and dyed boxwood.

Steamer chair Victorian folding chair for reclining, made extra stable by extending the seat frame at the back as additional legs. Often with quick-drying curved slats in the back and a caned seat.

Steatite *See* Soapstone.

Steel Hardened, toughened form of iron alloyed with carbon. Could be sawn, filed or chiselled to almost lace-like delicacy, associated with the locksmith's and gunsmith's costly crafts. In England chiselled and cut steel work was associated with Woodstock, Oxfordshire, long before it became an important cottage industry there, from about the 1740s (scissors, buckles, watch chains, sword hilts, jewellery, intricate and brightly polished) until overshadowed by the Soho, Birmingham, factory of Matthew Boulton. *See* Blued steel; Cut-steel.

Steel engraving From *c.*1820 onwards. A cold, closely detailed print taken (often in great numbers) from a plate of an improved hard steel instead of copper, then in short supply. By the 1840s an engraver often took a few prints from an engraved copper plate before it was steel-surfaced for a cheaper, longer run of prints.

Step cut. Emerald cut. Trap cut (Fig. 39) In jewellery, a jewel cut which displays a stone's richest colour rather than glitter. Oblong

234

or square cut with the facets cut as a series of sloping steps.

Stereoscope. Victorian entertainment especially of the 1850s–60s, dependent on the development of stereoscopic photography. Two slightly different views of the same scene, mounted on a card, were inserted into an adjustable stand fitted with eye-pieces so that the viewer's eyes combine them as a single picture vividly three-dimensional. The cards included views, sentimental scenes, portraits, etc., experiencing renewed popularity in the 1890s, on glossier paper.

Sterling (Fig. 140, 141) Pure silver alloyed with copper in the proportion 92.5% to 7.5%. Recognized from *c.*1300 and hallmarked with a lion passant gardant (walking with head turned) from 1544. London assay office from 1821 and eventually some provincial assay offices (Birmingham in 1875) changed the mark to a lion passant (looking straight ahead). *See* Britannia standard silver.

Steuben Glass Works Founded in 1903 by T. G. Hawkes and England born and trained Frederick Carder. Sold to Corning Glass Works in 1918. Made fine art glass until the 1930s, including iridescent pieces similar to Tiffany's Favrile glass.

Stevengraph *See* Picture ribbons.

Stick barometer *See* Barometers.

Stiles In furniture, the vertical rails to the sides of panels; when between panels they are known as muntins.

Stipple engraving Print often in red-and-brown or red-and-blue tints, popular from the 1760s for somewhat effeminate portraits after Gainsborough, etc. Dots or flecks instead of lines, acid-etched but usually touched up with a graving tool. Associated especially with F. Bartolozzi, in London from 1764.

Stirrup cup For the mounted horseman, so a footless drinking-vessel frequently shaped as the head of a fox, hound or fish or as a clenched fist. From about the 1760s in silver, followed by Derby porcelain, bone china, stoneware, earthenware, including fakes.

Stiven, Charles *See* Lauencekirk ware.

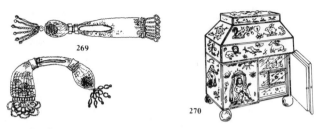

269 Stocking purses, open and closed. **270** Stumpwork casket.

Stocking purse. Miser purse Flexible (knitted, crocheted, buttonhole stitched, etc.) and shaped like a stocking leg with a central lengthways slit and two metal rings to slide up and down it. With the rings at the centre, coins could be inserted, falling to the ends and then secured when the rings were slid apart, beyond the extremities of the slit. Carried with the ends hanging down; ornament such as gilt metal and cut-steel bead tassels weighted them and distinguished the contents (sovereigns one end, silver coin the other.)

Stomacher Stiffened bib of a woman's bodice around 1700. Hence massive jewellery often tapering from a wide bow down to a pendant, worn above the waist through Georgian and early Victorian days, some separating into smaller units.

Stone china. New Stone Made by William Turner, *c.*1800 and by Josiah Spode from *c.*1805. Strong, compact feldspathic earthenware, heavy, with a blue-grey tint; paler, smoother from 1810 (marked New Stone, 1810–15; later New Japan Stone and Copeland Stone China). Other earthenware potters used such names as semi-porcelain, semi-china, opaque porcelain. *See* Ironstone china.

Stonewares Clay mixed with sand or flint, fired at greater heat than earthenware, making them strong, impervious to liquids. Made in the 17th century by Dwight and in Staffordshire.

Customary salt-glaze (*see* Glaze) left a slightly uneven 'orange skin' surface, but *brown stoneware* was used for bellarmines, jugs, tobacco-jars, etc. and was popular as a late 19th-century art ware (*see* Doulton; Martin brothers).

Refined *white stoneware*, slightly translucent, attempted imitation of Chinese porcelain. Too inelastic for the potter's wheel, but sharply moulded for teapots, etc. and decorated like porcelains by the 1750s. *See* Nottingham stoneware.

Stool Term covering a wide range of backless, armless seats and footrests, from the hearth-side cricket to the upholstered tabouret. *See* Backstool.

Storr, Paul (1771–1839). Notable silversmith associated with ornate, richly elegant work in Regency style.

Stourbridge glass West Midlands region including Dudley, Wordsley, etc., noted for glassmaking from the 17th century and continuing importantly to the present day. Associated with notable cameo glass, cased glass, rock crystal and other engraving and cutting styles, Victorian fancy glass, early pressed glass.

Straining spoon *See* Mote skimmer.

Strap hinge With a long leaf, plain or decorated, stretching across a cupboard door, etc. In 16th- to 17th-century iron and popular again (often in copper) with Voysey and other late 19th-century designers.

Strapwork 1. Scrolls, interlacing arabesques, cartouches, etc., taken from engravers' two-dimensional patterns and translated into low relief furniture-carving, silver-chasing, embroidery borders, often suggesting curls of cut parchment. Occasionally found in 16th- to early 17th-century furniture; more often Victorian. 2. In silver, applied ornament around tankards, etc., especially of the early 18th century.

Stras. Strass *See* Paste.

Strawberry dish Any small saucer-bowl, as in late 17th-century repoussé silver, that would present attractively the period's 'wild size' strawberries or other dessert.

Strawberry Hill Show villa at Twickenham furnished by Horace Walpole, 1747–53, that has given its name to a sophisticated mid Georgian style of mock-Medieval Gothic furnishings, not approved by serious Victorian Gothic revivalists.

Straw-shank. Stuck-shank. *See* Shank.

Straw work Tiny squares of split straw, some dyed or painted, glued to a hard surface (or to paper pasted on wood, etc.) so that their 'grain' contributes to the scintillating effect of geometrical patterns, scenes, etc. Of early ecclesiastical use and noted on furniture and in contemporary accounts from the 17th century; later a popular amateur hobby (on tea caddies, etc.) and a successful craft for Napoleonic prisoners-of-war.

Stretchers (Figs. 271, 317) In furniture, horizontal rails linking the legs of a chair or table. Were placed low as foot rests for Elizabethans, becoming ornate in walnut, but ill-suited to the cabriole leg and unnecessary to high quality work in sturdy mahogany. Popular in the late 19th century as numerous, extremely thin spindles.

Strike-light To kindle fire before friction matches. Neat form of mechanical tinder box resembling a flint-lock pistol. A 'spunk' (slip of wood sulphur-dipped) could be lit from smouldering tinder in the pistol pan when this was ignited by steel particles struck by the flint in 'firing' the pistol.

String box Only distinguishable when including a hole in the lid for the end from a ball of twine. From the 1820s and popular in later Victorian colour-printed tinware in imitative shapes.

Stringing 1. In furniture, very narrow square-section strips of wood for inlay or veneer patterns, sometimes chequered dark and light to suggest the 1800s' popular rope twist, sometimes in Regency brass. 2. In Victorian fancy glass, close twisting of glass threads, popular as ornament wound around handles, stems, etc., improved by Benjamin Richardson in the 1860s.

Stucco Plaster, at best composed of gypsum and pulverised marble, for walls, ceilings, etc.

Stuffed-over Furniture framework almost completely covered by upholstery, but not necessarily the thick padding implied by the modern term overstuffed.

Stump bed Common wooden framework on four short turned legs. If it had a head-board it was known as a stump-end bedstead.

Stumpwork (Fig. 270) Victorian name for the 17th century's raised embroidery, especially popular 1650s–80s as amateur ornament, mainly worked by children, for caskets, mirror frames, pictures. Figure scenes, especially from the Old Testament, with heraldic animals and other motifs from published patterns were worked in many different stitches and incorporating purls, spangles, seed pearls, all applied to white satin. Often some motifs were padded and details of dress partly detached.

Sucket glass (Figs. 93–95) For 'dry' sweetmeats such as candied fruits taken with the fingers or a small fork, included among fashionable dessert glasses, being a wide shallow bowl often with an elaborate fancy rim (impossible on a drinking-glass) on a tall stem.

Suffolk chair *See* Mendlesham chair.

Sugar crushers (Fig. 251) 1. Nippers for cutting sugar lumps from the sugar loaf. 2. Small glass pestles for use with rummer drinking-glasses.

Sugar tongs In silver, bow-shaped like a smoker's steel ember tongs from *c*.1690, but delicate to suit the small sugar lumps required in tiny teacups. Scissor-shape established by the 1730s, with a spring device to aid in gripping the sugar from the 1750s. A simpler, sturdier bow-shape from *c*.1760 with a springy U-shaped arch soldered to decorative arms, until the whole article was made out of a single strip of silver from *c*.1790. Some in the Regency with fiddle-shaped ends to match spoons.

Sulphides *See* Crystal cameos.

Summerly's Art Manufactures Attempt in 1846–50 to improve commercial products, launched by Henry Cole (1808–82) (later Sir Henry, first director of South Kensington Museum), as Felix

Summerly's Home Treasury Office. Artists' designs commissioned for inexpensive factory-wares, from papier mâché to painted table glass, sometimes recognisable by the mark FS.

Sunderland, Co. Durham Made *earthenware* through the second half of the 18th century including creamware, but is associated especially with cheap sailor gifts, etc., mainly early to mid 19th century, often decorated with black transfer-printing or colourful lustres. These included animals and other simple chimney ornaments; wall texts in colours and purplish pink-gold spattered lustre; frog mugs with views of Wearmouth bridge (opened 1796 and re-opened 1859) or portraits of the local Camperdown (1797) hero Jack Crawford. Many bore verses or personal inscriptions.

Also made *glass* remembered for, e.g., many goblets engraved with views of Wearmouth bridge and pressed glass such as the popular 'Gladstone for the million' plate with a stippled ground of raised dots registered in 1869 by the firm of Henry Greener.

Sung dynasty, China (AD 960–1279) Important to the west for celadon wares among a range of new ceramics (some true porcelain) that inspired 19th to 20th century studio potters. Also sensitive landscape painting.

Sunset-glow glass. Milk glass Evolved in the 1770s as a cheap substitute for enamel glass in blown-moulded vases, jugs, etc. Milky-white, opacified with arsenic or bone ash, giving it a fiery opalescence against the light.

Surface prints The inking of the printing plate (stone or metal) dependent on the chemical antipathy of oil and water instead of the physical surface-cutting required for both intaglio and relief prints. *See* Lithography.

Surfeit water drinking-glass Tall, very narrow flute on a wide foot, distinctively different from other Georgian cordial glasses. Probably intended for a potent brandy distillation described, 1738, as a 'costly physic for the ills of gluttony'. Sometimes now called a ratafia glass.

Sussex chair *See* Morris chairs.

Sutherland table (Fig. 295) Small space-saving gate-leg table with a very narrow top on trestle supports and wide, deep flaps. Named after Harriet, Duchess of Sutherland, d. 1868.

Swadlincote (Fig. 34) Derbyshire earthenware art pottery established by William Ault from Bretby in 1887, continuing through Edwardian days and since. Made 'Ault faience' with colour glazes in majolica style including splashed and broken colour effects. Conservatory vases and stands, ornaments, etc., including some designs commissioned from Christopher Dresser.

Swag (Figs. 86, 206) Popular ornament on Neo-classical furniture, silver, etc. Festoon of drapery, flowers or husks in a dipping curve between two end supports.

Swage Steel tool for shaping and patterning metal such as the moulded foot ring of a tankard or mug.

Swan-neck pediment Broken pediment consisting of two opposing S-scrolls usually flanking a central ornament.

Swansea porcelain *See* Nantgarw.

Swansea potteries Earthenwares, bone china, basaltes, etc., made at the Cambrian Pottery, 1760s–1870. Cow-shaped milk jugs associated with Glamorgan Pottery Works, 1815–39.

Swash turning. Twist turning (Fig. 115) For furniture. Later known descriptively as barley-sugar twist. Oblique cutting on turner's lathe, used on much late 17th-century furniture and popular with early Victorians, whose liking for symmetry required chair legs, etc., to show opposing twists. Introduced from Holland, but English work less tightly twisted.

Swinton *See* Rockingham.

Sycamore In Britain, species of maple or false-plane. Close-grained, white when young, yellowing with age, often with fine rippled grain. Used for turnery and veneers and stained as harewood. Also in Laurencekirk and Mauchline woodware.

Syllabub (Fig. 97) Stemmed glass for Georgians' frothy dessert of sweetened wine topped with whipped cream; hence a wide-mouthed bowl curving inwards in a double-ogee line on a decorative stem or knop above a small foot that allowed for close arrangement of such glasses on a pyramid.

S.Y.P. teapot (Fig. 286) 'Simple Yet Perfect'. Wedgwood novelty, 1913, reputedly designed by the Earl of Dundonald. Pot contained a perforated compartment for tea-leaves which were infused by hot water when the pot stood on its side. When the pot was righted for pouring this automatically strained the tea from the leaves, thus regulating the strength of the infusion.

Table 1. *See* Under separate headings: architect's, console, cricket, drum, games, gate-leg, harlequin, horseshoe, imperial, kidney, loo, Pembroke, piecrust, pier, pillar-and-claw, pouch, refectory, rent, Rudds, screen, social, work, writing. 2. In jewellery, the top flat facet of a cut gemstone; hence a table-cut stone, its rectangular top having bevelled edges.

Tablet In furniture, a small rectangular panel for an inscription.

Tabouret Round-topped upholstered stool; many Victorian. Introduced by Charles II from France where etiquette permitted privileged ladies to be thus seated in the king's presence.

Talbert, Bruce (Fig. 137) (1838–81) Dundee wood-carver turned architect and furniture-designer, in London from 1865, supporting the arts-and-crafts movement. His *Gothic Forms Applied to Furniture* published 1867 and *Examples of Ancient and Modern Furniture* 1876.

Talbotype *See* Calotype.

Talc *See* Mica.

Tallboy Double chest of drawers evolved in the 1700s from the chest of drawers on stand, the upper chest slightly narrower, often with canted corners.

Tables 271 Draw, *c.* 1600s. **272** Gate-leg, late 17th century. **273** Console (gilded), *c.* 1750. **274** Gate, early Georgian. **275** Spider-leg, *c.* 1760s. **276** Pembroke, *c.* 1790s. **277** Games-and-card, with two folding flaps and movable back leg, mid 18th century. **278** Card, *c.* 1830 (closed).

242

271

272

273

274

275

276

277

278

Tambour. Reed-top In late 18th-century furniture, a space-saving flexible desk lid or small cupboard door. Composed of a row of narrow convex mouldings glued across stiff fabric, their ends sliding in grooved runners that curve into the body of the piece. Thomas Shearer added 6d for a tambour lid to his costing of a desk (£3. 7s), but few have lasted.

Tambour embroidery. Tambour frame Frame with two circular hoops fitting inside each other to stretch fabric between them for embroidery. Often mounted on a stand, popular for late 18th-century tambour embroidery worked with a small hook in a looped chain-stitch on muslin, etc.

Tambour 'lace' Worked with a tambour hook over net. This work was stimulated by the 1830s boom in cheap bobbin net, made by machine, as a basis for lace effects in both tambour work and needle-run darning stitches. *See* Limerick 'lace'.

T'ang dynasty, China (AD 618–906) Commercially prosperous period showing much Buddhist influence. Sculpture included fiercely realistic animals, more important than minor commercial tomb figurines. Ceramics showed complicated patterns in lead glazes and in the 9th century some of the first high-fired porcelain. Also notable lacquer, metal work, etc.

Tankard Medieval vessel of staved wood becoming important from the Tudor period onwards in silver, pewter, etc., differentiated from a handled mug by its hinged lid raised by a massive thumbpiece. *See* Flagon.

Tantalus Mid 19th-century name taken from mythical king of Phrygia tantalised by the sight of inaccessible fruit and water. An open frame for a row of squares, locked in by a grooved bar passing over their stoppers.

Taper. Taperstick 1. Thin form of candle in appropriately graceful stick, made for the pipe-smoker, letter-writer's sealing wax, etc. Or a flexible wax taper made for the bougie box and wax-jack. 2. Shape gradually diminishing towards one extremity; hence the slender taper decanter (no shoulder shaping), 1760s–1800s.

Tapestry Framed-up warp (lengthwise) threads of flax or hemp hand-woven with weft (crosswise) threads of dyed wool, making elaborate patterned and pictorial wall hangings and upholstery. Subjects included pictorial scenes – Biblical, historical, battles, etc. and Medieval romance and chivalry – against closely patterned backgrounds of flowers and greenery (millefleurs and verdures). The ancient craft was practised in England under continental influence in Warwickshire (*see* Sheldon) from *c.*1560 and in and near London, including Mortlake and Soho, in the 1670s at Lambeth and for a few years around 1750 at Fulham. Out of fashion by the 1780s, but used for much 18th-century furniture upholstery. *See* William Morris. (Incorrect, but popular name for cross-stitch canvas embroidery.)

Tappit hen (Fig. 214) Scottish measure vessel like a lidded flagon with a long incurving waist. Term formerly indicated three-pint size (one Scottish pint) with chopin and mutchkin for medium and small sizes.

Tartan wares Widely popular ornament (textiles, furniture, ceramics, etc.) when Queen Victoria acquired Balmoral, 1852. *See* Mauchline ware.

Tassie glass James Tassie (1735–99) and nephew John, to 1840, made wax portraits and from these, using plaster moulds, cast medallions in soft white glass suggesting the layered work of cameos. These sold cheaply for seals, rings, etc., but lacked the undercut detail of jasper ware.

Tatting French *de la frivolité*. Thread work with a three-inch shuttle and often a hairpin-type hook, to make dress trimmings, etc., composed of small loops and picots often combined with crochet or lace stitches. The shuttle often of piqué tortoiseshell or ivory. Popular from the late 18th century and especially from the 1850s onwards. High-backed 'tatting or sewing chairs' advertised in the 1870s.

Tazza Wide shallow bowl on a footed stem. Plural tazze.

Tea-board *See* Trays.

Tea caddy. Canister 1. Closely lidded box for dry tea-leaves in use from *c.* 1680 in silver and other decorative materials in formal, Rococo, chinoiserie, naturalistic (pear, etc.) shapes. Matching pair for green and bohea tea might be accompanied by a glass bowl for the tea-blender to mix the leaves in front of guests before ladling them into the teapot, adding boiling water from the accompanying tea kettle. While tea was very expensive caddies were strongly locked — another key for milady's chatelaine. 2. From the late 18th century the name was applied also to the tea chest.

Tea-caddy ladle Small decorated scoop, mostly from the 1770s onwards, for spooning dry tea-leaves into the teapot. Found in many collectable shapes, some with enamelled crests (mainly 20th century).

Tea chest In the early 18th century, a foil-lined wooden box (tea trunk) often covered with waterproof shagreen or morocco leather. From *c.* 1730, chest-shaped, velvet-lined, partitioned to hold two caddies and a mixing or sugar vessel. Handsome, following contemporary furniture styles.

Tea jar Porcelain (Worcester, etc.) en suite with tea ware sometimes used in place of a silver caddy for dry tea-leaves. Simple oviform vessel with a small neck and domed lid.

Teapot From the late 17th century. Collectors note increasing size and range of treatment through the 18th and 19th centuries as tea became less costly. For unusual designs *see* Barge ware; Cadogan; Double-spouted; Royle's self-pouring; S.Y.P.

Teapoy Term that changed its meaning. 1. To Georgians it was a

Teapots. 279 New Hall china 'silver shape', often imitated. **280** Scottish silver bullet, *c.* 1730s. **281** Doulton's Royle. **282** Spode's Cadogan. **283** Barge ware. **284** Liberty pewter. **285** Britannia metal (revived Rococo style). **286** Wedgwood S.Y.P. in position for brewing the leaves and (smaller detail) for pouring the tea. **287** C. Dresser design from his *Principles of Decorative Design*, 1873.

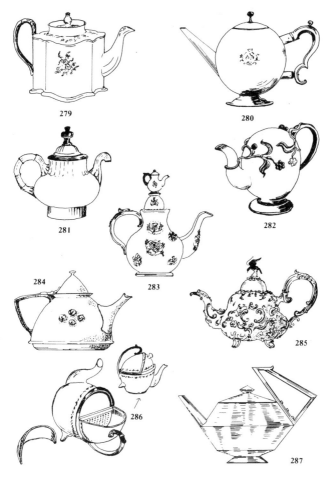

279

280

281

282

283

284

285

286

287

247

small light table usually pillar-and-claw, for the tea-drinker's cup and saucer. 2. This proved useful for the hostess's tea chest, etc. and the Regency–Victorian teapoy or tea-stand might consist of a tea chest permanently attached to such a stand in wood, papier mâché, Tunbridge ware, etc.

Tear In glass, air introduced into hot glass by the glassman who could draw the spherical bubble into an elongated drop while shaping, e.g., an early baluster wine-glass stem.

Tea or coffee urn Neo-classical urn or vase shape with a tap near the base for pouring without lifting. Silver, Sheffield plate, from *c*. 1760s; copper seldom before *c*. 1820. At first it might keep hot over a charcoal brazier, possible alternatives being a box iron from the 1770s or a spirit lamp, mainly from the 1830s onwards. In ceramics, included richly ornamented heat-resistant vitreous stoneware from *c*. 1850.

Tea and coffee 'machines' in Sheffield plate and silver were made mainly 1790s–1800s. In these, a large urn heated by a box iron or spirit lamp held the hot water (six pints or more) and swivelled so that its tap could supply either of two smaller urns (for tea and coffee), all arranged on a galleried stand with a drip bowl. Less ornate designs were made during the Regency.

Teak Brown oily wood, very hard, tool-blunting, heavy and durable for joinery, and ship and garden furniture.

Telescopic candlestick Sliding candlestick, popular for 50 years from the 1790s, but may pass unrecognised today. Stumpy straight-bodied pillar stick containing from one to five extensions above a weighted square, circular or – from *c*. 1810 – lobed base. Made in pairs and sets, some silver and brass, but mainly Sheffield plate. From the mid 19th century some were spring-loaded, to push up the candle as it burned.

Tenon *See* Mortise-and-tenon joint.

Tent bed. Sparver bed Simple version of the field bed with four posts and a domed or arched canopy covered with a tester cloth. Especially popular in the late 18th and early 19th centuries.

248

Tent stitch. Petit point Wear-resistant ground-covering embroidery consisting of rows of close diagonal stitches, one over every crossing of the fabric's warp and weft. Worked with a backward slant, thus greatly strengthening the customary linen fabric for furniture panels, firescreens, etc. Name implied working on a stretching frame (from terms associated with the cloth-maker – tenter hooks, etc.) From the mid 16th century onwards.

Term *See* Therm.

Terracotta 'Baked earth' – soft, unglazed, slightly porous earthenware, its colour largely dependent on choice of clay, usually reddish (sprayed with ferric chloride solution before firing for a richer red) or yellow-brown. Ancient material used by sculptors to sketch future work by modelling the wet clay. As earthenware it was popular in Victorian conservatories etc., its slightly glossy surface often painted with warrior figures in the 'Etruscan' manner. Many 19th-century makers, including T. Battam (1840s–60s) who decorated huge vases in black, or in red on a black ground, for M. H. Blanchard; W. & T. Wills (suggesting carved lacquer); F. & R. Pratt; Watcombe Co., Torquay; Coalbrookdale Co. More than 100 large buff terracotta scenic panels, for York Minster, etc., some 4 feet high, were made by notable George Tinworth (1843–1913) who worked at Doultons from 1866.

Terret *See* Horse bells.

Tesselated. Tessera *See* Mosaic work.

Tester Wooden canopy of a standing bedstead supported by a headboard and two posts at the bed-foot or by four posts. Term used from the 16th century; sometimes confused with the early fabric celure (or selour) hanging at the bed-head until this was replaced by panelling.

Therm. Term Strictly the head and armless bust of a figure rising from an inverted obelisk shape as support for a lamp, etc., or at a bed-head. More generally means a pedestal, square on plan; hence, *thermed leg* in furniture, square on plan as distinct from a round, turned leg, and *thermed foot* or *spade foot*, a square-section, tapering foot.

Thimble Ancient Roman, in bronze or stitched leather. Elegant from *c.*16th century in gold or silver; in the 18th century some jewelled with hardstone caps and in painted enamels; in the 19th century, bone china, stamped silver (very long, with views or other decoration), as well as ivory, mother-of-pearl, etc. For hard work many from *c.*1600 were short and thick, in brass or steel; cast brass through the 18th century, or stamped from the 1790s; also timeless bone, wood.

Thistle silver mark *See* Scottish silver.

Thistle spirit measure In use from the early 19th century, but discontinued from 1907.

Thonet, Michael *See* Bentwood furniture.

Threading 1. In silver, engraved lines as an ornamental border, e.g. in the thread-and-shell pattern popular on fiddle-stem spoons. 2. In glass, *see* Stringing.

Three-piece drinking-glass (Fig. 103) With bowl, stem and foot made separately and invisibly joined under heat.

Throwing In ceramics, shaping on a potter's wheel (clay slammed onto it to clear it of air bubbles). *See* Turnery.

Thumb mould Rounded projecting edge to a table top. Also a repetitive pattern of small gouge cuts on the edge of a chest, etc.

Thumb-piece. Lever. Purchase (Fig. 214) Projection from the hinge on the lid of a tankard or flagon pressed with the thumb to hold the lid open while drinking. Many ornamental.

Thuya wood Warm golden brown, from a North African tree, its curled and spotted burrwood used as veneer. Different from thuja of the cedar family.

Tiara Ornamental headdress.

Tiffany, Louis Comfort (1848–1933) New York jeweller's son who founded his decor business 1879, leading to art-glass work. Had his own glass works from 1893, his commercial art-glass studios producing many thousands of items, no two identical,

1896–1920. Familiar for flowing Art-Nouveau plant motifs, such as flower-shaped glass lamp-shades. Made notable iridescent glass (*see* Favrile); some cameo glass; enamels and other metalwork and some furniture. Letter marks dating some wares included the valued X mark (not for sale). Few signed by Tiffany, some by Arthur Nash from Stratford-on-Avon who was in U.S. from 1892.

Tiger ware Early stoneware with mottled glaze.

Tiles Widely collected in earthenware variously decorated for fireplaces, walls, etc. Notable in delftware from 17th-century Bristol, London and Liverpool. Main production followed Herbert Minton's rediscovery of encaustic floor tiles. Victorian and Edwardian wall tiles were moulded in plastic clay or compressed from dry clay between metal dies. Ornament included: hand-painting, freehand or over transfer-printed outlines; raised outlines (tube lining) around colour glazes; colour-shadow effects in deeply hollowed relief work flooded with colour; photographic prints, etc. Subjects ranged from Wedgwood Kate Greenaway figures and Doulton nursery-rhyme characters for hospital tiling to William de Morgan's grotesques and ambitious scenic panels by Gordon Forsyth of Pilkington's, etc. *See* Encaustic ornament.

Till From the 16th century a small furniture drawer associated with storing money.

Timepiece (Fig. 68) Clock with no striking mechanism, as, e.g., a coaching-inn clock.

Tin Silvery white metal taking a high polish. Domestic work especially from the 16th to mid 19th centuries. Tin workers were subject to Pewterers' Guild authority, but by 1800 were more numerous in London than pewterers, making lamps, ewers, table-wares, etc., often marked ENGLISH BLOCK TIN. Being corrosion-resistant, the metal was widely applied to iron. *See* Japanning; Pontypool and Usk ware. Also used in such alloys as bronze and pewter and to opacify glass and ceramic glazes. *See* Champlevé enamel; Delftware; Enamel glass; Enamels.

Tinder box Essential for fire-lighting before Victorian friction matches. Of brass or tinned iron, large or pocket size, to hold the flint and steel (for making a spark), the tinder (usually freshly scorched linen or cotton fabric or 'touchwood', fanned into a flame to light accompanying sulphur matches) and a damper to extinguish the tinder after use. *See* Strike-light.

Tin-enamelled ware. Tin-glazed ware *See* Delftware.

Tinsel Cheap glittering base-metal substitutes for early gold and silver tissues. Collectors are mainly interested in *tinsel pictures*, generally of the 1820s–60s, developed from the hobby of pasting fabric snippets on fashion plates (revived this century). Prints of stage celebrities in theatrical poses against painted backgrounds had their costumes replaced from behind with shaded fabrics and, most conspicuously, accoutrements, ornaments, etc., added using punched-metal foil scraps sold, paper-backed, for the purpose. Reproductions are common.

Tinworth, George *See* Terracotta.

Tipstaff Staff carried as an official badge, the office identified by details on its metal cap or tip.

Toasting glass Mainly late 17th to 18th centuries, for drinking a lady's health. Stem $\frac{1}{8}$ to $\frac{1}{4}$ inch in diameter, so that it could be snapped rather than have the glass demeaned by subsequent lesser toasts.

Toastmaster's glass Georgian, with a deceptively small bowl, so that a caller of toasts could remain sober. *See* Sham-dram.

Toastrack In silver, etc., from *c*. 1770 onwards, as a series of wire or ribbon arches on a flat platform; Victorians might make it part of a holder for eggcups, spoons and salt cellar. Some shaped in the letters TOAST.

Tobacco box Brass, copper, pewter, lead, including fancy shapes such as a man's head, its purpose often identified by inclusion of a moisture-retaining inner lid or press. Jars in 19th-century brown stoneware often with sprigged ornament, from Denby pottery and elsewhere. *See below.*

Toby jug Name from Toby Fillpot, nickname of Henry Elwes, recorded on a print published on his death, 1761 and later. Applied as sprigged-on ornament on stoneware tobacco-jars, etc., and as a figure jug for strong ale. At first a corpulent, dour old man with lank hair under his spout hat. May have been modelled by John Voyez for the potter Ralph Wood. Several variants, such as Martha Gunn. Treatments included mingled colour glazes, enamel colours, 'Pratt ware', Rockingham glaze, brown salt-glaze ware, followed by many reproductions.

Toddy glasses 1. Sturdy type of rummer, *q.v.*, for drinking hot toddy (usually rum or whisky, hot water, lemon, nutmeg, sugar) from the 1770s onwards. 2. A larger goblet ($1\frac{1}{2}$ pints or more) for preparing this drink with an ovoid bowl followed by bucket and barrel shapes – often splendidly engraved – on a thick short stem and a thick foot, often square. *See* Toddy lifter.

Toddy lifter (Fig. 251) For serving toddy from the large mixing goblet. Pipette in a long-necked bottle shape with a hole each end. Immersed in the toddy then lifted with a thumb over the top hole so as to retain the contents until released into the drinking glass. About 1790s–1840s.

Toft ware Slipware such as huge wall plates very crudely decorated with heraldic lions, mermaids, royalty, etc., often within criss-cross borders; some bearing the name of Thomas Toft (father and son, d. 1689 and 1703), Ralph Simpson or William Talor, etc.

Toile de Jouy Linen cloth printed near Paris. *See* Printed fabrics.

Token Piece of metal used in payment instead of money, the issuer undertaking to give money or goods to match its nominal value as its stamped marking indicated. Issued from the 1780s and again around 1810 during shortages of official coinage. Many with interesting illustrations of factories or people at work; others political, etc.

Tôle peinte Term favoured by some collectors for an often highly skilled French equivalent of japanned tin-plate (often japanned pewter, with a tendency to craze). *See* Japanning; Pontypool and Usk wares.

Tompion, Thomas (1639–1713) Extremely important English maker of watches and spring-driven and weight-driven clocks, related to George Graham. His clocks were numbered, from 1 to 542, starting in the 1680s. Early clocks show his name in full in script; later in printed lettering with the first name as *Tho*.

Tongue-and-groove joint For joining side edges of planks, with a ridge along one plank fitting a hollow in the next. Used, e.g., for smooth carcase work under veneer. Also used sometimes for the flap-junction in a gate-leg table, until ousted by the rule joint.

Topaz Crystal gemstone, warmer yellow than citrine and harder (and much more valuable), taking a higher, lustrous polish. Occasionally green or sky blue; sometimes heated to a pink tone. Found in the Cairngorms and Mourne mountains.

Torond, Francis (1743–1812) French Huguenot miniaturist turned silhouettist, in London from 1784 working in Indian ink on card to create tiny conversation pieces, which have been copied.

Tortoiseshell Horny plates mainly from the outer shell of the hawksbill sea turtle, translucent yellow, attractively mottled, light-weight, taking a lustrous polish and immune from odour and tarnish – ideal for snuffboxes, fan sticks, combs, etc. Under heat the shell could be embossed in relief or welded into large sheets for veneers, over foil, on furniture, etc. *See* Boule; Piqué.

Tortoiseshell ware In earthenware, cloudy effects imitating the then-popular shell, developed by Thomas Whieldon, *c*.1750, by tinting the biscuit with metallic oxide colours and applying a liquid glaze. Firing produced mingled mottled effects in a colour-range of green, yellow, slate blue, dark brown, grey. Often known as Whieldon ware, but widely made by others in Staffordshire, Liverpool, Leeds, etc. into the early 19th century.

Touch Stamped trademark on pewter indicating maker and/or quality (but not an assayer's mark). More frequent on Continental pewter and of little help to the collector.

Touchstone Blackish quartz, jasper, basalts, etc. Gold or silver articles rubbed upon it made streaks that to the expert indicated their quality.

Tourmaline Translucent crystal gemstone in a wide range of colour including red, pink, black and deep green and changing colour when viewed against the light from different angles.

Toys A term long implying small charming playthings for adults, e.g., the painted enamel snuffboxes, tiny porcelain smelling bottles and similar elegancies made by specialist 18th-century toymen.

Trade cards Advertisements widely issued by retailers, listing their goods and services. Many splendid 18th-century examples remain, their Rococo scrolls framing tiny illustrations of contemporary furniture, glass, silver, etc.

Trade mark On ceramics, etc., the words being introduced into manufacturers' marks only from 1862 onwards (after the passing of the Trade Mark Act) – often much later.

Trafalgar fashion Reflected rejoicing over the 1805 naval victory. Included, e.g.: in *ceramics*, Nelson mugs, jugs and other portrait souvenirs; in gilded *silver*, a series of two-handled vases designed by Flaxman for Lloyds Patriotic Fund, to be given to 66 senior officers present at the battle; in *furniture*, the notable London makers, Morgan & Sanders, changed the name of their establishment to Trafalgar House and in 1806 launched their Trafalgar dining-table (this opened on a 'lazy tongs' frame for insertion of extra leaves and, when closed, fitted into the sideboard opening). Many typical sabre-legged Regency chairs were given cable-twist side-rails or crestings (Fig 290); Sheraton suggested greater elaboration with anchors and other nautical symbols. Collectors are reminded of possible confusion with centenary commemorative souvenirs issued 1905.

Trailed ornament 1. In glass, heated ribbons of clear or coloured glass applied in loops and blobs over the surface of ornaments and around the rims of sweetmeat glasses, etc. Thicker than threading. 2. In ceramics. *See* Slipware.

firm's Cymric silver, and including striking designs by Archibald Knox.

Tula ware *See* Niello.

Tulip shape Usual term for vessels in curving waisted baluster outline such as some 18th-century tankards.

Tulipwood French *bois de rose* and thus often confused with related rosewood. Hard, heavy, light pinkish-brown with yellow-grey and brown streaks. Found in late 18th- and early 19th-century veneers and bandings.

Tumbler 1. Glass drinking-vessel, originally self-righting with a heavy rounded base. 2. Later a short handleless cylinder, straight-sided, with a heavy flat base.

Tunbridge ware Important souvenir wood-wares from the late 17th century, associated with Tonbridge and Tunbridge Wells. Developed as elaborate forms of marquetry on boxes, even small tables, teapoys, etc. by the 19th century, using native woods in their natural contrasting colours.

Parquetry patterns of diamond shapes in different woods, arranged so that they appeared to be three-dimensional cubes, were popular by the 1800s.

These were followed by Victorian *'mosaics'* such as local

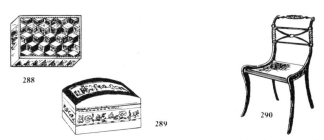

Tunbridge-ware boxes. **288** Cube marquetry. **289** Mosaic view and flower border. **290** Trafalgar chair with cable moulding.

scenes in flower borders, suggesting Berlin wool work. Collectors do not always realise how the pattern for the mosaic had to be assembled line by line from strips of coloured woods, glued and sliced and finally glued again into the block representing the full pattern or view. This could then be sawn into a number of identical thin slices each showing the full pattern expressed in small squares of end-grain wood, to be glued on boxes, etc.

Turkey work Tufted woollen upholstery for chairs, etc., commercially manufactured mainly from the late 16th to the early 18th centuries, the pile hand-knotted in formal flower patterns; later carpet-woven.

Turkish style. Moorish style Mid 19th-century furnishing fashion, especially for men's smoking-rooms, penetrating into other late Victorian rooms in such details as elaborate little pearl-inlaid and beaded coffee tables and cosy corners. *See* Divan.

Turnbuckle For fastening a cupboard door, a short strip of wood or metal turning on a single central screw.

Turnery Furniture or treen assembled (with dowelled joints) from members (cleft, for strength, rather than sawn) shaped by tools while being turned in a lathe. This might be a throw-lathe motivated by a wheel-boy, or a pole-lathe or bow-lathe kept in motion by a foot treadle. Ancient craft noted in, e.g. gate-leg tables; also fine 18th-century work, such as the tops and pillars of claw tables, made at a period when turnery was also a rich people's hobby, in ivory, amber, etc. By the late 18th century, better steel tools may have been one reason for the return to fashion of turned furniture legs. Much poor Victorian work, with merely slight surface incisions. *See* Bobbin turning; Swash turning; Wassail bowl.

Turquoise Precious stone, sky blue to blue-green, usually almost opaque. Age may turn it a dirty translucent green. Treasured from time immemorial, and much favoured in 19th-century jewellery, especially pavé set and in uncut pebble shapes harnessed with gold or silver for Art-Nouveau effects.

260

Tuscan order *See* Orders of architecture.

Tutenag Term now applied either to zinc or to a white-metal alloy composed of zinc and copper. Sometimes confused with paktong.

Twist *See* Air twist glass; Swash turning; Turnery.

Tyg 1. Staffordshire name for a porringer. 2. Now a collector's name for a slipware mug with two or more handles for communal drinking.

Ultramarine 1. Costly blue colour prepared from lapis lazuli, sparingly used on porcelain. 2. *Artificial ultramarine* developed *c.* 1800 and widely used, e.g. on Staffordshire earthenware figures of the 1830s–70s.

Underglaze colours *See* High temperature colours.

Upholder. Upholsterer Basically concerned with soft furnishings, but in the 18th century became involved in the whole business of house furnishing so that important firms such as the various Chippendale partnerships usually specified that they were both cabinet-makers and upholsterers. Most old fabrics on antique furniture today date from the 19th century when their range was spectacularly wide.

Uranium Rare metallic element, its oxide used for colouring Victorian glass and ceramics in greenish-yellow tones and later for orange and vermilion ceramic glazes, being prohibited for a time as a health hazard. *See* Queen's Burmese glass.

Urn (Fig. 164) Classical vase shape with a wide mouth, a shouldered body tapering to a spreading foot and frequently two arching handles. During Neo-classical fashions this was a widely popular shape for, e.g. silver and Sheffield plate hot-water vessels for making tea or coffee (with a tap at the back); wooden knife boxes; sets of porcelain mantelpiece vases (garnitures); candlesticks and their sockets; also as a motif in furniture marquetry. *See* Krater.

Usk japanning *See* Pontypool and Usk.

Uxbridge chair Regency name for a large mahogany cane-backed easy chair.

Valances 1. Narrow bands of drapery hiding curtain tops around a bedstead tester (linked at the corners by cantons) or across a window. 2. In wooden furniture, an alternative name for apron.

Valentine Ancient traditions associated with February 14 (St Valentine's day) developed into sending of anonymous greetings, the first commercially prepared verses and pictures – on flimsy folded quarto sheets of paper – dating to the 1760s. Lavish early Victorian paper lace, tinsel, dried flowers, etc., often elaborated into transformation scenes and other surprises built up in layers on tiny concealed paper springs and presented in special boxes. Penny post in 1840 permitted greater anonymity, prompting a spate of cheaper printed work including some cruel and vulgar. Designs resembling postal orders (for £LOVE) and bank notes were prohibited from 1872.

Varnish Clear liquid drying to a hard protective surface. Earliest had linseed or other oil base. From the late 17th century included spirit varnishes (shellac and spirits of wine) heat-hardened before intensive polishing. *See* French polish; Japanning; Vernis Martin.

Vase Tall vessel with a swelling body tapering to a narrow foot, circular on plan, the basic shape of a potter's wheel-thrown ornaments and much lathe-turned woodwork.

Vaseline glass Named for its greenish-yellow tone resembling the ointment introduced in 1872. *See* Uranium.

Vauxhall glass London glasshouse founded 1615 to make drinking-glasses, windows and mirror plate. Revived 1665, continuing to 1780, its early mirror plate very thin with wide bevels.

Veilleuse (Fig. 109) Food-warmer for bedside or invalid use, in delftware, creamware, stoneware, bone china, etc. (including hard-paste porcelain reproductions). A small lidded pot for soup or caudle resting on a cylindrical pedestal which housed a small lamp heater. Frequently, as an additional unit, a bowl of water was fitted between pot and lamp to keep the contents from sticking as it heated. Variants included a lid with a taper socket and a pot with handle and spout. Georgian and Victorian.

Vellum *See* Parchment.

Velvet Silk fabric with a close upstanding pile. Italian imports from the 14th century and widely used for furnishings from the later 17th century.

Velveteen Resembling velvet, but made of cotton.

Veneer Ancient craft rediscovered in the 17th century. Carcase furniture strongly made in plain deal, etc., could thus be covered in attractive contrived patterns of grain including knotty burr woods unsuited to structural stresses. Involved highly skilled shaping and glueing of veneers often less than $\frac{1}{8}$ inch thick. The notion of veneers as shoddy stems from poor Victorian work.

Venetian frame Horizontal mirror in three sections, the central one arched. Long popular over the mantelshelf, its name taken from the 18th century's 'Venetian window' in this shape.

Venetian glass Brilliantly successful handling of fragile soda glass in intricate shapes and patterns, the craft being concentrated on the island of Murano from 1291. Renowned from the late 15th century for its comparative clarity when very thinly blown, likened to rock crystal. Products included white-opaque, coloured and gilded glass and much clever manipulative work such as the familiar pincered winged glass stems; a decline in quality began in the late 17th century when English flint-glass proved superior for table-ware. Its 19th-century revival was the inspiration for much Victorian fancy glass, following exhibitions of the 1850s–60s, including lace glass, millefiori paperweights, stringing.

Venetian lace Brought to England from 1500 onwards, in gold and silver, black silk and white thread.

Associated specially with guipure and rose (raised) needlepoint or *gros point de Venise* in sculptured effects, supreme in the 17th century.

Venison dish Large oval dish with channels to drain the juices.

Verdigris 1. The green deposit found on corroding surfaces of copper and copper alloys such as brass. 2. Colour for dyeing, etc., made with acetic acid applied to copper.

Verdure *See* Tapestry.

Vermicular pattern Closely spaced meandering lines often used as a background on porcelain, japanned tin-plate, etc., sometimes called the Stormont pattern.

Vernis Martin Generic term for fine quality transparent varnish such as that patented (but adapted rather than invented) by four French coach-painter brothers led by Robert Martin (1706–65).

Verre églomisé Glass such as mirror borders and furniture and snuffbox panels decorated on the underside with patterns or scenes engraved through gold or silver leaf and backed with red, blue, green or black pigment. An alternative method was to paint on the underside of the glass and back this with metal foil. An ancient form of ornament, in fashion around 1700 and again in the Regency, for overmantel mirrors. *See* Glass prints.

Verzelini, G. (1522–1606) From Venice, at work in London, 1570s–92, introducing the manufacture of thin soda glass table-wares now known as Anglo-Venetian glass.

Vesica pattern (Fig. 175) Associated especially with cut decoration on Irish table glass – a Gothic pattern of pointed ovals formed by a series of intersecting circles.

Vesta boxes *See* Match boxes.

Vickers metal Form of hard leadless pewter developed by John Vickers of Sheffield from the 1770s. Silvery-white when new, with a finer texture than his Britannia metal. Until 1817 he used a small mark, *I Vickers*. From 1837 his successors added the address *Britannia Place, Sheffield*.

Victorian period (Figs. 21, 58, 89, 103, 114, 136, 137, 184–190, 195–197, 201, 217, 228–233, 287, 289) (1837–1901). Usually

Victorian furniture. 291 Buttoned armchair. **292** Papier mâché work-table (typical small capacity). **293** Prie-dieu chair. **294** 'Piano desk' development of davenport, 1860s. **295** Sutherland table. **296** C. Eastlake design for writing-cabinet from his *Hints on Household Taste*. **297** Japanese influence in E. W. Goodwin design, *c.* 1867. **298** Liberty chair designed by Richard Reimerschmid, *c.* 1900.

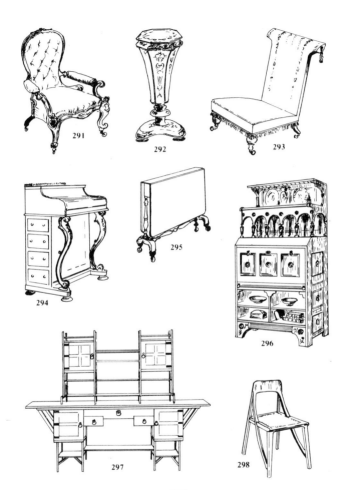

291

292

293

294

295

296

297

298

defined as: Early Victorian, 1837–55; Mid or High Victorian, 1850s–1880; Late Victorian, 1880–1901. But there were no sharp divisions. Many early Victorian characteristics were established by 1830. Escapist romanticism prompted great copying of earlier styles often disastrously 'improved' – Gothic, Rococo, 'Louis XV', 'Renaissance' and 'Elizabethan' (in fact more suggestive of massive Jacobean furnishings). High Victorians admired the bold angular lines of Louis XVI design, loading their furniture with marquetry, ormolu and china plaques, defying cheap imitation. William Morris was a major influence in leading a reaction in favour of rugged craftsmanship and there was widespread effort to improve public taste. Period also saw rediscovery of Japan and the remarkably widespread Arts and Crafts movement; also, among late Victorians, a brief welcome for the original notions of Art Nouveau, some commercialised as 'quaint'. Despite ubiquitous shallow mechanical carving and other price-cutting practices much fine craftsmanship continued, including increasingly exact copying of 18th-century work, to baffle today's beginner collectors.

Vignette Originally Gothic architectural vine ornament, adapted for manuscript decoration, becoming a term for any small view, portrait or decorative motif that shades off towards the edges without definite borders. Associated with the renowned wood-engraver Thomas Bewick (1753–1828) and frequently filling hated blank spaces at the beginnings and ends of book chapters; also fashionable on mid 19th-century writing-paper.

Vile, William With his partner John Cobb, pre-eminent cabinet-makers and upholsterers to George III, much of their work now identified. After Vile's death, 1767, the business was continued by Cobb until his own death in 1778.

Vinaigrette Developed from pomander and pouncet box. Tiny closely-lidded container for a scrap of sponge soaked in the period's improved aromatic vinegar, fashionable *c*. 1770s–1880s. Typically a silver box, its ornamental hinged lid opening to reveal

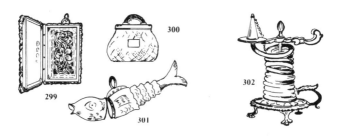

Vinaigrettes, silver. 299 Open to show inner grill. **300** Purse design.
301 Flexible fish. **302** Wax jack.

an inner gilded grill, highly decorative in early work when the
whole box might be less than an inch long. Also found in gold,
jewelled, etc., and in many imitative shapes, from walnut to
flexible fish. *See* Double scent bottle.

Vincennes porcelain *See* Sèvres.

Violet wood *See* Kingwood.

Virginal English musical instrument from about the 15th century
in a rectangular case with a keyboard and plucked strings.

Virginia walnut wood *See* Black walnut wood.

Vitrine Glazed display cabinet. Victorian name for a furnishing
introduced around the mid 18th century.

Vitro-porcelain The name given by the firm of J. G. Sowerby to
opaque glass resembling china, but shaped and decorated like
other Victorian pressed glass. Comment of the period noted white
and turquoise blue, but differentiated it from the firm's closely
veined malachite glass and other coloured glass such as their
patent queen's ware glass. products included children's nursery-
rhyme scenes as well as innumerable ornaments.

Vitruvian scroll. Wave pattern Series of S-scrolls found on heavy
early Georgian furnishings. Vitruvius was a Roman architect of
the Augustan age.

Voider In the 16th to 17th centuries a receptacle for clearing the dining-table after a meal, replaced by 18th-century trays.

Voyez, John Ceramic modeller associated with characterful, but ugly, figures, coarse-lipped and with wrinkled eyes. Worked for Wedgwood, Ralph Wood, H. Palmer, in the 1760s–90s. *See* Toby jugs.

Voysey, C. F. A. (Fig. 199) (1857–1941) Important designer of simple, popular Art-Nouveau furniture, mostly in plain oak in tall slender outlines with handsome metal handles and hinges.

Vulcanite. Ebonite Short-lived mid Victorian imitation of jet, made by heating india-rubber with sulphur, its black tone eventually turning brown.

Wafer Small disc of gelatine, etc., for sealing letters; hence small wafer boxes on inkstands. Name comes from the very thin wafers prepared for church use, and more widely for quick open-fire home cooking (using eggs and flour) between the discs of wafer tongs.

Wafer tongs Long-handled wrought iron tongs ending in flat discs covered on the inner sides with incised patterns. Medieval to early 19th century.

Wainscot From Medieval days, meant oak quarter-cut and adze-trimmed, making boards 8–10 inches wide, much imported from Northern Europe and Low Countries for furniture and panelling. Smaller billets of split oak were known as clapboard. By the 18th century imported wainscot billets could be of deal.

Waiter *See* Trays.

Wall, Dr A partner in the Worcester porcelain company from its founding in 1751 to his death, 1776, although collectors when referring to Worcester's brilliant early 'Dr Wall' period also include the years 1776–83, under works manager William Davis.

Walnut wood Golden brown with fine markings, English and European but unobtainable from France from 1720. Used for high quality furniture from the 16th century and immensely popular after 1660 in solid and veneers including burr wood. Only gradually ousted by Georgian mahogany and widely used by Victorians. *See* Black walnut wood.

Walton, John At work *c.*1806–35 as a maker of cheap brittle earthenware figures, Biblical groups, farm animals, remembered because his work was often marked with WALTON impressed on a raised scroll on the figure's tall rustic base. Figures frequently supported by branches of brightly coloured oak leaves. Ralph Salt (1782–1846) made figures in similar style.

Wardian case Domed close-fitting glass case which became popular with mid Victorians for growing moisture-loving plants, named after Nathaniel Ward; hence mid Victorian fashion for fern patterns.

Wardrobe Meaning changed from closet to large clothes cupboard (clothes press until the late 18th century). With a mirror on the door from about the 1860s.

Warming-pan Long-handled pan with a perforated lid holding heated charcoal to be passed between the bed-sheets, taking off chill. Typically brass until the 18th century when lighter in weight and might be of copper. 'Beefeater hat' lid changed in the late 18th century to a curved lid fitting inside the rim of a still lighter, shallower ember pan. In its final phase, the sealed pan had a screw-in handle, for filling with hot water and could be left in bed.

Warwick frame From the early 18th century, a cruet stand for five vessels (three castors and oil-and-vinegar bottles) with a lobed platform and guard ring, lifted by a loop handle on a central column. Became more elaborate late in the century, often with a circular platform and four feet.

Warwick school of carving Recorded in carved sideboards and other furniture showing the early Victorian love of intricate detail expressed in story-telling historical and hunting scenes. Style originated among a small group of carvers in Warwickshire, *c.*1840s, (most notably William Cookes) developing also in Bath and on Tyneside.

Warwick vase Classical vase in marble, some 5 feet tall, from

Tivoli excavation taken to Warwick Castle in 1774. Bronze replicas were manufactured by Edward Thomason, *c.*1820. Smaller copies were widely made, e.g., in silver by Paul Storr (1812) and in Sheffield plate by I. & I. Waterhouse, as wine coolers, etc.

Wash-hand-stand *See* Basin stand.

Wassail bowl Turned wooden bowl customary for Christmas festivities, the huge stemmed and footed vessel standing on a tray surrounded by smaller matching wooden tumblers. When lignum vitae wood became commercially available, it could have a capacity as great as 5 gallons – probably from early in the 18th century – following traditional patterns (and still being made this century). Some silver-mounted and occasionally lidded.

Wasters Found on sites of old potteries – pieces discarded for faults during manufacture.

Watch disc Circular paper (sometimes silk or satin) to fit inside the outer case at the back of a gentleman's watch. Might be printed with an advertisement, but occasionally was embroidered with a monogram or other personal motif in hair or silk, or included a tiny silhouette portrait framed by a conventional printed design, associated with the 1840s.

Watch fob (Fig. 3) Small pocket in the waistband of men's breeches for watch, money, etc.; hence moiré silk fob ribbons or fob chain attached to watch, often, for security, threaded through a buttonhole to dangle outside the pocket. The ribbon or chain essentially linked the watch with its key, but became showy with the fashion for shorter waistcoats from *c.*1770, when often two watches were carried, the fob ribbons being hung with watch, keys, seals and other trinkets, a fashion continued in the 19th century. *See* Albert.

Watch stand Decorative stand for bedside or desk for a watch to do duty as a clock. From the late 18th century onwards in wood, papier mâché, ceramics, often in an imitative shape such as a grandfather clock or supported by flat-back figures.

Watcombe *See* Terracotta.

Waterford glass, Ireland Under G. & W. Penrose and successors, 1783–1851. Their manager, John Hill, brought skilled employees from Stourbridge, making table-wares in fine flint-glass more brilliant than that of Cork or Dublin, but indistinguishable from English work except for a tendency to massive design. As in English glass their use of fine Derbyshire lead oxide gave a variable trace of blue tint avoidable from *c.* 1810. The firm also made coloured glass and some glass made at Waterford was cut elsewhere. Occasional marks. *See* Irish glass.

Water gilding *See* Gilding.

Waterloo leg *See* Sabre leg.

Watermarks Visible in texture of paper held up to the light — makers' symbols, letters, numbers, useful dates, introduced during manufacture.

Wax jack (Fig. 302) To hold a flexible wax taper, providing a safe tiny light for the smoker, soon going out if unattended. Consisted of an open frame with a central vertical or horizontal spool and above it a spring clip with horizontal arms to hold the taper end; often also with a cone extinguisher on a chain. In 18th-century silver, Sheffield plate, brass. *See* Bougie box.

Wax portraits Ancient craft using beeswax for memorial work and becoming an important art form in 15th to 16th-century Italy. In England fashionable for portraits, *c.* 1750s–1840s, plaster casts from original models providing duplicates as required, mounted on glass, velvet or silk under convex glass. The wax might be whitened and tinted and late work might include such details as seed pearls. Many were unsigned, but notable artists included: Samuel Percy, 1750?–1820 of Dublin, working in high relief, including figure groups; Huguenot Isaac Gosset, 1711–99; James Tassie using pinkish wax on blue glass; American Patricia Wright, 1725–86, in London from 1772; Peter Rouw; R. C. Lucas, 1801–83. *See* Tassie glass.

Wedgewood (sic) *See* Wedgwood marks.

Wedgwood, Josiah (1730–95) Celebrated English potter. Remembered for his early green-glaze ware, queen's ware, pearl ware, jasper, basaltes and other fine-stonewares and marbled glazes. His successors also made bone china, 1812–22 and again from 1878; English majolica, etc. Used the mark *Wedgewood & Bentley* or *W & B* from *c*.1769 to 1780, but the usual mark was WEDGWOOD or *Wedgwood*, with impressed date letters from 1860 (and *England* from 1891). Compare other Wedgwood marks below. Notable contributors to Wedgwood wares included artist Emile Lessore, 1859–75, and modellers William Hackwood, 1769–1832, John Voyez, 1768–9, and, on a freelance basis, John Flaxman, R.A., 1775–1800, George Stubbs, A.R.A., 1780–90, James Tassie, 1769–91. *See* Etruria; Whieldon.

Wedgwood marks Other potteries using confusingly similar marks to those of Josiah Wedgwood & Sons included: 1. *Wedgwood & Co.* (Fig. 73), of Tunstall from 1860 (distinguishable by the inclusion of *& Co.*, but may have used a *Wedgwood* mark while the firm was styled Podmore, Walker & Wedgwood from *c*.1850. 2. *Ralph Wedgwood & Co.*, at Burslem 1780s–96 and at Knottingley, Yorks, *c*.1796–1801. 3. *J* (for John) *Wedge Wood*, Burslem and Tunstall, 1841–60. 4. *W. S. & Co's Wedgewood*, a mark used to avoid legal trouble by William Smith & Co., Stockton-on-Tees, *c*.1825–55, with *Vedgwood* as an alternative.

Wednesbury painted enamels. Source of many enamel toys now ascribed to Bilston. Important centre for this minor craft, under Samuel Yardley, from the 1770s into the 19th century. Quickly made press-embossed enamel-dipped snuffboxes, etc., attractively ornamented with hand colouring or transfer-prints. *See* Enamels.

Weights and measures marks Measures for drinks, shellfish, etc., may offer a clue to their dating by the style of marks that denote official testing. Thus in pottery such as mocha ware the potter's own capacity mark might be confirmed by a metal plug under a vessel's lip or a zinc band around the handle. The Imperial system of measures was introduced in 1824 and tested vessels were stamped with a local badge or emblem and year letters or figures. In 1878 the Board of Trade established a standard mark of a royal crown over the monarch's cypher, with a number to indicate the county or borough – 522 for London, etc. Eventually acid or sand blasting was used to apply a stencilled mark including the vessel's capacity.

Wellings, William Silhouettist working in London in the 1790s, remembered for conversation pieces (full length figures) painted with delicate detail on card in tones of black, grey and brown.

Wellington chair Curious name for a chair inlaid with lines of ebony or other black wood, a Regency fashion later associated with mourning for the Duke of Wellington, d. 1852.

Wellington chest Probably contemporary name (compare Trafalgar fashion) for a small chest of drawers, *c.* 2 feet wide, secured by a single lock. To one side of the chest's framework a hinged extension could close to cover the drawer edges, being fastened top and bottom by a locking device.

Welsh dresser Popular late Victorian name for a handsome 18th- to 19th-century dresser, often comparable in its decoration with provincial longcase clocks. Frequently with curving profiles to the shelves' side supports and a canopy frieze matched by a frieze below the row of drawers in the central table section. Turned spindles might link this section to a low pot-board above substantial feet. There might be decorative small cupboards in the upper, shelved, section and often cupboarding to fill the lower section – too narrowly defined as a North Wales feature. *See* 'Tridarn'.

Welsh ware Generic term for large oblong meat dishes in coarse earthenware slip-covered and ornamented with parallel lines in darker slip combed into wavy stripes. Associated especially with the early 19th century, but continued into the 20th.

Welted foot *See* Folded foot.

Whalebone *See* Scrimshaw.

Whatnot. Etagère. Omnium Moveable stand mainly for displaying tiny treasures, its three or four open shelves often edged with low galleries and typically with corner supports of neatly turned spindles resting on castors. In use from the 1790s (in Gillow firm's records), but mainly Victorian, in mahogany, rosewood, walnut, sometimes with one or two low drawers. Rectangular and, from the 1850s, also in a three-sided corner shape, the front of each shelf attractively curved.

Wheel barometer. Dial barometer (Figs. 14, 15) With its essential mercury tube entirely concealed in a wooden case, the mercury's movements activating a pointer on a circular numbered dial harmonising with clock furniture. Devised in the 1660s, but seldom made until about the 1760s, becoming widely popular in the late 18th century when the frame might be shaped in curving outlines such as the familiar 'banjo', often with a hygrometer and thermometer above the dial and a spirit level below as it had to hang straight. Aneroid barometers were often housed in these handsome cases. *See* Hallifax barometers.

Wheel engraving *See* Engraved glass.

Whieldon, Thomas (*c.*1719–95) Important Staffordshire potter whose apprentices included Josiah Spode and who was partner to Josiah Wedgwood (1754–9). Important to the development of agate ware, mingled colour glazes including tortoiseshell ware, and green-glaze ware including cauliflower ware, so that his name has become a generic term for these (unmarked) wares.

White embroidery. Ayrshire embroidery. Flowering (Fig. 244) Poorly paid professional work widespread among thousands of cottagers (formerly home spinners) of West Scotland and Northern Ireland from the late 18th century, following the development of cotton muslin weaving. By the 1820s firmer muslins were covered with ambitious lacy flower embroideries including pulled work and frequently introducing cut-work fillings of exquisite needlepoint lace; used for christening robes, fichu

303 White embroidery: shoulder-wrap known as pelerine and details of typical 'flowering'. **304** Quilting: detail from 18th-century petticoat.

capes, pelerines, berthas, collars, etc. By the 1850s, strongly threatened by the work of embroidery machines (Swiss 1828 invention) so that hand-work deteriorated into speedier, cheaper ornament such as broderie anglaise and richelieu work.

Whitefriars Glassworks (Fig. 90) Important London makers of flint-glass table-wares from the early 18th century, becoming James Powell & Sons in 1733. Designs by Philip Webb were sold by the William Morris firm. Whitefriars glass was widely admired at exhibitions through Victorian and Edwardian days, Harry Powell putting the firm in the forefront of glass design, including stained glass cathedral windows.

White-line engraving *See* Wood engraving.

White metal Metal alloys suggesting silver when new. *See* Britannia metal; Nickel silver; Paktong; Vickers metal.

Whitewood 1. *See* Spruce. 2. Term might also imply furniture left unstained and unpainted, as in the 19th century's widely distributed white-Wycombe chairs in cheap styles for bedroom and kitchen.

Wigstand Simple turned wood pillar suggesting a candlestick but topped by a mushroom dome. Not to be confused with the early basin stand.

275

William and Mary period Term for William III's reign, 1689–1702 (his wife, Mary II d. 1694), covering the transition from the flamboyant restoration years to the curvilinear grace of the Queen Anne period. Much foreign influence through William's Dutch interests and the activities of Huguenot refugees.

Williamite glass Confusing portraits of William III (William of Orange) and inscriptions such as 'To the glorious memory' commemorating the battle of the Boyne on decanters and drinking-glasses mainly produced after 1780, following the establishment of the political Orange Institution. The equestrian portraits on glasses (taken from Van Nost's statue) were associated with the 1822 appointment of the Duke of York as the Institution's grand master. Engravers often added to the confusion by preferring to work on 18th-century glass.

Willow pattern Imagined Chinese design widely used from the early 19th century onwards for blue underglaze ornament on table-wares. Thomas Turner of Caughley was associated with an early variant (no bridge or figures) and the theme was explored by Minton, Spode, Leeds, Herculaneum and many other potteries making slight variations on a basic pattern of willow tree, pagoda, bluebirds and two or three figures on a bridge.

Willow wood White to pinkish, soft, but tough and light, polishing well. Often dyed black as an ebony substitute for small work. Its twigs used for wickerwork.

Wilton carpet Generic term for pile carpets, as made at Wilton, Wiltshire, with a Brussels loop weave (the close pile surface trimmed like velvet) from the 1740s. Knotted pile carpets also made there when Axminster works were taken over from 1835.

Windsor chair Name has been traced to the 1720s and production continues. Long favoured for coffee-house and farmhouse kitchen and for garden use among the well-to-do, meeting the need for uncushioned comfort and tough resilience under rough handling on hard floors. Cheaply made because largely depended on turners' pole-lathe work, often prepared in bulk in suitable woodlands. The basic solid block of the saddle seat was bored to receive the back and arm verticals and, on the underside, four out-jutting legs. Resilience was aided by the use of steam-heated curved members, most attractively in springy yew-wood for the vertical hoop of the back, the horizontal hoop of the arm rests,

Windsor chairs. 305 Comb-back. **306** High-back hoop. **307** Brace-back.
308 'Lancashire'. **309** 'Gothic'.

following the rounded curve of the seat and, in early work, for a backward-curved 'cow's horn' front stretcher. Main varieties include: 1. The earliest *comb-back* continuing through the 18th century with a back composed of nine or ten plain spindles supporting a comb-shaped crest-rail. A single-piece arm-rest encircling the back strengthened the spindles and prompted development of *hoop-back* varieties with a single vertical arching hoop to frame the whole back. 2. Of these the *low-back* Windsor was made with the arching hoop bedded in the seat. 3. On the *high-back* the hoop rose from the horizontal arm hoop. Within the hoop, vertical spindles usually flanked a central splat ('wheel splat' from the end of the 18th century). Shaped laths instead of spindles added to Victorian comfort. 4. In the *brace-back* variety the raking back was supported by stays – two spindles running from high in the arching back-rail to a small projection (bob-tail) at the back of the seat. Some use of ungainly cabriole legs in the wake of fashion, but leg ornament consisted mainly of baluster turning. 5. Heavy work sometimes wholly of yew has been associated with the north of England – the so-called *Lancashire* Windsors. 6. Some fashionable *'Gothic'* Windsors were made from the 1760s onwards with church-window shaping in the hoop and splat. In the 19th century the large-scale factory assembly of Windsors and simple variants catered mainly for a cheap market. *See* Mendlesham chair; Smoker's bow; Whitewood.

Wine bottle. Some of the earliest 'wanded bottles' had rounded bases originally sheathed in osier. More for collectors in thick glass from the 17th century were in tall-necked shaft-and-globe shapes made by blowing and tooling the dark glass. From *c*. 1730 shorter-necked cylindrical bottles were blown-moulded (showing a slightly dappled surface from the metal mould). Through the 18th century bottles gradually became thinner and taller and in the early 19th century the string-rim gave way to a broad sloping lip. Mechanical shaping from the 1840s. Mineral-water bottles were developed from early in the 19th century. Air-tight stoppers included a screw type from 1872 and a marble type from 1875. *See* Kick; Sealed bottles.

Wine coaster. Slider (Fig. 256) In silver, Sheffield plate, turned wood, for easy movement of 18th- to 19th-century decanters and wine bottles on polished tables. The base flat, baize covered, supporting a low vertical rim variously ornamented and often ornate from the 1790s onwards, for richly cut decanters. Including wheeled double-coasters, some made as carts or wagons with the beer wagon as a variant, shaped to hold jug and glasses.

Wine cooler. Wine cistern From Tudor to Victorian days, for ice and water to keep wine bottles cool in a hot candle-lit dining-room. Lead-lined, in silver, marble, granite, or solid mahogany. Had to be massive until about the 1760s to hold wide wine bottles and then increasingly deep. Many from the late 18th century were in mahogany of brass-bound staved construction with brass lion-mask handles; many in the early 19th century in sarcophagus shape, some with fixed linings of rolled zinc from the 1820s. By then alternatives included the ice pail.

Wine-glass cooler Individual bowl for each diner, in use *c.*1750s–1850s, in glass, often blue from the 1780s, green or red from the 1820s. Was an alternative to the communal monteith with one or two pinched beak shapings in the rim to hold the stems of glasses inverted into the iced water, thus differing from smooth-rimmed finger bowls.

Wine label. Bottle ticket In silver, etc., for hanging by a chain

Wine labels. 310, 311 Late 18th century. **312, 313** 1820s.

279

round the neck of a bottle or decanter. Plain from the 1720s, becoming ornate from the 1770s including late 18th-century die-stampings and massive 19th-century castings. Single-letter labels and perforated lettering in vine leaves from the 1820s. Alternatives to silver included painted enamels (many fakes), ivory, mother-of-pearl, china.

Wine measures (Fig. 215) Made in thick ley-metal pewter to a specified pattern kept by the Pewterers' Company from early in the 17th century so that consumers could see that they received full measure. The vessel's lid, thick lip, vertical rim, baluster-shaped body and flat base would show up any deliberate indentations (and prevented insertion of a false bottom). In the mid 18th century lines were added around body and lid, to show if the rim was cut down. The maker's touch mark, if any, was struck on the rim, but many were unmarked, might be of over-leaded pewter and might give short 'Birmingham measure'. After introduction of the Imperial system of measures in 1824 these vessels were usually made without lids. *See* Weights and measures marks.

Wine table *See* Horseshoe table.

Wine waiter Comparable with a canterbury, but partitioned for bottles. Resembled a castor-mounted stool supporting a low decorative gallery with cross-partitions and a central raised hand hole. Intended for use during informal, servant-free meals.

Wing chair High-backed upholstered chair with forward-projecting wings at head height to protect its occupant from draughts. Made from the late 17th century onwards.

Winged furniture Case furniture such as a sideboard, wardrobe, etc., in which the main central section is flanked by smaller sections, frequently in breakfront form. *See* Break, broken.

Wirework 1. Gold, silver or other metal drawn through a series of diminishing holes until it was of the required thickness of round-section wire or flattened ribbon for filigree work, jewellery or more substantial table-baskets, etc. Notably popular in *Sheffield plate*, (Fig. 254) being drawn from the billet of fused copper and silver. This was used at first, *c.* 1780s, in short pieces, the repetitive shapes soldered into position, but later in longer curving patterns, for épergnes, cruet stands, etc. 2. For embroidery, mainly worked either in gilded silver wire or in silk closely wrapped in silver-gilt ribbon, for couching, and in early professionally embroidered gloves, etc., to take the rub of wear. *See* Pinched plate; Purls.

Witch ball Evolved from traditional spherical flask for holy water: by the early 19th century balls of 'Nailsea' glass had become popular cottage ornaments, comparable with rolling pins. Might be in thick dark glass flecked and spotted, some looped with strands of fused-in coloured glass before being fully inflated by the glassblower. Some in clearer glass were coloured inside in marbled patterns, sometimes as a backing for transfer-printed ornament. Some early balls were silvered inside as reflective watch balls and new silvering methods were devised in the 1840s and 1850s. Many balls were sealed, associating them with the common glass net floats used by fishermen.

Wolverhampton style (Fig. 201) Decorative technique developed at the Old Hall factory of Frederick Walton & Co. in the 1840s by Fred Perks and others for the period's popular japanned ornaments, especially picture trays of papier mâché and of tinned plate, cheaper than Pontypool ware, and known as Wolverhampton ware. Bronze powders combined with oil colours were used to achieve striking atmospheric effects such as sunlight streaming into a church through gothic windows or moonlight on picturesque ruins among dark trees.

Wood *See* Treen, and under individual headings – Acacia, etc.

Woodcut Style of relief print using the side-grain of easily worked wood. The background was cut away by knife to leave a raised pattern for printing clear-cut outlines suitable for cheap work on rough paper and associated with early printed books, broadsides, etc. *See* Wood engraving.

Wood engraving Refinement of the woodcut, worked on the end-grain of a hard wood such as box, but still a relief print. Taken by inking the projections in the wood surface left when the engraver had cut away the lines and areas he wished to appear white in the print. But in the skilled hands of, e.g., Thomas Bewick (*c*.1753–1828) using the thrusting strokes of the metal engraver's burins, the method allowed considerable subtleties of tone and texture. Even a luminous sky might be suggested with parallel lines of graduated widths and facial shadows might be varied with white criss-cross contour lines.

In *white line engraving* the engraver expressed his design mainly in the lines cut away (white in the print) against the shadow-mass printed from the close end-grain wood.

Wood family Staffordshire potters. Included the brothers Ralph (1715–72) important figure-maker and Aaron (1717–85), celebrated block-cutter and modeller. Ralph's son and grandson, both also Ralph (1748–95) and (1781–1801), worked as figure-makers. Aaron's sons William (1746–1808) and Enoch (1759–1840) worked as modellers, as did their cousin Ephraim (1773–1830s). Enoch's sons (cousins to the youngest Ralph) were Enoch, Joseph, Edward and Thomas, all potters through much of the 19th century. Collectors look especially for figures and toby jugs by the Ralph Woods, coloured at first in stained glazes and later in overglaze enamels; also for notable portrait figures (Wesley, William IV, etc.) and large groups as well as toby variants from the elder Enoch Wood. Enoch also made basaltes, creamwares, fine blue-printed wares, etc. He was in partnership, *c*.1790–1818, as Wood & Caldwell and the firm continued as Enoch Wood & Sons to 1846.

Wool weights Flattish bronze discs in stirrup or shield outline weighing a tod (28 lb.) or a half or quarter tod, carried by the travelling tronager whose job was to check local trons or weighing beams required to assess the immensely important revenue tax on wool. Manufactured from 1494 onwards, but remained state property to be recalled and melted down when new ones were

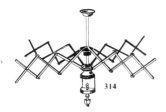

314 Wool winder. **315** Wool weight (George III) showing punch marks on rim.

issued (e.g. three issues during the reign of William III); hence their rarity apart from fakes. Their main feature is a representation of the royal arms – cast in relief from 1587 – but collectors look also for the Founders' Company punch-marks, like silver assay marks, and a letter and emblem indicating each tronager's work-area. No new weights after 1795, but re-testings were punch-marked and from 1826 all those re-tested were dated.

Wool winder A light framework, typically of Victorian walnut, with four expanding arms around a central vertical metal shaft rising either from a weighted stand or from a clamp for fixing to the table edge. A screw at the top held the arms sufficiently expanded to stretch the skein of wool and they revolved as the wool was pulled and rolled into a ball.

Worcester porcelains Ceramics made in Worcester from 1751 to the present day. Founded as the Worcester Tonquin Manufactory by Dr John Wall and partners, probably taking over the early Lund and Miller Bristol porcelain venture, and becoming the Royal Worcester Porcelain Company in 1788.

Brilliant early period to 1783, making soapstone porcelain ornaments and table-wares in magnificent patterns and colours including celebrated blue and other coloured grounds. Also much blue-painting and notably early transfer-printing, with many jugs, plates, etc., also patterned in low relief with overlapping leaves.

Followed by the Flight period, *q.v.* to 1840, production including bone china from *c.*1800, still mainly ornaments and table-wares of great brilliance, including vases painted with picturesque views and celebrated 'japans'.

The firm was then acquired by the rival Chamberlain factory. From 1852 under W. H. Kerr and art director R. W. Binns the factory was modernised, becoming the Worcester Royal Porcelain Co. in 1862. Products included parian ware and successful ornament suggesting Limoges enamels (associated especially with Thomas Bott, d. 1870, and his son T. J. Bott), built up in washes of somewhat translucent white enamel on glazed blue grounds. Ivory porcelain was made from 1856; remarkable pierced ornaments by George Owen suggesting carved ivory; and new end-of-century glaze effects in Sabrina art ware. In the past there has been confusion between marks from Worcester and Caughley. *See* Doughty birds.

Work table *See* Pouch table.

Woven Coventry ribbons *See* Picture ribbons.

Wreathings Spiral ridges sometimes discernable inside hollow-ware such as early stoneware, delftware and Plymouth porcelain. These strengthened the vessel against possible collapse in the firing kiln.

Wright & Mansfield Cabinet-makers, 1860–86, remembered for handsome Neo-classical satinwood furniture enriched with marquetry, ceramic plaques, etc.

Writhen (Fig. 258) Twisted or plaited. 1. In silver, a term applied to knops in twisted shapes as on early spoons. 2. In glass, applied to surface-twisting of a drinking-glass stem or to swirled ribbing or fluting on the lower part of the bowl (suggesting early Venetian influence, but practical too in obscuring the sediment in early 18th-century liquors.)

Writing screen *See* Screen writing-table.

Wrotham, Kent Important pottery centre, *c.*1610–1740, making slipware, some handsome pieces having survived. Production included jugs, tygs, posset pots, candlesticks, usually of lead-glazed red clay decorated with inscribed pads of white clay, or with slip trailing, the motifs occasionally suggesting needlework stitching.

Wrought iron. Malleable iron Purest form of iron, tough, strong, corrosion-resistant, for the early blacksmith's hammered work. Important in Medieval, Baroque and Rococo furnishings, from locks and hinges to weather-vanes and park gates, becoming the decorative artist's medium under such leaders as Huguenot refugee Jean Tijou, at work in London around 1700, his *New Booke of Drawings* published 1693. *See* Cast iron.

Wych elm *See* Elm.

Wycombe chairs Associated with High Wycombe, Buckinghamshire chair-making centre from the 18th century, becoming extremely important from Victorian days for a wide range of light chairs – balloon backs, lath backs, etc. and variants of the Windsor. *See* White wood.

X-chair With a seat slung between side-rails that linked the two rounded X-shapes formed by the back legs and the front legs which were continued upward as back and arm supports, often finished with small pummels of metal or wood. Mainly associated with rich 17th-century households, the difficult curved shaping masked by leather or rich fabric secured by the cofferer's brass-headed nails.

Xylography Printing from wood. *See* Woodcuts; Wood engraving.

Xylopyrography Developed from pokerwork. The surface of, e.g., chestnut wood was charred all over and the darkness cut away to achieve varying lighter tones somewhat suggesting a sepia drawing. The technique recalled that of the mezzotint engraver working on his roughened copper plate and mezzotints were copied (e.g. among the items shown at the 1851 Exhibition).

Yard-arm, Diagonal or Signpost barometer From 1670, for more exact readings of air pressure variation. Realising that this is observable in the top few inches of the vertical mercury tube (*see*

Barometers) Sir Samuel Morland bent the tube when about 28 inches high, extending the measurement area to 18 inches or more, spread out almost horizontally. Popular in the 18th century, often mounted in mirror framing.

Yard-of-ale glass Drinking-vessel holding about a quart that had to be drained at a single draught. With a flaring mouth and narrow tubular body that, in 18th-century examples, ended in a ball knop and a domed, welted foot. Became flat-footed and knopless in the 19th century when a popular trick variant of the 1830s–40s ended with a hollow bulb at the base, intended to splash the drinker's face.

Yellow ware Comparable with green-glaze ware developed by Josiah Wedgwood in the 1750s using a lustrous yellow glaze, often applied over earthenwares moulded in low relief.

Yew wood Hard, close-grained golden brown to reddish brown, a native wood long used by turners (*see* Windsor chairs.) Its fine figure, especially in burr wood, was used for veneers.

Yorkshire/Derbyshire/Lancashire chair Modern name for a single chair widely made in the 17th century, conspicuous only for the treatment of the open back. This consisted of straight side-

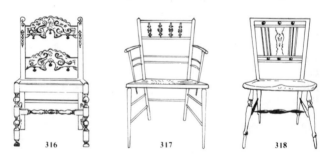

Regional chairs. 316 Yorkshire–Derbyshire–Lancashire style.
317 Morris Sussex chair. **318** Mendlesham.

rails topped by small outward-turning scroll finials and between them a broad, carved, arching top-rail and similar cross-rail, both with pendant knobs. Alternatively, an arcaded top-rail might be linked to a narrow cross-rail by two or three decorative spindles. Often this chair had a squab seat.

Yorkshire dresser Popular name for a widely-made style of 18th- and 19th-century dresser with a centrally placed clock dividing the high shelving.

Zaffre blue For colouring glass, ceramics, etc. Prepared from cobalt, coming in ancient times from Persia; discovered in Saxony in 1545, becoming a monopoly and unobtainable briefly during Saxony's war with Prussia, 1756–63. Some minor use of Cornish cobalt, especially in the early 19th century. As a colour it was vastly important in ceramic decoration because it could withstand the glazing kiln heat and proved excellent for underglaze painted and transfer-printed wares. *See* Blue and white; Blue glass; Bristol blue; High temperature colours; King's blue; Mazarine; Powder blue; Smalt; Ultramarine.

Zebra wood. Tiger wood Strong reddish brown with dark stripes used mainly for banding in the late 18th to 19th centuries, but occasionally as a striking veneer covering a whole article of furniture.

Zinc Brittle, bluish-white metal much used in alloys (brass, etc.) and for spelter castings.

Zircon Hard, brilliant, transparent gemstone, a variety of brown or greyish zirconite. When colourless or smoky it is known as jargoon. It may be heated to an attractive blue but this is liable to fade or discolour. *See* Hyacinth; Jacinth.